ENCOURAGING REFLECTIVE PRACTICE IN EDUCATION

An Analysis of Issues and Programs

ENCOURAGING REFLECTIVE PRACTICE IN EDUCATION

An Analysis of Issues and Programs

RENEE T. CLIFT
W. ROBERT HOUSTON
MARLEEN C. PUGACH

Editors

Teachers College, Columbia University
New York and London

Published by Teachers College Press, 1234 Amsterdam Avenue
New York, NY 10027

Library of Congress Cataloging-in-Publication Data

Encouraging reflective practice in education : an analysis of issues
  and programs / Renee T. Clift, W. Robert Houston, Marleen C. Pugach,
  editors.
      p. cm.
  Papers of a working conference on reflection in teaching and
  teacher education sponsored by the University of Houston and the
  United States Dept. of Education, Office of Educational Research
  and Improvement, held in Houston, Oct. 1987.
    Includes bibliographical references.
    ISBN 0-8077-2991-4 (alk. paper). — ISBN 0-8077-2990-6 (pbk. : alk. paper)
    1. Teachers—Training of—United States—Congresses. 2. Teaching—
  Vocational guidance—United States—Congresses. 3. Reflection
  (Philosophy)—Congresses. I. Clift, Renee Tipton. II. Houston, W.
  Robert. III. Pugach, Marleen Carol, 1949- . IV. University of
  Houston. V. United States. Office of Educational Research and
  Improvement.
  LB1715.E66 1990
  370'.71—dc20   89-27205
                                                                       CIP

    ISBN 0-8077-2990-6 (pbk.)
         0-8077-2991-4

Printed on acid-free paper

Manufactured in the United States of America

97 96 95 94 93 92 91 90   8 7 6 5 4 3 2 1

Contents

Foreword

- Is reflective practice just the latest educators' fad or is it a potential cornerstone of efforts to unify the vast array of educational reform initiatives that will lead us into the 21st century?
- What is reflective practice intended to accomplish, and why is it receiving so much attention lately?
- On what are practitioners to reflect?
- What, specifically, is reflective practice, and why are there so many different interpretations of what it should look like?
- How is it similar to and different from what goes on in schools and universities today?
- What have we learned from prior and present efforts to bring about reflective practice?
- What resources and conditions are needed to support reflective practice?
- What difference is reflective practice likely to make in educators' and, ultimately, students' knowledge, skills, attitudes and behavior?

If any or all of these questions are of interest to you, this volume should serve you well. One of its most important contributions may be that it raises these and other very basic questions, strongly encouraging the reader to explore each of them thoroughly before making any judgments about the desirability and feasibility of reflective practice.

The authors draw extensively from both theory and practice to make their cases. More than 50 years of writing and thinking, from John Dewey to Donald Schön, serve as food for thought. Readers will find valuable syntheses and analyses—admittedly condensed but not superficial—heretofore unavailable in a single volume. From the realm of practice, you will read descriptions and assessments of ongoing programs, lessons learned from prior efforts to bring about reflective practice, and projections for the future. Several of the writers draw from

While the author is an employee of the United States Department of Education, the opinions expressed herein are solely those of the individual and do not represent any judgments, positions or policies of the United States Department of Education.

their recent experiences in research-based teacher education improvement projects funded by the U.S. Department of Education's Office of Educational Research and Improvement. Others look at reflective practice within the context of approaches such as the school-based decision-making models espoused by the current educational reform movement.

There is important information here for persons at all levels of educational responsibility. Much of the discussion focuses on how teacher educators and prospective and practicing teachers can interact to bring about reflective practice, but there are clear implications for many others as well. School district, university, and state-level policy-makers will be interested in the resources and conditions essential for reflective practice, as well as in the outcomes likely to be derived. Curriculum developers will want to better understand the dilemmas faced in decisions about the content of reflective practice. Parents will want to examine how reflective practices will influence their children's learning and development, and to look at the expectations for parent and student roles in supporting and benefitting from reflective practice. Researchers will find a multitude of issues worthy of study, potential hypotheses that might focus those studies, and heightened emphasis on the need to better integrate research and practice as critical elements of reflection. The reader will encounter optimism and skepticism; opinion and fact; grand visions and very focused activities; emphases on moral, ethical and political considerations in reflective practice, as well as an emphasis on acquiring teaching skills and behaviors; and distinctly different views of the purposes of learning, teaching, and schooling.

What the reader will not encounter are definitive answers to questions such as, "Should I unequivocally endorse reflective practice?" or "What's the best way to do it?" The authors are generally in agreement that there has been a great deal of rhetoric about reflective practice, but far too little serious consideration and debate of alternative purposes for and approaches to reflective practice. There has been even less in the way of well-conceived, systematic, carefully planned and implemented, and rigorously studied initiatives to convert the rhetoric into reality. The authors are, in a sense, trying to get the reader to think before acting, to learn from history, to realize that reflective practice will, by definition, mean different things for different purposes and settings, and to understand what reflective practice may or may not be able to accomplish.

The authors do not want the reader to be an "accidental tourist" in the land of reflective practice. They attempt to describe the history as well as the cultural and physical geography of the region, in order to provide you with enough information to see how and why the region developed, to decide whether or not you want to go there, and, if you do, how to explore and develop the region by making creative use of its resources and coping with or compensating for its limitations.

It is not just the authors who believe that getting the lay of the land is important. In recent months, I have participated in a variety of forums ranging from a national symposium of state-level policymakers, on the topic of "Preparing Teachers Today for Teaching Tomorrow," to a regional meeting of school and university-based educators, on "Developing Inquiring Professionals". Many of the discussions in these sessions began by focusing on how to "make" our schools and universities and the people in them more reflective. Participants arrive with questions of "How do I do it?" What becomes evident quickly is that they have very different views of (1) what "it" is, (2) what purposes can best be served by reflective practice, and (3) the intended and unintended effects that are likely to be brought to bear on people, norms, activities, and the local educational system, as a result of moving toward reflective practice.

With surprising regularity these discussions often evolve to the point of addressing many of the same philosophical and conceptual issues that are addressed by several chapters in this volume. The rush to a conclusion about operational and feasibility questions is justifiably slowed by the realization that there are critical questions that must be asked first. It is not likely that these practitioners and policymakers have suddenly been overcome with altruistic pinings to explore reflective practice in any idealistic or philosophical sense. Rather, it is more likely that, in having experienced decades and dozens of "movements" in American education, these persons recognize the possibility that perhaps we have not been asking enough fundamental questions of ourselves about what we wish education, schools, teachers and students to accomplish. Reflective practice well done demands that we ask exactly those fundamental questions, as the foundation for all else. The potential utility of reflective practice as a means by which fundamental educational change could be realized is what draws together so many diverse actors upon the education stage. When one sees (as was the case for the "Developing Inquiring Professionals" conference mentioned above) a major school district, a national research university, and a teachers union cosponsoring a push for reflective practice, it is hard to deny the unifying potential of the theme.

So it is that policymakers and practitioners, theoreticians and education philosophers, along with the contributors to this book, seem to begin to converge on several major points of concentration. They have realized that there is no single appropriate definition of reflective practice and no single set of strategies that best exemplifies it. Reflective practice is as much a state of mind as it is a set of activities. This means that reflective practice must be internalized by those who are to practice it, and they must believe in its worth and utility for making things better. Clearly, one cannot "make" this happen by edict and enforcement. Furthermore, while reflective practice may be essential for every individual educator to undertake, its greatest potential for producing change and improvement is as a collective, collegial activity. An individual can promote his or her excellence, but a collectivity can better promote the excellence of a system.

Technical skills, knowledge, and behavior are all essential elements of reflective practice, but they do not compose its whole. Value-laden issues such as moral, ethical, and political judgments must be brought to bear at the local level on what is to be taught, to whom, and how. These are the "front-end" judgments of reflective practice, where the decisions about what content is to be reflected upon are made. Until this has been appropriately addressed, decisions about ways by which to transform that content into knowledge, understanding, and action by teachers and students will be premature and insignificant. Teachers, along with parents, students, administrators, teachers' unions, school boards, and community, business, and industry representatives must be informed about and involved in such decisions. Teachers are but one link in the chain of responsibililty for reflective practice.

It is also beginning to be generally recognized that the complexity, ambiguity, and immediacy of teaching require teachers who are adept and flexible. Teachers must constantly adjust and extend their teaching to students, situations, content, and purposes that vary. As one author suggests, these teachers "improvise," much in the manner of an artist such as an exceptional musician who is so skilled and confident that she willingly and consistently seeks new challenges, venturing into previously uncharted territories in search of new opportunities for excellence, and moves her audience to new levels of excitement, appreciation, and involvement. This teacher/artist must be able, as Schön describes, to reflect-in-action as well as reflect-on-action.

These then are the visions, hopes, and issues that are confronting those who wish to move beyond merely the rhetoric of reflective practice. This volume makes it clear that there is nothing magical or inherently wonderful about reflective practice. As the authors of several chapters indicate, much has been done poorly in the name of reflective practice, and may yet be done, that will have little if any benefit for education. Worse, reflective practice done in bad faith, poorly, or in an incomplete fashion can leave residual frustration, bitterness, or distrust across many levels of a system, for a very long time. It is probably safe to say that unless the reasons for pursuing reflective practice are important, clear, and agreed upon—and there is a strong and long-term commitment to providing resources and conditions that support reflective practice—one would be better off not trying it at all. Reflective practice requires much change, much support, and much patience.

I hope that I have motivated you to continue reading. If you do, I believe you will find yourself challenged to think about whether or not reflective practice is worth pursuing. Given the many different perspectives presented, the reader will undoubtedly agree with some and disagree with others. To return to an earlier metaphor, reflective practice is now much like an underdeveloped land: its potential for growth will be determined by the diligence, rigor, and wisdom that comes from within the teacher, and the nurturance and opportunities it receives from without. This book should help you decide whether or not there is sufficient substance and worth in the concept to warrant further exploration and development.

JOSEPH C. VAUGHAN
United States Department of Education
Office of Educational Research and Improvement

Introduction

This book is the product of a working conference on Reflection in Teaching and Teacher Education sponsored by the University of Houston and the United States Department of Education, Office of Educational Research and Improvement (OERI), held in Houston in October 1987. Originally, the conference was called because those of us who had contracted to create demonstration teacher education programs for OERI felt that we needed some time to meet and to talk about our endeavors in program development—particularly those programs that were labeled "reflective" in nature.

As we began to explore the possibility of a working conference, we became aware of other teacher education programs around the United States and Canada that were exploring the potential of encouraging both experienced and novice teachers to be more reflective. Whenever we learned of people who were so involved, we invited them to join us for a conversation on the nature of reflective practice and its implications for teacher education at all levels of experience.

In the weekend we spent together, it became very obvious that there was no consensus regarding the definition of reflection, conceptions of reflective practice, or the ways in which teacher educators or schools might encourage reflective thinking. There were even those among us who raised questions about the value of reflective practice, suggesting that people could become too reflective and, therefore, incapable of decisive action. Indeed, the only thing that was agreed upon was that this topic is complex and that it deserves further discussion and careful examination. With the publication of this book we invite an even wider audience to join our conversation.

The first section of the book, Chapters 1 through 5, presents a variety of conceptual issues in reflective practice and includes different theoretical orientations to the nature of reflective thinking. When the term *reflection* is heard by different people, it is understood in many different ways. These five chapters offer a sample of multiple understandings of reflection with no attempt to promote one over another. Chapters 6 through 10 present examples of programs designed to encourage reflective practice. This section of the book includes teacher educators' accounts of the successes and problems inherent in the practical implementation of the abstract concept of "reflection." These chapters further elaborate upon the complexity introduced in the first five chapters by highlighting the gaps between rhetoric and practice. The final chapter discusses the importance of continual inquiry into our own practices as teacher educators in the context of reflection. In it readers are encouraged to examine external factors that shape teaching and teacher education and to consider how those factors encourage or discourage different kinds of practices. With this book we envision a lively continuation of the discussions begun in Houston and extended at a 1988 working conference at the University of Florida. We hope the exchange of ideas and spirited debate will be sustained at future meetings as well.

The original conference in Houston, and this book, would not have been possible without the support and encouragement of the Office of Educational Research and Improvement, although this text in no way represents either the official views of the U.S. Department of Education or those of any of the officials within that department. We would particularly like to acknowledge Joe Vaughan's encouragement and advice. We would also like to thank the late Marianne Amarel, and Hilda Borko, Gene Hall, Alan Tom, and Marsha Weil for helping us pull together themes that emerged from the Houston conference and that helped shape the form and content of this book.

We are indebted to Sarah Biondello and Ron Galbraith from Teachers College Press for their support from the initial conception of the book all the way through publication. Cathymae Nelson at the University of Wisconsin–Milwaukee carefully typed the entire manuscript and provided initial proofreading, thereby making our task of editing all the easier. Most of all we would like to thank each chapter author for meeting deadlines (a rarity in most edited volumes) and, more important, for providing us with such a rich diversity of well-thought-out material. We hope that you will receive as much intellectual stimulation in reading this text as we did in editing it.

RENEE T. CLIFT
W. ROBERT HOUSTON
MARLEEN C. PUGACH

ENCOURAGING REFLECTIVE PRACTICE IN EDUCATION

An Analysis of Issues and Programs

PART I

**REFLECTING ON THE CONCEPT
OF REFLECTION IN
TEACHER EDUCATION**

1 The Evolution of Reflective Teaching and Teacher Education

VIRGINIA RICHARDSON
University of Arizona

As often happens in education, a new (or not so new) term begins to show up in the literature and catches on with amazing speed. It enters the consciousness of a large number of people in a short period of time and drives program development and reform in both classroom instruction and teacher education. This phenomenon contrasts with the lament that certain aspects of schooling and teaching never change (Cuban, 1984) and that teachers and teacher educators do not keep up with the literature or research.

Reflection is one of those terms. Donald Schön's book, *The Reflective Practitioner*, appeared in 1983. Just three years later, the 1986 American Educational Research Association conference program could have been called "The Reflective Teacher Program"; and one can hardly read an article about teaching without mention of reflection. Schön has been flown from campus to conference to workshop to discuss the meaning of reflective practice and its implications for education, and many teacher education programs include as a major goal the preparation of reflective teachers.

Reflective thinking and teaching are not new ideas. Dewey (1909/1933), for example, describes the concept and how it would operate in an individual who is deliberating within a practical action setting. In such a case, he suggests, a moral individual would treat professional actions as experimental and reflect upon the actions and their consequences. However, when Schön's *Reflective Practitioner* struck the consciousness of educationists in the mid-1980s, it was not always as a re-embracing of Dewey's notion, but as the discovery of a new concept.

As I see how the term is taking hold in educational discourse, it concerns me that the reflective concept could become another slogan used to drive supposedly new programs that eventually (and inevitably) fail to live up to their expectations. Such failure could discredit the original concept. I wonder if the term was ever envisioned by Schön as a driving metaphor for a particular type of program.

3

I also wonder why the concept of the reflective practitioner caught on so quickly in the teaching world. What did it replace? Are there lessons we can learn from other such concepts that quickly entered the thinking and discourse of teaching scholars and teacher educators? Perhaps we in teacher education are asking too much of the reflection concept.

The purpose of this chapter is to examine the reasons that the notion of the reflective teacher has such an appeal to teaching scholars and teacher educators and to present some potential problems with the use of reflective teaching in developing teacher education programs. In order to do so, I will examine parallel examples of two other popular concepts that strongly affected the development and discussion of teacher education programs in the 1970s and early 1980s: competency-based education and the teacher as decision maker. As will be made clear in this discussion, the topic cannot be approached without also examining the relationship between the evolution of research on teaching paradigms and the concepts that drive teacher education reform.

COMPETENCY-BASED TEACHER EDUCATION

Haberman and Stinnett (1973) describe the competency-based teacher education (CBTE) and performance-based teacher education (PBTE) movement as alternatives to the prevailing experience-based teacher education programs. The experience-based programs assume that when students successfully complete a certain number of courses and the student teaching experience, they are ready to teach. The CBTE or PBTE movement assumes, instead, that a certain number of behaviors are necessary for teaching to be effective and that teachers should be able to demonstrate that they can perform these behaviors prior to teaching. In many instances the behaviors are those identified by researchers on teaching effectiveness as being related to student achievement on standardized tests of the *process* of teaching and student products, such as successful test performance or positive attitudes. Both CBTE and PBTE program developers emphasize the importance of the process-product research base.

While different proponents use either PBTE or CBTE and often emphasize differences between them, the distinctions blur when they are analyzed. As Haberman and Stinnett state: "We found no basis for distinguishing between the ways in which both terms are used" (p. 93). Thus the term CBTE will be used in this chapter to refer to both approaches.

The CBTE concept is similar to the competency-based curriculum programs for elementary and secondary students, with several exceptions. Competency-based curriculum programs for students are based on notions of scope and sequence of knowledge and skill attainment derived from the knowledge structure of the particular subject matter. In CBTE, however, the skills and knowledge relate to pedagogy; a knowledge base that is not fully developed and that certainly does not yield prescriptions for sequence. Nonetheless, required pedagogical knowledge and skills are separated, delineated, and addressed in learning modules. Preservice teachers are required to demonstrate knowledge of and/or ability to perform the behaviors in one module before moving on to the next. Each prospective teacher proceeds at his or her own pace. The experience is individualized. Research on teaching is meant to provide teacher educators with the competencies known to positively affect student learning.

CBTE was seen as a response to the calls for accountability in public expenditures that began in the mid-1960s. Proponents of CBTE could state exactly what skills students of teaching were learning, and could relate each to increasing student achievement in elementary and secondary schools. Haberman and Stinnett (1973) point out that the concept appealed to the new and increasing numbers of research-oriented faculty who had begun to teach in college programs. Thus began, as Doyle (1988) recently described, the psychologizing of teacher education. By incorporating behavioral psychology, the training of teachers could be seen within the university setting as a legitimate science, thus, it is to be hoped, improving the status of teaching and teacher education.

In 1974, a conference titled "Competency Assessment, Research, and Evaluation," sponsored by a number of agencies within the Office of Education in conjunction with other organizations concerned with teacher education, was held in Houston, Texas. The purpose of the conference, the proceedings of which were later published (Houston, 1974), was to explore the research needs that surrounded the CBTE concept. While a number of CBTE programs were in operation at the time, the major question addressed at the conference was discussed by Fred McDonald (1974): "What is the nature of teaching competence?" (p. 12). He goes on to state that "I have chosen to place the description of competence as the critical problem on which research must be done" (p. 18) and suggest that it cannot be measured before we know what it is. McDonald's and many of the subsequent chapters, however, deal with how teacher competencies would be identified and measured and how this information could be used in teacher education. The process-product researchers were there in force, suggesting that the processes explored in their research could be considered as competencies (e.g., Gage, 1974; Gustafson & Powell, 1974; Soar, 1974).

Houston (1987) suggested more than a decade later that this conference and others like it did little to spur the type of research necessary to support CBTE. He feels that the lack of research, more than anything else, limited the potential for further development and infusion of CBTE into teacher education programs.

> What makes this shortcoming so apparent in CBTE is the expressed need for research by those supporting the movement. The future of CBTE was inextricably tied to an empirical base for teacher education. Critical in this process was the identification of valid competencies of effective teachers. Second, CBTE implied the determination of appropriate teacher-education curricula and methods that would modify behaviors of trainees so that they would demonstrate such competencies. Third, it implied that adequate assessment procedures were available or could be constructed to measure sensitively the changes in behavior. Finally, it assumed that institutions would devote the needed resources to research and refine competencies, programs, assessments, and research. (p. 90)

However, as discussed below, the problem seems less one of an inadequate research base than one of the questionable validity of the assumptions of the education/research paradigm that spawned CBTE.

Although Houston (1987) estimates that there were still a total of 80 institutions in 1980 reporting full-scale operation of CBTE, and another 284 operating small-scale programs, he suggests that "the period of infusion has passed—and perhaps the period of greatest effectiveness and growth" (p. 94).

Critiques of CBTE and Process-Product Research

One set of critics of CBTE in the mid-1970s referred, as did Houston (1987), to the lack of a sound research base (e.g., Cooper, Jones, & Weber, 1973; Haberman & Stinnett, 1973; Shalock, 1974). This criticism, however, was usually leveled by those involved in the movement.

Another set of critics was identified as the "humanists," and their criticisms of CBTE revolved around the seemingly mechanistic, technician view of the teacher who is trained to perform a number of skills and then, somehow, puts them together in the context of the classroom. Broudy (1972), for example, suggests that these disconnected and mechanistic performances are provided to the students without an overall normative view of humans, the universe, and education. Broudy (1984) later suggested that the major problem with CBTE is that it equates competency with test performance: "Controversy arises at the point where teaching as the unified act of a person exercising a skill is equated with the overt behaviors to which it has been reduced" (p. 4).

Dewey's work provided a basis for the humanist criticism. His views on teacher education are in opposition to the assumption in CBTE that there is a set of correct behaviors in teaching. Teacher education should be pointed toward "making the professional student thoughtful about his work in the light of principles, rather than to induce in him a recognition that certain special methods are good, and certain other special methods are bad" (Dewey, 1904/1962, p. 22).

Competency-based teacher education is closely related, paradigmatically, to the process-product research that was being conducted in the mid-1970s. In fact, regardless of the critics' charges, there is a research base for CBTE: the large-scale studies that attempt to link teaching behaviors with student learning, recently summarized by Brophy and Good (1986). This research is highly behavioral and positivistic. The early process-product research assumed a one-way causal relationship between teacher behaviors and student learning, as indicated by gains on standardized achievement tests. The identification of these effective teacher processes—behaviors—could be thought of as competencies to be turned into prespecified behaviors in which to train teachers in CBTE programs. It is not surprising that the criticism directed at CBTE is similar to that directed at process-product research, although the critics of the latter are not necessarily labeled as humanists.

The criticisms of process-product research revolve around conceptual and methodological issues. The conceptual problems concern the highly behaviorist, context-generic approaches to the description of teaching in process-product research. For Fenstermacher (1979), process-product research ignores the fact that "the school situation is made up of persons who act intentionally within a complex social system" (p. 159). Shulman and others at the 1974 National Conference on Studies in Teaching (National Institute of Education, 1975a, 1975b) point out that teacher behaviors, like those in other professions, such as medicine, are driven by decisions and judgments made in uncertain, complex environments. Thus studies of teacher behaviors alone are not useful for either descriptive or prescriptive purposes. For Doyle (1977), the process-product paradigm ignored classroom history, students, context, and teachers. More recently, Doyle (1988) has suggested that although the psychologizing of teaching through process-product research was, in part, an attempt at building academic status, it has functioned as a means of controlling teacher behavior by policy makers and administrators. The many methodological complaints of inadequate measures, assumptions of causality in correlational research, and so forth have been summarized elsewhere (e.g., Heath & Nielson, 1974; Koehler, 1978).

The educational research paradigm that spawned competency-based teacher education and its knowledge base, process-product research, is deemed by many as inadequate in its potential to describe teaching validly or to provide the content of teacher education. The inadequacy of the research base of CBTE, then, is not in its quantity of studies, but in its conception of the teaching-learning process. What, then, took its place?

THE TEACHER AS THINKER: THE DECISION MAKER

In 1973, a conference was convened by the National Institute of Education to map the field of research on teaching and develop a comprehensive research agenda. The field was broken into ten areas for panel discussion. The panels represented very different ways of thinking about teaching, and several involved concepts and methodologies representing disciplines different from those traditionally employed in the study of classrooms and teaching. For example, the panel on Teaching as Information Processing (National Institute of Education, 1975a), chaired by Lee Shulman, proposed the application of cognitive psychology to the study of classrooms and teaching.

This panel report was turned into a request for proposals for the Institute for Research on Teaching, won by Michigan State University. A new approach to the study of teaching was launched. This work has been summarized by a number of scholars, notably Shavelson and Stern (1981), Clark and Peterson (1986), Borko and Niles (1987), and, more recently, Borko and Shavelson (in press). The teacher decision-making research includes studies of teacher planning, interactive decision making, and judgments. One important outcome of this work emphasizes that teachers make many decisions in the course of one day and that these decision-making processes are similar to those employed by executives (Berliner, 1983). Another important finding is that expert teachers do not use the Tyler model of planning that is taught during preservice teacher education (Yinger, 1979). The Tyler model suggests a linear process of planning that begins with behavioral objectives, moves to determining alternative approaches to fulfilling the objectives, and culminates in selecting among them (Tyler, 1950).

In attempting to capture the "wisdom of the practitioner" (Shulman

& Lanier, 1976) and indicating that teachers are like highly paid executives, this work was thought to enhance the status of teaching. It failed, however, in terms of validity. The decision-making work still fit within the positivist, technical research paradigm exemplified by process-product research. Decision making merely became a step, or series of steps, taken before teachers behave effectively or ineffectively in the classroom. The decision-making model developed by Shavelson and Stern (1981), for example, suggests that teachers operate automatically within well-established routines and make decisions at the point when something unacceptable occurs during the routines. They first observe a cue, then decide whether the cue is within tolerance and whether immediate action is necessary; if action is deemed necessary, they determine what action is appropriate and whether to store the information (or knowledge) regarding this particular decision. These steps all precede a deliberate and unplanned change in routine. As Shulman (1986) suggested, these researchers

> have implicitly accepted the process-product model of teaching as exemplified in the Dunkin-Biddle model, and have treated teachers' thoughts as processes that precede teacher behavior. Since the behavior in question is the same behavior deemed important in the process-product program, then the kinds of thoughts that are understood become those germane to the predominantly classroom-management behavior of teachers studied by that program. (p. 25)

Further, Yinger (1986) questions the stimulated recall technique, the methodology generally used to determine teachers' interactive decisions. Its validity, he suggests, is based on Bloom's (1953) research demonstrating that students listening to an audiorecording of an activity in which they had participated could predict the next event if the recording were stopped. Bloom (as reported in Yinger, 1986) feels that since the recall of events is similar to the recall of private conscious thought, stimulated recall is a valid method for determining conscious thought processes preceding actions. However, Yinger makes a strong case, based on recent cognitive psychology, for doubting "the validity of stimulated recall as a means for accurately reporting interactive thinking" (p. 9).

It has been difficult to figure out how to use the decision-making work in teacher education. The finding that experts do not plan according to the Tyler model may lead one to the following conclusions:

1. Teachers have not been trained well enough in the Tyler model (a conclusion reached by Brophy [1980]). Perhaps, then, we should

spend more time teaching planning to teacher education students in methods courses.

2. Beginning teachers have planning needs different from those of experienced teachers (Borko & Niles, 1987; Morine & Vallance, 1976). Therefore we should continue as usual to train preservice teachers in the Tyler model and inservice teachers with a different model.

3. We should train beginning teachers in the models used by experienced teachers in order to move them more quickly toward expertise. The models used by experienced teachers have been described by Yinger and Clark (1982) as cyclical in nature. Unfortunately, experienced teachers rely heavily on knowledge about the context of a particular classroom and are affected by teachers' planning style (Clark & Yinger, 1979). It is difficult to determine how this way of thinking about teachers' planning can become an element of a teacher education program. Therefore, the Tyler model of planning still prevails in most preservice methods courses.

The information-processing model, then, enhanced the status of teaching, but to date it has not been convincing as a valid description of the way teachers think in practice. From a positivist perspective, the methodological problems inherent in the decision-making research seem insoluble. Further, the model has not appeared to affect teacher education practice, except for using the metaphor of the teacher as decision maker to describe programs that supply teachers with one way of thinking about teaching and an accompanying language for the analysis of teaching (e.g., Madeline Hunter's [1976] "essential elements of instruction").

THE TEACHER AS THINKER: THE REFLECTIVE PRACTITIONER

The concept of the reflective teacher has been in the literature for some time. Throughout the 1970s, a small number of international scholars and teacher educators were interested in reflection and inquiry, based, in large part, on Dewey's (1909/1933) concept of reflective teaching (e.g., Feiman, 1979; Korthagen, 1985; Schaefer, 1967; Tom, 1985; Zeichner & Liston, 1987). This way of thinking presented an alternative to the fixed, positivist conceptions of the CBTE and decision researchers. However, these views were not incorporated within a particular research paradigm. Thus Dewey's alternative of reflection and inquiry was a vague ideal in opposition to the CBTE advocates' concrete, linear, operationalized, and seemingly rational way of thinking, conducting research, and implementing practice.

During the mid to late 1970s, qualitative research methodologies for studying teaching became more accepted, particularly those borrowed from anthropology. Ethnographic research was not only a different methodology; it represented an alternative paradigm for understanding human behavior within the complex culture of the school (Erickson, 1986). The interactive nature of the teaching-learning process in relation to the beliefs and understandings of teachers could therefore be explored. Thus the time was ripe for introducing a way to approach teachers' thinking and action that matched the ideals of Dewey and presented an intuitively valid description of praxis and practical thinking, while also enhancing the status of the teaching profession.

Schön (1987, 8–12) provided a powerful argument against the research paradigm that produced CBTE. He suggests that the technical rationality approach to the development and implementation of knowledge is not useful for practice. His alternative is an "epistemology of practice implicit in the artistic, intuitive processes which some practitioners do bring to situations of uncertainty, instability, uniqueness, and value conflict" (1983, p. 49). While Schön wrote about engineers, town planners, architects, managers, and clinical psychologists, with few references to teachers per se, both the architect and the clinical psychologist encounter teaching situations in their work. The relevance of his concepts to teaching are quite clear.

Schön's argument against the positivist paradigm is particularly powerful because he proposes an alternative way of describing practitioner thinking that is intuitively valid. The important concept in Schön's work is "knowledge-in-action." As compared to the decision-making models or even Dewey's notion of reflection, this type of knowledge/action activity does not rely on a series of conscious steps in a decision-making process. The knowledge is inherent, instead, in the action; it is based, in part, on the past experiences of the practitioner interacting with the particular situation. Interacting with a situation brings forth and expands upon a type of tacit knowledge in an individual that is not consciously articulated at the time. Thus it may not be possible for a practitioner to describe the decision-making processes that led to an action. This way of thinking cannot be described or explained within a technical rationality thinking/action model, since it is neither linear nor conscious.

The knowledge-in-action concept legitimizes a way of thinking that seems to go on constantly in teaching as well as other professions. Further, it does not imply that forgetting the cognitive bases on which one's professional actions are based is a problem, nor does it suggest a lower status for the occupation in which thinking/action goes on. For Schön, knowledge-in-action is an essential element of the epistemology of all professional practice. Teachers, then, join with other professionals in this particular epistemology. Thus Schön found intelligence in the act itself rather than in attempting to make the act seem intelligent.

Knowledge-in-action cannot, by definition, be ascertained by talking with a practitioner, since it is not a conscious process. It may be possible to infer knowledge-in-action from observations of action. However, such observation does not tell us about how the practitioner's experience interacts with the situation. To determine expert knowledge, we need to examine another cognitive process. Schön calls this process, wherein the practitioner consciously interacts with a problematic situation, converses and experiments with it, as "reflection-in-action." It is, at times, possible to observe teachers, supervisors, or mentors reflect-in-action, as Schön did with a number of professionals.

Knowledge and reflection-in-action, as valid and status-building concepts, appeal to teaching scholars and teacher educators and have led to considerations of reflective teacher education programs (see, for example, MacKinnon, 1987; Russell, 1988). The next section examines the potential of reflective teaching concepts for affecting teacher education.

Competencies, Reflection, and Teacher Education

The development of competent and reflective teachers is a value toward which most teacher educators would strive. The problems develop in the ways in which this value is translated into programs designed to produce such teachers. In the CBTE model, the logical relationship between teacher competencies as described in research and the content of teacher education programs is quite clear. The first and most important task is the identification of those competencies held by effective teachers; it then follows logically that the teacher education program should train preservice students in those competencies.

Given this logic, it is understandable that the failure of CBTE would be blamed on the failure of the competency identification task. However, contrary to Houston's (1987) sense that CBTE failed because its research base was not developed, I would suggest that it failed because the model itself was not valid to many teacher educators. The notion that teaching consists of a large number of competencies, identified as behaviors that can be trained in preservice teacher education students, is an inadequate conception for the development of teacher education programs.

In a seminar conducted with teacher educators at the University of Maryland, one conclusion reached was that we could probably train our students in most behavioral competencies with one exception: acting appropriately. Acting appropriately requires judgments, assessments of, and some experience with, the situation. This is what it is difficult to "teach" in preservice teacher education. Competency-based teacher education was not the success expected by its proponents, not because of a poor research base, but because the behavioral, technical translation of a value—the desirability of competent teachers—into a teacher education model was not valid to many teacher educators or teachers.

The relationship between either Dewey's or Schön's concept of reflection and teacher education is less than completely clear. To say that we want teachers who are reflective does not, as in the CBTE model, translate directly into the content of a teacher education program. Schön (1987) himself could only speculate on how reflection-in-action might be developed. He suggests a three-stage process that moves from providing students with technical training, to helping them think like professionals, to enabling them to develop new forms of understanding and action (p. 40). Schön's ambivalence in deciding whether reflection-in-action is a descriptive or a prescriptive concept (Fenstermacher, 1988) contributes to the problem of using it to guide teacher education programs.

The number of reflective teacher education programs have, nonetheless, been increasing in the 1980s (see Calderhead, 1988; Tom, 1985). These programs range from quite technical approaches (Cruickshank & Applegate, 1981) to Deweyan ones (Korthagen, 1985; Zeichner & Liston, 1987) to those based on Schön (Russell, 1988). The difficulty with the latter two types seems to be in developing and sustaining the kind of intellectual energy required to promote reflection-in-action among both teacher education faculty and students. The habits of reflection desired in teacher education students should also be apparent in their teacher educators: reflection by teacher educators on their actions as teacher educators. Such sustained involvement with students and reflective approaches to teaching are not always rewarded in higher education institutions that require scholarly publication, especially when descriptions of programs are not easily published or disseminated. Developing reflective teachers appears to be a difficult task, and program developers feel that their programs are less than completely successful (Korthagen, 1985; Zeichner & Liston, 1987).

I see two threats to the development and implementation of reflective teacher education programs based on Schön or Dewey. The first is a process that seems to take place in education any time a major new idea catches on. This process leads to a "technologizing" of an idea or a program. Based on a positivist, linear conception of the educational and teacher education process, this process operationalizes an abstract value, such as competency or reflection, into a behavior that is generalizable, observable, and teachable. Wise (1979) calls this process "hyperrationalization," and Richardson-Koehler (1988) suggests that the process is guided by efforts to control knowledge and behavior. Such a technical approach could turn reflection into a behavioral competency to be trained in a CBTE program. Cruickshank's (1981) reflective teaching program has been described by Zeichner (1983) and Gore (1987) as technical in nature. The programs that provide students with a language for analyzing teaching and that train teachers in how to observe by using the analysis scheme are also technical in nature. Missing from these programs are the second two elements of learning to reflect-in-action described by Schön: learning to think like a teacher and "making new sense of uncertain, unique or conflicted situations of practice" (1987, p. 39).

The second threat to the development of reflection-in-action programs is the use of a positivist research paradigm with which to conduct research and evaluations around reflective teacher education programs. The kinds of questions asked at conferences focusing on reflective teaching are similar to those asked about CBTE: What is reflection? How can it be measured? Is a reflective teacher more effective than an unreflective teacher? What is the best way to develop reflective teachers? I am not suggesting that these questions are unimportant. They are, however, embedded within a positivist research approach and imply erroneously that answers to such questions through research will provide the form and substance of reflective teacher education programs. What is needed, then, is a way of looking at the concept of reflection-in-action, at how teachers learn such reflection, and at programs designed to develop such learning that match the paradigm inherent in the concept.

More important, however, to the development of reflective teacher education programs is to go beyond Schön's concept of reflection-in-action. Schön's is a descriptive concept, quite empty of content. On what are teachers to reflect? Schön's notions of reflection-in-action is similar to Dewey's reflective action (see, also, Clandinin & Connelly, 1986). Like Dewey's reflective practitioner, Schön's reflection-in-action practitioner focuses on a problem and experiments with the situation. Schön, however, focuses strictly on a thinking/action process, whereas for Dewey (1909/1933) the moral teacher is one who is reflective. Zeichner (1983) points out that Dewey's view suggests that teacher education should involve preparing teachers to be reflective about "the moral, technical and political issues, as well as the instrumental issues, that are embedded in their everyday thinking and practice" (p. 6). As Scheffler (1968) states:

Teachers cannot restrict their attention to the classroom alone, leaving the larger setting and purposes of schooling to be determined by others. They must take active responsibility for the goals to which they are committed, and for the social setting in which these goals may prosper. If they are not to be mere agents of others, of the state, of the military, of the media, of the experts and bureaucrats, they need to determine their own agency through a critical and continual evaluation of the purposes, the consequences and the social context of their calling. (p. 11)

Dewey's critical sense of reflective action is still the one to which we must return to provide the content of teacher education.

CONCLUSIONS

In this analysis of three descriptive/normative concepts of teaching, three conditions have emerged as being necessary for the concepts to be generally accepted in the world of teacher educators and used to drive teacher education practice. The conditions are the potential for the improvement of the status of teaching; the validity of the concept for the ways teachers view themselves and teacher educators view teaching; and a normative view of teaching that projects a content for teacher education that goes beyond a description of the processes of teaching.

The first concept, the competent teacher, evolved into competency-based teacher education programs. While CBTE met the first and third conditions, it failed because of its lack of validity for teacher educators. That is, the nature of teaching seemed more than the sum of a set of behaviors learned in teacher education programs, even though those behaviors were shown to be performed by effective teachers. Many teacher educators find it difficult to accept CBTE because of their practical knowledge that it is just as important for teachers to learn when and how to use a behavior as it is to learn an individual skill in isolation. Such learning requires judgment, experience, and a theoretical sense of the goals of educaton.

The second concept is the teacher as decision maker. A reaction to the behavioral approaches in CBTE, the decision-making research attempted to tap the wisdom of the practitioner. By tying the research approaches to those undertaken in the medical profession, and suggesting that the types of decisions made by teachers are similar to those of executives, this approach met the status-enhancing condition. However, because the decision theorists still operated within the linear, positivist framework of the process-product researchers, there were validity and methodological problems. Further, the decision framework did not provide much guidance for teacher education programs, since the research work was descriptive rather than normative or improvement orientated.

Schön's concepts of knowledge and reflection-in-action have both validating and legitimizing qualities. They describe a way of thinking in action that makes sense to practitioners and that applies to practitioners in many different professions, not just teaching. Schön's conceptualization of reflection does not (nor was intended to) provide the normative aspect necessary for selecting the substance of teacher education. Dewey's concept of reflective action, however, is useful in this respect. Thus a combination of the simultaneous knowledge/action and reflection/action processes described by Schön and Dewey's critical approach to reflection should meet the three conditions necessary for providing an effective basis for teacher education programs.

There is a relationship between the acceptance of a conception of education and the availability of a research approach with compatible assumptions. A tentative and partial answer to the question of why Schön's reflective practitioner has been widely accepted is that qualitative research paradigms have opened our minds to accepting and using very different conceptions of the teaching-learning process.

However, the road in front of us is rocky. We must avoid turning the notion of the reflective teacher into a technical approach to teacher education, as well as resist pressure for research and evaluation approaches that examine the reflective teacher education process in a positivist manner. We in teacher education should, instead, concern ourselves with the content of teachers' reflection, with what teachers will view as problematic. Only then will we develop teachers who are, as Scheffler (1968) suggests, "a class of intellectuals vital to a free society" (p. 11).

REFERENCES

Berliner, D. (1983). The executive functions of teaching. *Instructor, 93,* 29–39.
Bloom, B. S. (1953). Thought processes in lectures and discussions. *Journal of General Education, 7,* 160–169.
Borko, H., & Niles, J. (1987). Planning. In V. Richardson-Koehler (Ed.), *Educators' handbook: A research perspective* (pp. 167–187). New York: Longman.
Borko, H., & Shavelson, R. J. (in press). Teacher decision making. In B. Jones & L. Idol (Eds.), *Dimensions of thinking and cognitive instruction.* Hillsdale, NJ: Erlbaum.

Brophy, J. (1980, July). *Teachers' cognitive activities and overt behaviors.* Paper presented at the International Research Project on Basic Components in the Education of Mathematics Teachers, Michigan State University, East Lansing.

Brophy, J., & Good, T. (1986). Teacher behavior and student achievement. In M. Wittrock (Ed.), *Handbook of research on teaching* (3rd ed.) (pp. 328–375). New York: Macmillan.

Broudy, H. S. (1972). *A critique of PBTE.* Washington, DC: American Association of Colleges for Teacher Education.

Broudy, H. S. (1984). The university and the preparation of teachers. In L. Katz & J. D. Raths (Eds.), *Advances in teacher education* (Vol. 1) (pp. 1–7). Norwood, NJ: Ablex.

Calderhead, J. (1988, April). *Reflective teaching and teacher education.* Paper presented at the annual meeting of the American Educational Research Association, New Orleans.

Clandinin, J., & Connelly, F. M. (1986). The reflective practitioner and practitioners' narrative unities. *Canadian Journal of Education, 11*(2), 184–198.

Clark, C., & Peterson, P. (1986). Teachers' thought processes. In M. C. Wittrock (Ed.), *Handbook of research on teaching* (3rd ed.) (pp. 255–296). New York: Macmillan.

Clark, C., & Yinger, R. (1979). *Three studies of teacher planning* (Research Series No. 55). East Lansing: Institute for Research on Teaching, Michigan State University.

Cooper, J., Jones, H. L., & Weber, W. A. (1973). Specifying teacher competencies. *Journal of Teacher Education, 1*(24), 23.

Cruickshank, D. R., & Applegate, J. H. (1981). Reflective teaching as a strategy for teacher growth. *Educational Leadership, 38*(7), 553–554.

Cuban, L. (1984). *How teachers taught: Constancy and change in American classrooms: 1890–1980.* New York: Longman.

Dewey, J. (1933). *How we think.* Boston: Heath. (Original work published 1909).

Dewey, J. (1962). *The relation of theory to practice in education.* Cedar Falls, IA: Association for Student Teaching. (Original work published 1904)

Doyle, W. (1977). Paradigms for research on teacher effectiveness. In L. Shulman (Ed.), *Review of research in education* (pp. 163–198). Itasca, IL: Peacock.

Doyle, W. (1988, April). *Curriculum in teacher education.* Paper presented at the annual meeting of the American Educational Research Association, New Orleans.

Erickson, F. (1986). Qualitative methods in research on teaching. In M. Wittrock (Ed.), *Handbook of research on teaching* (3rd ed.) (pp. 119–161). New York: Macmillan.

Feiman, S. (1979). Technique and inquiry in teacher education: A curricular case study. *Curriculum Inquiry, 9*(1), 63–79.

Fenstermacher, G. D. (1979). A philosophical consideration of recent research on teacher effectiveness. In L. S. Shulman (Ed.), *Review of research in education 6* (pp. 157–185). Itasca, IL: Peacock.

Fenstermacher, G. (1988). The place of science and epistemology in Schön's conception of reflective practice. In P. P. Grimmett & G. L. Erickson (Eds.), *Reflection in teacher education* (pp. 36–46). New York: Teachers College Press.

Gage, N. (1974). Evaluating ways to help teachers to behave desirably. In W. R. Houston (Ed.), *Competency assessment, research, and evaluation* (pp. 173–185). Syracuse, NY: National Dissemination Center for Performance-Based Education.

Gore, J. (1987). Reflecting on reflective teaching. *Journal of Teacher Education, 38*(2), 33–39.

Gustafson, G., & Powell, M. (1974). A practical approach to a complex problem. In R. W. Houston (Ed.), *Competency assessment, research, and evaluation* (pp. 88–99). Syracuse, NY: National Dissemination Center for Performance-Based Education.

Haberman, M., & Stinnett, T. M. (1973). *Teacher education and the new profession of teaching.* Berkeley, CA: McCutchan.

Heath, R. W., & Nielson, M. (1974). Performance-based teacher education. *Review of Educational Research, 44,* 463–484.

Houston, W. R. (Ed.). (1974). *Competency assessment, research, and evaluation.* Syracuse, NY: National Dissemination Center for Performance-Based Education.

Houston, W. R. (1987). Competency-based teacher education. In M. J. Dunkin (Ed.), *The international encyclopedia of teaching and teacher education* (pp. 86–94). New York: Pergamon.

Hunter, M. (1976). *Prescription for improved instruction.* El Segundo, CA: Teacher Improvement Program.

Koehler, V. (1978). Classroom process research: Present and future. *Journal of Classroom Interaction, 13*(2), 3–11.

Korthagen, F. A. G. (1985). Reflective teaching and preservice teacher education in the Netherlands. *Journal of Teacher Education, 36*(5), 11–15.

MacKinnon, A. M. (1987). Detecting reflection-in-action among preservice elementary science teachers. *Teaching and Teacher Education, 3*(2), 135–146.

McDonald, F. J. (1974). Conceptual model of R&D for CBE. In W. R. Houston (Ed.), *Competency assessment, research, and evaluation* (pp. 11–21). Syracuse, NY: National Dissemination Center for Performance-Based Education.

Morine, G., & Vallance, E. (1976). *Teacher planning.* Beginning Teacher Evaluation Study Technical Report. Special Study C. San Francisco: Far West Laboratory for Education R&D.

National Institute of Education. (1975a). *Teaching as clinical information processing* (Report of Panel 6, National Conference on Studies in Teaching). Washington, DC: Author.

National Institute of Education. (1975b). *Teaching as a linguistic process in a cultural setting* (Report of Panel 5, National Conference on Studies in Teaching). Washington, DC: Author.

Richardson-Koehler, V. (1988). *What works does and doesn't. Journal of Curriculum Studies, 20*(1), 71–79.

Russell, T. (1988). From pre-service teacher education to first year of teaching: A study of theory and practice. In J. Calderhead (Ed.), *Teachers' professional learning*. London: Falmer.

Schaefer, R. J. (1967). *The school as a center of inquiry*. New York: Harper & Row.

Scheffler, I. (1968). University scholarship and the education of teachers. *Teachers College Record, 70*(1), 1–12.

Schön, D. (1983). *The reflective practitioner*. New York: Basic Books.

Schön, D. (1987). *Educating the reflective practitioner*. San Francisco: Jossey-Bass.

Shalock, H. D. (1974). Closing the knowledge gap. In W. R. Houston (Ed.), *Competency assessment, research, and evaluation* (pp. 34–60). Syracuse, NY: National Dissemination Center for Performance-Based Education.

Shavelson, R., & Stern, P. (1981). Research on teachers' pedagogical thoughts, judgments, decisions, and behavior. *Review of Educational Research, 51*, 455–498.

Shulman, L. S. (1986). Paradigms and research programs in the study of teaching: A contemporary perspective. In M. C. Wittrock (Ed.), *Handbook of research on teaching* (3rd ed.) (pp. 3–36). New York: Macmillan.

Shulman, L., & Lanier, J. (1976). *Institute for Research on Teaching Technical Proposal*. East Lansing: Michigan State University.

Soar, R. (1974). Classroom observation. In W. R. Houston (Ed.), *Competency assessment, research, and evaluation* (pp. 100–111). Syracuse, NY: National Dissemination Center for Performance-Based Education.

Tom, A. R. (1985). Inquiring into inquiry-oriented teacher education. *Journal of Teacher Education, 36*(5), 35–44.

Tyler, R. W. (1950). *Basic principles of curriculum and instruction*. Chicago: University of Chicago Press.

Wise, A. (1979). *Legislated learning*. Berkeley: University of California Press.

Yinger, R. (1979). *A study of teacher planning: Descriptions and theory development using ethnographic and information processing methods*. Unpublished doctoral dissertation, Michigan State University.

Yinger, R. (1986, April). *Examining thought in action: A theoretical and methodological critique of research on interactive teaching*. Paper presented at the annual meeting of the American Educational Research Association, San Francisco.

Yinger, R., & Clark, C. (1982). *Understanding teachers' judgments about instruction: The task, the method, and the meaning* (Research Series No. 121). East Lansing: Institute for Research on Teaching, Michigan State University.

Zeichner, K. (1983). Alternative paradigms of teacher education. *Journal of Teacher Education, 34*(3), 3–9.

Zeichner, K., & Liston, D. (1987). Theory and practice in the evolution of an inquiry-oriented student teaching program. *Harvard Education Review, 57*, 23–48.

2 Reflective Practice in Teacher Education

PETER P. GRIMMETT
University of British Columbia

ALLAN M. MACKINNON
University of Toronto

GAALEN L. ERICKSON
University of British Columbia

THEODORE J. RIECKEN
University of Victoria

There is currently considerable interest and debate about the notion of "reflective practice" in the field of teacher education. While much of the recent debate has been stimulated by Schön's (1983, 1987, 1988) writings, other scholars have provided extensive practical and theoretical accounts of how this construct might be utilized in conceptualizing teaching practice in a variety of contexts. Close examination of this rapidly accumulating body of literature on the nature of reflective teaching reveals a diversity of meanings that are attached to this and similar terms; further, it reveals little agreement on what conditions may be required to foster reflective teaching.

This circumstance of a burgeoning but diverse literature calls for clarification of both the usage of terms and the nature of the underlying assumptions operative in the various research programs spawned from alternative perspectives. This chapter is one attempt at such conceptual clarification.

The study of reflective practice in teacher education is essentially concerned with how educators make sense of the phenomena of experience that puzzle or perplex them. The purpose of the endeavor is the pursuit of meaning as distinct from the pursuit of truth or fact (Donmoyer, 1985). Because teaching involves the interaction of complex human beings capable of creating an inordinate number of ways of characterizing phenomena experienced within a diverse social and linguistic culture, questions of meaning precede questions of truth. In accentuating this point, Guba (1981) writes:

> Human behavior is rarely, if ever, context-free; hence knowledge of human behavior individually or in groups is necessarily idiographic, and differences are at least as important as similarities to an understanding of what is happening. (p. 78)

In other words, how subjects attribute meaning to phenomena is an important object of inquiry. One form of knowledge, then, in this research genre represents the explication of educators' meanings and understandings as they engage both in the actual practice of teaching and in the process of examining the practice of others. The purpose is neither prediction nor explanation; rather, it is to explore phenomenologically how educators create what Shulman (1987) describes as the "wisdom of practice" within the complex and dynamic world of teaching.

CONCEPTIONS OF REFLECTION

The recent surge of interest in this topic has seen many scholars of diverse traditions and backgrounds beginning to craft ideas around the concept of reflection. A brief examination of two recent review articles will provide the reader with an overview of some of the issues in this domain and the way in which they have been conceptualized.

Zeichner's (1986) review focuses on selected research reports outlining various approaches to the preparation of reflective teachers during preservice education. He observes that, while most of the reports describe the types of strategies used in their respective programs, they vary considerably in terms of the degree to which the reported programs are explicitly justified in a theoretical stance. He classifies these reports according to the level at which a reflective intervention is directed. In some cases, entire teacher education programs have been revised; in others, individual courses have been altered without modifying the overall program.

Tom (1985) describes his conceptualization of the literature in this field in terms of inquiry-oriented teacher education. He identifies three dimensions. The first dimension has to do with the *scope of inquiry*. Some approaches are more narrow in scope, delimiting teaching to technical aspects; while others are broader, in that they focus on making problematic the moral and political contexts within which teaching is embedded. The second dimension considers these approaches according to the *model of inquiry* employed. Distinctions are based on the rigor of the model being used and the projected outcomes of the program. The third dimension makes an *ontological distinction* between those approaches that view educational phenomena as objective, or basically value neutral, and those that view reality as being socially constructed.

Both these reviews illustrate that, while many teacher educators use terms and employ approaches that initially appear to be very similar, there may indeed be little shared meaning about either reflective teaching or inquiry-oriented teacher education. There appears to be even less agreement on what characterizes the content of reflective inquiry and on what kinds of contexts could best foster such a process. Nevertheless, many teacher educators seem to be persuaded that reflection (however they understand and operationalize the term) is a worthy aim in teacher education.

In summary, scholars who have dealt with the concept of reflection—whether they have focused on its philosophic origins or on its value in teacher education programs—have used somewhat different definitions of the concept. The purpose of this review, then, is to extend the thinking of Zeichner and Tom by developing a more extensive system of categorization for examining studies of reflection in teacher education. In so doing we hope to clarify some of the assumptions underlying researchers' and program developers' conception of reflection; equally importantly, we will attempt to explicate the stance taken toward the role that knowledge plays in the development of teacher education programs. Thus, this chapter conceptualizes research on reflective practice according to three basic perspectives derived from the question: How is knowledge, whether derived from research or practice, viewed in terms of its contribution to the education of teachers? Put differently, is this knowledge seen as an external source for mediating action in the sense that it *directs* teachers in their practice; or is such knowledge regarded as *informing* practice as teachers deliberate among competing alternatives for action; or does such knowledge constitute one source of information that teachers use metaphorically to *apprehend* practice as they reconstruct their classroom experiences?

We argue that the categories presented below distinguish between and among three different perspectives on reflection, based on the epistemological stance each represents. We examine the presuppositions about the nature of the knowledge that structures the general conception of reflection represented by each perspective. For each perspective we consider the relationship between knowledge and reflection in terms of three basic categories: (1) the source of the knowledge that is reflected upon; (2) the mode of knowing represented by the particular conception of reflection; and (3) the use to which that knowledge is put as a result of the reflective process.

Three caveats need to be made here. First, this review is not exhaustive; rather, it represents the variety of thinking and empirical work that has been carried out and reported in a rapidly increasing body of literature. Further, we focus most of our attention on the third perspective on reflection because, as an emerging conception, it has received little attention in the literature to date. The first two perspectives are discussed only briefly; the purpose is to illustrate these, so as to provide a comparative frame for the third perspective. Second, we do not claim that the perspectives are either exhaustive or mutually exclusive. They appear to offer a fruitful way of analyzing the differences in the research studies examined, but they should be construed as only one among many possibilities for sorting and making sense of this literature. Finally, it must be acknowledged that the reflective process, whether it be described by a practitioner or by a researcher, is dependent on the context, on the richness of repertoire that a person brings to that context, and on his or her ability to draw on a level of reflection appropriate to that context. Hence the nature of the description emanating from these studies must necessarily be incomplete and occasionally fragmented. Caution is required when attempting to generalize across settings in studies of this nature.

PERSPECTIVES ON REFLECTION

The term *perspective* is not intended to refer to a deep psychological or philosophical conception that represents a general worldview or an intellectual lineage that encompasses the full range of a person's lived experiences. Rather, *perspective* is used here simply to describe a cluster of studies that appear to possess similar epistemological commitments regarding the roles and purposes assigned to a knowledge base in the reflective process. Accordingly, we have grouped studies of reflective practice around the three perspectives of instrumental mediation of action, deliberation among competing views of teaching, and the reconstruction of experience.

Reflection as Instrumental Mediation of Action

This first perspective represents a view of reflection as a process that leads to thoughtful, mediated action, usually involving the putting into practice of research findings and theoretical formulations of education. From this perspective, the purpose of reflection is *instrumental* in that the reflective process is used to help teachers replicate classroom practices that empirical research has found to be effective. The knowledge source in this type of reflection is usually that of an external authority. Educational researchers, journal articles, and research-tested theories of education, rather than actual situations of classroom practice, are regarded as knowledge sources. Given the source of this knowledge, it must be represented primarily in a propositional format; hence the mode of knowing is *technological* (Zumwalt, 1982). Propositional knowledge is reflected upon and then applied to practice in an instrumental manner. Within this conception of reflection, knowledge is used to *direct* practice. One example of this perspective can be obtained from the writings of Cruickshank (1985), who views reflective teaching as a form of laboratory experience similar to micro-teaching—suitable for use not only in preservice teacher education but also in inservice training, graduate education, and research on teaching. In the preservice setting it is used in methods courses to help "prospective teachers to gain knowledge of theory and then to learn to apply this knowledge under controlled, laboratory conditions" (p. 705). An example of this would be teaching preservice or inservice teachers about a learning theory or motivation theory and "then [asking them to] use Reflective Teaching to see how well students can apply this knowledge in the act of teaching" (p. 705). This form of laboratory exercise begins with a micro-teaching session, after which small groups of peers observe and then discuss the videotaped lessons, the performance of the teachers, and pupil learning. Drawing from Cruickshank's work, Peters (1985) investigated the outcomes of the reflective teaching model, claiming, among other things, that "students will identify [a] greater number and wider variety of variables present during the act of teaching" (p. 61).

In summary, this perspective describes a conception of reflection as thoughtfulness about action—contemplation that leads to conscious, deliberate moves, usually taken to apply research findings or educational theory in practice. The use of the word *apply* is significant here, for those who subscribe to this conception of reflection seem to hold an associated view of educational theory and research findings about teaching that is technological in character. It is a view of reflection wherein one could expect the knower (in this case the person reflecting on the knowledge) to use knowledge to *direct*, or *control*, practice. Put differently, one could expect the knower to ensure that his or her practice *conforms* to what research has found to have positive effects on student learning. The group of researchers espousing this perspective are optimistic in the sense that they assume changes in teachers' practice can be brought about through this kind of reflection. They do, however, refer to technical limitations in bringing about reflectivity among education students, such as the lack of time afforded in teacher education programs. A further distinguishing feature of this perspective is the view that new information comes solely from authorities who publish in journals, rather than from the practice situation itself.

Reflection as Deliberating among Competing Views of Teaching

A second perspective in teacher education proposes a conception of reflection based on deliberation and choice among competing versions of good teaching. This involves consideration of educational events in context. Reflective activity includes anticipation of the consequences following from different lines of action, which are derived from these competing versions of good teaching. In this perspective, external authority is also regarded as a source of knowledge, but with the difference that the understanding of that knowledge is usually mediated through teaching colleagues and the context of the actual teaching situation. The mode of knowing is deliberative (Zumwalt, 1982). Knowledge about teaching is viewed as having a relativistic quality. The practitioner uses an "informed eclecticism" (Schwab, 1969) in his or her practice. Research knowledge in this kind of reflective process is used not to direct practice, but to inform it.

In a study that illustrates the importance of context in reflection, Trumbull (1986) examined teachers' responses to a microcomputer simulation designed to illustrate different classroom management strategies. She found a wide variation in teachers' interpretations of hypothetical classroom management problems that were presented as part of the simulation. Teachers often cited the importance of context in relation to decision making in classroom settings. For these teachers, context and personal experience were an important part of understanding the problem situation. She writes:

> Their remarks indicate that they were not comfortable ascribing meanings to the characteristics mentioned in the descriptions. . . . [They] often referred to their own experience to interpret the problem situations. These references can be seen as attempts to provide context that would give meaning. (p. 143)

Grimmett (1984) and Grimmett and Crehan (1987) found that the reflective process embedded within instructional supervision of in-service teachers became actualized only when both supervisor and teacher are capable of functioning conceptually at a highly complex level (Schroder, Driver, & Streufert, 1967). Where one of the participants' conceptual functioning was low, reflection and the deriving of insight from the framing and reframing of classroom events rarely occurred. By analyzing the content of conference dialogues, Grimmett explored the conditions that accompanied instances of teacher reflection and insight. When supervisor and teacher freely exchanged views and regarded feedback as a source of information to be evaluated critically, reflective dialogue was promoted. Supervisors framed research knowledge in the form of questions that apprised teachers of information considered useful for deriving insightful appreciation of the lesson under discussion. Indeed, the criteria on which Grimmett judged the conference dialogue to be reflective was whether it brought fresh insights to bear on the teacher's lesson and facilitated the teacher's viewing of his or her behavior as a causal factor in his or her professional development.

Focusing on the world of action as experienced by practicing teachers, Sanders and McCutcheon (1986) describe a process of practice-centered inquiry in which surprise or perplexity can initiate reflection. They comment that "when teachers get surprised by a set of exams, or an unexpected student response, they ask themselves why it happened, and what factors might have contributed to it" (p. 65). Sanders and McCutcheon suggest that teachers address these practice-centered questions by being thoughtful and seeking out all the information they can before deciding what to do to improve the situation. Based on these deliberations and actions in the practice setting, Sanders and McCutcheon argue that practitioners are able to develop an extensive repertoire of practical knowledge of "practical theories of teaching" that primarily take the form of "rules of thumb" and sets of expectations. Practice-centered inquiry is used widely by teachers, many of whom engage consciously in the process. Sanders and McCutcheon argue that teachers and administrators can use the basic structure of practice-centered inquiry as a set of tools to engage in cooperative deliberation about teaching.

Those who subscribe to this perspective on reflection are distinguished by their attention to the context of educational events and by the idea that, in reflecting about particular events in context, one deliberates between and among competing views of teaching and examines each in light of the consequences of the action it entails. Thus there is a tendency for those who espouse this perspective to subscribe to an eclectic view of knowledge, the test of which is whether it benefits student learning.

Reflection as Reconstructing Experience

A third perspective in teacher education includes conceptions of reflection as the *reorganization* or *reconstruction of experience*. This leads to new understandings of:

- action situations
- self-as-teacher, in terms of the cultural milieu of teaching
- taken-for-granted assumptions about teaching (derived from a critical-theoretical stance)

For each of these aspects, the source of knowledge for reflection is found in both the context of the action setting and in the practical application of personal knowledge. Puzzlement and subsequent reflection about a practice situation or the presuppositions that guide action in it lead to a mode of knowing that could be described as dialectical. In this view of the reflective process, knowledge is seen as emergent and often depicted as being metaphorical in nature (Lakoff & Johnson, 1980). That is, understanding a situation is often a matter of "seeing-as," a process in which practitioners recast, reframe, and reconstruct past understandings in such a way as to *generate fresh appreciations* of the puzzlement or surprise inherent in a practice situation. In this perspective, knowledge, including personal understandings of practice situations, is used to *transform* practice. Each of the three aspects subsumed under this perspective is dealt with below.

Reconstructing action situations. The chief feature of this aspect is the degree to which the *act* of problem setting in an action situation is made problematic in and of itself. Here, reflection is seen as a way in which a teacher can either attend to features of the situation that were previously ignored or assign new significance to features that were previously identified. In either case, reflection involves recasting situations once they have been clarified, rethinking the assumptions on which initial understandings of a problematic issue were based, and beginning to reconsider the range of possible responses a teacher might use (Pugach & Johnson, Chapter 10, this volume).

MacKinnon (1987) developed a scheme for detecting reflection-in-action among preservice teachers enrolled in a science methods course. Drawing from Fuller and Bown's (1975) developmental conceptualization of teacher concerns and Schön's (1983) analysis of reflection-in-action, he examined the manner in which methods students made sense of their teaching performance in the context of clinical supervision by their methods instructor. MacKinnon's criteria for detecting reflection are built around Schön's concepts of problem setting and reframing and Fuller and Bown's notion that, while interpreting classroom events from pupil-centered perspectives is an indication of an education student's developing into a teacher, such students nevertheless tend to rely on their personal experience as learners in constructing meaning from classroom events. MacKinnon argues that, when preservice teachers are guided through a "cycle of reflection" consisting of problem setting, reframing, and resolution, they become reflective in the analysis of their own teaching.

The reconstruction of practice situations that occurs in student teachers is the focus of a case study by Laboskey and Wilson (1987), which investigated the potential effects that becoming a "researcher in practice context" (Schön, 1983, p. 63) had on the student teachers' development of reflection. Student teachers were presented with opportunities to do case study research on themselves as teachers. They were asked to spend a period of three weeks looking carefully at their teaching in order to identify and explore an issue of interest. To aid in the process, they kept a journal and were observed and debriefed by their supervisor and a peer. The cases produced by the student teachers fell into three general categories: descriptive, problem setting, and problem solving. Twenty-three of the forty-five cases analyzed had problem-setting characteristics—that is, they identified, scrutinized, and clarified a problem that the student teachers had encountered in teaching. These cases were essentially exemplars of student teachers' framing and reframing the problematic situation.

Within this problem-setting category, Laboskey and Wilson identified two types of cases. One consisted of the framing of a problem around self-in-a-situation, while the other consisted of framing a problem around a *concept*, such as humor, continuity, risk taking, flexibility, and accountability. In the latter cases, they argued that the student teachers had focused on a principle they had abstracted from their practice and, in doing so, had begun to reframe a problem situation in a manner that led them to new insights about teaching.

The sort of experience that Laboskey and Wilson recount on the part of the student teachers in their program seems to be what Garman (1986) had in mind when she wrote about reflection as being at the heart of clinical supervision, indeed the process of inquiry within the teacher's practice. Garman discusses techniques designed to encourage a practitioner to understand his or her own frames of reference through "theorizing in the context of practice"—understanding and depicting meaningful human action for the purpose of guiding practice. She represents the process in five steps:

1. involvement in a scenario;
2. a record of the scenario;
3. making sense of the records:

4. making an "educational-construal"—an abbreviated, manageable rendering of events and meanings for future use;
5. a confirmation—a way to determine whether the construal has meaning to other practitioners.

Studies reported in this aspect of the reconstruction of experience perspective on reflection address the degree to which the act of problem setting in an action situation is made problematic. In this process of reframing the practice setting, teachers are able to bring new meanings and ways of seeing to problems in their practice. As such, the role that knowledge plays in this particular conception is one that provides the knower with metaphors that permit him or her to *appreciate* and *transform* practice situations.

Reconstructing self-as-teacher. Literature reviewed in this aspect of reflection focuses on the individual's view of himself or herself as a teacher rather than on a reconstruction of the practice setting. Because much of the work in this genre expects teachers to become more aware of the cultural milieu in which they operate, the studies tend to be phenomenological or hermeneutic in orientation, aimed at providing interpretive accounts of the way teachers structure their knowledge and their worlds of practice.

Van Manen is an educational theorist who has written extensively about the nature of reflection in educational settings. His writings, and those of writers who draw on his work, can be located in this conception of reflection. In drawing on German and Dutch scholars whose work has come to be known as *Geisteswissenschaftliche Pädagogik* (human science pedagogy), Van Manen (1987) has articulated a conception of pedagogy that includes as one of its principles, that of "self-reflection of life." He describes three ways in which the idea of life's reflectivity has been used in hermeneutic pedagogy: self-reflection as an ontological phenomenon, self-reflection as a life philosophy, and self-reflection as a methodological concept. As an ontological phenomenon, self-reflection is concerned with ways of being in the world. It is concerned with the nature of being human and how we come to understand our own existence. Human beings acquire an understanding of themselves through self-reflection, and it is only through life that one can understand life. In using the concepts of self-reflection as a life philosophy and self-reflection as a *methodology*, Van Manen seeks to gain insights into the action of teachers, not only as educators but also as adults who share a lived reality with children. To be self-reflective in this sense is to be attentive to the relationship between theory and action. From a methodological point of view, he writes:

> Pedagogy's task is to practise an active self-reflection (a thoughtfulness) on the reality in which adults live with children in order to be able to offer those adults (parents, teachers, and other educators) insights or understandings. (p. 13)

Hultgren (1987a) is one of those who has drawn upon Van Manen's framework in her phenomenological study of student teachers' experiences. She was interested in understanding what it meant to be a student teacher, what it was like to experience student teaching. The conception of reflection that she aimed to engender in her student teachers is described in her course syllabus in terms of reflective teaching. Learning to become a reflective teacher entails a series of experiences in both the course and practicum settings wherein the students "come to understand [their] own lifeworlds and how these are connected with taking action in the everyday lifeworld of teaching" (p. 37). Becoming reflective

> entails a personal search, a search for meaning wherein a central question for you will be—what, in my existence as a person, in my relations with others, in my work as a teacher, is of real concern to me and what sense can I make of it? (p. 38)

Coming from a somewhat different theoretical perspective, Munby (1987) used Schön's (1983) conceptions of the role of metaphor and "seeing-as" in practical action to examine metaphors in teachers' language and the role that they might play in teachers' professional actions. Through his analyses of teachers' linguistic patterns, he investigated the way in which teachers construct their professional realities, documenting how metaphors evolve through time and influence the development of practical knowledge. Munby comments on some of the assumptions that appear to separate and confound the realities of actual practice and those of teacher education programs: "We are involved in trying to document and analyze developments in professional knowledge that have been masked or obscured by the assumptions that dominate existing teacher education programs" (p. 9). He goes on to argue that these assumptions range from the belief that research knowledge in the form of propositional statements can be applied directly to the practice setting to the belief that the primary purpose of the practicum is to obtain a set of teaching skills through applying this propositional knowledge in a nonreflective manner.

A similar theoretical focus guided the work of Russell (1987) in his examination of teachers' views of the relationship between theory and practice. Interested in the changes that occur in teachers' perspectives on their work over time, Russell interviewed fifteen teachers with varying teaching experience. He notes a disparity between the way in which experienced and inexperienced teachers view theory and practice. He concludes:

> The picture that emerges suggests that learning to teach is *not* a two-step process of (1) learning theory and (2) putting theory into practice. Yet our culture in general and our universities in particular use the phrase theory into practice so easily and freely that it would be surprising if those electing programs of teacher education did not *see their own learning as* a two-step proces. (p. 9)

Using a phenomenological conception of knowledge construction and use, Elbaz (1981, 1983) presents a case study of one teacher's practical knowledge in which she described the influences that setting and personal history had on this teacher's practice. She argues that although decisions are unique to their circumstances, making decisions involves a process of deliberation involving the use of rules of practice, practical principles, and images. Elbaz's concept of image is a composite of a teacher's beliefs, values, needs, and feelings, often encapsulated in terms of brief metaphoric statements relating her ideas about teaching. Images, then, allow teachers to

> marshall experience, theoretical knowledge and school folklore . . . to guide the teacher's thinking and to organize knowledge in the relevant area. The image is generally imbued with a judgement of value and constitutes a guide to the intuitive realization of the teacher's purposes. (1981, p. 61)

In summary, those who hold to this conception of reflection argue that experience, as embodied in one's personal biography, constitutes both the content and consequence of reflective thinking. That is, reflection shapes and restructures one's personal knowledge about teaching as well as about life. Such reconstruction of self-as-teacher enables the knower to *appreciate* and *transform* his or her understanding of the cultural milieu in which he or she attempts to practice pedagogy.

Reconstructing taken-for-granted assumptions about teaching. This final conception of reflection in teacher education consists of reconstructing taken-for-granted assumptions about teaching. Reflection, according to this literature, is a means by which critical theory (Habermas, 1971) can be practiced with an emancipatory intent—that is, it allows a practitioner to identify and address the social, political, and cultural conditions that frustrate and constrain self-understanding. Critical reflection, then, begins with such questions as to what ends and in whose interest knowledge is being used.

Drawing on the critical social theory of Habermas, the early Van Manen (1977) argued that, within the notion of self-reflection, there can be different levels of reflectivity. These levels of reflectivity correspond to three forms of knowledge and the associated cognitive interests, among which Habermas distinguishes the empirical-analytic, the hermeneutic-phenomenological, and the critical-theoretical. The empirical-analytic level of reflectivity is concerned with ends-means questions and the relationships between theory and practice. At the hermeneutic-phenomenological level, reflective concerns focus on the nature of lived experience and understanding the life-worlds of those with whom one interacts. Van Manen distinguished these two levels from the critical-theoretical level, which employs an *emancipatory* theory of truth. This latter view of truth is "the deliberative rationality of formulating norms, roles, and knowledge about possible ways of life undistorted by repressive forms of authority, privilege and the vested interests of exploitation" (Van Manen, 1977, p. 222). In an educational context, then, this third level of reflectivity requires one to examine and reflect upon the underlying assumptions, norms, and rules that constrain and shape one's practice. It is only through a process of reflective reconstruction of these taken-for-granted assumptions that one can be emancipated from possible forms of exploitation.

Smyth (1986) and Carr and Kemmis (1983) have been major proponents of the view of reflection that draws on a critical-theoretical perspective. These researchers draw explicitly from Habermas and Van Manen the notion that critical reflection "endorses the self-reflective stance of the 'practical' in explicating the aims and values of adopted moral positions in education and schooling" (Smyth, 1986, p. 18). They argue that critical reflection is necessary to identify the means by which educational goals and practices become "distorted" and "constrained" by structural forces in educational systems. Furthermore, through critical reflection one is able to develop emancipatory strategies in an attempt to obtain a greater degree of justice and wisdom in one's educational practice.

Considerable empirical research has been conducted in this particular genre of reflection studies. Drawing on Van Manen's "levels of reflectivity," Goodman (1986) developed a social studies methods course that taught students to develop and implement curricula from a critical perspective. An early field experience program that took place in conjunction with this course was designed to help methods students develop some degree of critical reflectivity. With assistance, these students were able to develop and teach such units as:

- "Super Views of the News"—a grade-six unit that critically examined the role of the mass media in shaping our lives
- "The Fifties: A Decade of Fun and Fear"—a grade-five unit that critically studied American life in the 1950s, focusing on the civil rights movement, McCarthyism, and particular forms of entertainment

Other examples of this type of work can be found in reports by Ross and Hannay (1986), who recommend the adoption of a critical-reflective stance in preservice social studies teacher education. They advocate cooperation among teacher educators, institutions, and classroom teachers in integrating the ideal of critical thinking and reflective inquiry into the everyday world of teaching and teacher education. They write that:

> Preservice students must be encouraged to reflect on the knowledge and skills overtly and covertly perpetuated through such taken-for-granted facets of everyday school life as textbooks, school organization, student tasks, or interaction patterns. (p. 12)

Likewise, Wedman and Martin (1986) argue that student teachers who have developed and practiced reflective skills through journal writing may be better able to overcome some of the negative effects currently associated with field experiences by questioning and examining routinized instructional practices and institutional procedures.

Hultgren (1987b) describes a similar conception of reflection in the context of a graduate course on critical thinking in which students were encouraged to learn about critical-reflective thinking. Some of the insights her graduate students came to as they grappled with their lived knowledge included understanding that critical thinking is more than a cognitive skill to be mastered, that critical thinking is not reserved for the gifted and talented, and that teachers are not naturally critical thinkers merely because they are engaged in fostering learning. More importantly, they came to conclude that critical thinking is not an intellectual process that can be imposed in schools whose environments do not support emancipatory learning; rather, "it is a way of being that must evolve as a way of being with others" (Hultgren, 1987b, p. 30).

Oberg (1986) and Oberg and Field (1986) describe the reflective activities of experienced teachers enrolled in a graduate-level curriculum course. As part of a course she teaches, Oberg guides her students through a process of self-reflection that focuses on teachers' experiences drawn from actual practice. By involving teachers in a practice-based kind of reflection, Oberg aims to have teachers make explicit for themselves the intentions and underlying assumptions, knowledge, values, and sensitivities that guide their practice. Oberg and Field comment:

> It is the teacher's own interpretation of theoretical and empirical knowledge, which along with her skills and practical wisdom, determine how she acts in any given situation. One way for the teacher to . . . understand explicitly the reasons for her actions is to reflect on her practice and to attempt to identify the assumptions underlying it. (p. 7)

As used by Oberg and her students, the conduct of reflection has four broad *moves* and uses four *vehicles* to facilitate the process. The first move consists of analyzing oneself as a practitioner by focusing on one's own professional actions. The second move involves an analysis of the meaning one associates with such professional actions. The third move consists of unraveling the underlying assumptions of the meaning one constructs around one's actions in order to perform the fourth move—reconsidering one's practices in light of those assumptions.

The four vehicles used to aid the development of teachers' self-reflection are readings that represent alternative views of the educational process; journal writings in which teachers record actual events of practice; written assignments designed to coalesce the journal writing and the reflective process; and dialogues in which Oberg and her students discuss their journal entries and reflective thinking. She describes the changes this process brought about in some of her students:

> In the course of their reflections, these teachers and others like them began to identify specific ways in which their practice might become more educative, that is, more consistent with their beliefs and values, their idea of the educational good. (Oberg, 1986, p. 31)

In summary, literature included in this third aspect of the perspective viewing reflection as the reconstruction of experience has focused on how teachers explicate the taken-for-granted assumptions and humanly constructed distortions that constrain and frustrate practice. All forms of knowledge, but especially personal knowledge, are regarded as "the social reconstruction of reality" (Berger & Luckman, 1967), the uncovering of which is essential for human emancipation. Reflection is the process by which such emancipation occurs through the explication of previously taken-for-granted assumptions. Knowledge in this conception provides the metaphors that *transform* one's understanding of the political, institutional, social, and moral constraints that impinge on the practice of teaching.

CONCLUDING NOTE

This review has examined selected studies in the field of teacher education that have used some notion of reflection as the primary theoretical construct in design and/or interpretation of findings. We have found it useful to identify three distinct perspectives based primarily on an analysis of the following questions: (1) *What* is being reflected upon?, (2) *How* is the reflective process engaged?, and (3) What is the *purpose* of reflection? A summary of how the three perspectives differ in responding to these three questions is presented in Figure 2.1.

Although we do not claim that these perspectives represent anything more than a useful schematic or heuristic for bringing some clarity to this field of inquiry, we think that this sort of conceptual mapping can have some important consequences. First, it can be used to orient

FIGURE 2.1 Summary of Epistemological Commitments for Three Perspectives on Reflection in Teacher Education

	Perspectives on Reflection	Source of Knowledge for Reflection	Mode of Reflective Knowing	Purpose of Reflection
1.	Reflection as instrumental mediation of action	External authority (mediated through action)	Technical	Directs
2.	Reflection as deliberating among competing views of teaching	External authority (mediated through context)	Deliberative	Informs
3.	Reflection as reconstructing experience	Context (mediated through colleagues/self)	Dialectical	Apprehends and transforms

the novice to this somewhat difficult and confusing terrain. Second, it can also provide a sense of direction for those who are already exploring this territory. By pointing out some of the significant epistemological landmarks and providing a brief description of the most salient features of those landmarks, we hope that even seasoned travelers may see features that they had previously overlooked. Finally, we hope that our initial endeavor at mapping will spur others into this important activity—leading to improvement and further clarification of our modest attempts and to the identification of new features and the charting of new territories. It is through the nurturing and sustaining of exploratory work *along with* the conceptual mapping of its findings that a field of inquiry will prove to be both habitable and fruitful for those who seek to live and work there.

REFERENCES

Berger, P. L., & Luckmann, T. (1967). *The social construction of reality: A treatise in the sociology of knowledge.* New York: Doubleday.

Carr, C., & Kemmis, S. (1983). *Becoming critical: Knowing through action research.* Victoria, Australia: Deakin University Press.

Cruickshank, D. R. (1985). Uses and benefits of reflective teaching. *Phi Delta Kappan, 66*(10), 704–706.

Donmoyer, R. (1985). The rescue from relativism: Two failed attempts and an alternative strategy. *Educational Researcher, 14*(10), 13–20.

Elbaz, F. (1981). The teacher's practical knowledge: Report of a case study. *Curriculum Inquiry, 11*(1), 43–71.

Elbaz, F. (1983). *Teacher thinking: A study of practical knowledge.* London: Croom Helm.

Fuller, F. F., & Bown, O. H. (1975). Becoming a teacher. In K. Ryan (Ed.), *Teacher education* (NSSE 74th Yearbook) (pp. 25–52). Chicago: University of Chicago Press.

Garman, N. B. (1986). Reflection, the heart of clinical supervision: A modern rationale for professional practice. *Journal of Curriculum and Supervision, 2*(1), 1–24.

Goodman, J. (1986). Making early field experience meaningful: A critical approach. *Journal of Education for Teaching, 12*(2), 109–125.

Grimmett, P. P. (1984). The supervision conference: An investigation of supervisory effectiveness through analysis of participants' conceptual functioning. In P. P. Grimmett (Ed.), *Research in teacher education: Current problems and future prospects in Canada* (pp. 131–166). Vancouver: CSTE/CSCI Publications.

Grimmett, P. O., & Crehan, E. P. (1987, June). *A study of the effects of supervisors' intervention on teacher classroom management performance.* Paper presented at the annual meeting of the Canadian Society for the Study of Education, Hamilton, Ontario.

Guba, E. G. (1981). Criteria for assessing the trustworthiness of naturalistic inquiries. *Educational Communications and Technological Journal, 29*(2), 75–91.

Habermas, J. (1971). *Knowledge and human interests* (J. Shapiro, Trans.). Boston: Beacon Press.

Hultgren, F. H. (1987a). The student teacher as person: Reflections on pedagogy and being. *Phenomenology and Pedagogy, 5*(1), 35–50.

Hultgren, F. H. (1987b). *What does it mean to experience critical thinking? An interpretive-critical perspective.* Paper presented at the annual meeting of the American Educational Research Association, Washington, DC.

Laboskey, V. K., & Wilson, S. M. (1987, April). *Case writing as a method in preservice teacher education.* Paper presented at the annual meeting of the American Educational Research Association, Washington, DC.

Lakoff, G., & Johnson, M. (1980). *Metaphors we live by.* Chicago: University of Chicago Press.

MacKinnon, A. M. (1987). Detecting reflection-in-action among preservice elementary science teachers. *Teaching and Teacher Education, 3*(2), 135–145.

Munby, H. (1987, April). *Metaphors, puzzles, and teachers' professional knowledge.* Paper presented at the annual meeting of the American Educational Research Association, Washington, DC.

Oberg, A. (1986, April). *Staff development through individual reflection on practice.* Paper presented at the annual meeting of the American Educational Research Association, San Francisco, CA.

Oberg, A., & Field, R. (1986). Teacher development through reflection on practice. Unpublished manuscript, University of Victoria.

Peters, J. L. (1985). Research on reflective teaching: A form of laboratory teaching experience. *Journal of Research and Development in Education, 18*(3), 55–62.

Ross, W., & Hannay, L. M. (1986). Towards a critical theory of reflective inquiry. *Journal of Teacher Education, 37*(4), 9–15.

Russell, T. L. (1987, April). *Learning the professional knowledge of teaching: Views of the relationship between "theory" and "practice."* Paper presented at the annual meeting of the American Educational Research Association, Washington, DC.

Sanders, D. P., & McCutcheon, G. (1986). The development of practical theories of teaching. *Journal of Curriculum and Supervision, 2*(1), 50–67.

Schön, D. A. (1983). *The reflective practitioner: How professionals think in action.* New York: Basic Books.

Schön, D. A. (1987). *Educating the reflective practitioner: Toward a new design for teaching and learning in the professions.* San Francisco: Jossey-Bass.

Schön, D. A. (1988). Coaching reflective teaching. In P. P. Grimmett & G. L. Erickson (Eds.), *Reflection in teacher education* (pp. 19–29). New York: Teachers College Press.

Schroder, H. M., Driver, M. J., & Streufert, S. (1967). *Human information pro-*

cessing: Individuals and groups functioning in complex social situations. New York: Holt, Rinehart & Winston.

Schwab, J. (1969). *The practical: A language for curriculum.* Washington, DC: National Education Association.

Shulman, L. S. (1987). The wisdom of practice: Managing complexity in medicine and teaching. In D. C. Berliner & B. V. Rosenshine (Eds.), *Talks to teachers* (pp. 369–386). New York: Random House.

Smyth, W. J. (1986). *Reflection in action.* Geelong, Australia: Deakin University Press.

Tom, A. (1985). Inquiring into inquiry-oriented teacher education. *Journal of Teacher Education, 36*(5), 35–44.

Trumbull, D. J. (1986). Teachers' envisioning: A foundation for artistry. *Teaching and Teacher Education, 2*(2), 139–144.

Van Manen, M. (1977). Linking ways of knowing with ways of being practical. *Curriculum Inquiry, 6*(3), 205–228.

Van Manen, M. (1987, June). *Human science and the study of pedagogy.* Paper presented at the annual meeting of the Canadian Society for the Study of Education, Hamilton, Ontario.

Wedman, J. M., & Martin, M. W. (1986). Exploring the development of reflective thinking through journal writing. *Reading Improvement, 23*(1), 68–71.

Zeichner, K. M. (1986). Preparing reflective teachers: An overview of instructional strategies which have been employed in preservice teacher education. *International Journal of Educational Research, 11*(5), 565–575.

Zumwalt, K. K. (1982). Research on teaching: Policy implications for teacher education. In A. Lieberman & M. McLaughlin (Eds.), *Policy making in education* (pp. 215–248). Chicago: National Society for the Study of Education.

3 Moral Approaches to Reflective Practice

LINDA VALLI
The Catholic University of America

Educators have suggested assorted images to describe the reflective teacher: teachers as problem solvers, scholar teachers, self-monitoring teachers, teachers as hypothesis makers, self-analytic teachers, teachers as action researchers, adaptive teachers, teachers as inquirers, and so forth (Zeichner, 1983; Tom, 1985). These images capture the sense that life in classrooms is dynamic and uncertain, that answers to teaching problems are not a simple process of rule application, and that teachers must exercise the wisdom of practice. The images also evoke Dewey's advice that education programs should produce students of teaching who are thoughtful about educational theory and principles rather than skilled only in the routine, mere technicians and "copiers, followers of tradition and example" (Dewey, 1904/1964, p. 325).

What is often missing in these images, however, is the notion that teaching is a moral as well as an analytic enterprise, that teaching complexities have ethical aspects, and that educational decisions are inevitably based on beliefs, however tacit, about what is good or desirable. This situation is ironic and regrettable, since most educators would agree with Shulman (1986) that "norms, values, ideological or philosophical commitments of justice, fairness, equity, and the like . . . occupy the very heart of what we mean by teacher knowledge" (p. 11). As Noddings (1987) argues, only recently have the goals of schooling, such as teaching academic skills, been detached from the development of character and explicitly moral aims.

CONTRASTING MORAL APPROACHES

This chapter describes three approaches to reflective teacher education that emphasize the moral foundations of teaching. These approaches—

I would like to thank Alan Tom for his comments on an earlier draft of this chapter. This work was supported by a grant from the U.S. Department of Education, Office of Educational Research and Improvement (Grant No. 400-85-1062).

the deliberative, relational, and critical—are similar to one another in that they

> express a concern for helping prospective teachers assume a greater role in shaping the direction of educational environments according to purposes of which they are aware and which can be justified in moral and ethical as well as instrumental terms. . . . Questions about what ought to be done take on primary importance and the process of critical inquiry is viewed as a necessary supplement to the ability to carry out the tasks themselves. (Zeichner 1983, p. 6)

Each approach is concerned with developing reflective processes and dispositions. Each emphasizes moral aspects of teaching and relates reflection to classroom practice. And each uses instructional strategies found in other approaches: journal keeping, questioning, action research projects, supervisory conferences, and so forth.

But the approaches are strikingly different in their theoretical underpinnings, purposes, content, and evaluative criteria. After an overview of each approach, the three are compared through the following questions: What is the purpose of reflection in that approach? What content is considered worthy of reflection? Upon what basis does the approach judge ethical teaching behavior? These questions reveal contrasting beliefs, with profound implications for reflective teaching, about the nature of morality and the good society.

The Deliberative Approach

Since deliberation means a thoughtful consideration of an issue, teacher education programs that use a deliberative approach have obvious links to reflectivity. An apt metaphor for this approach is Tom's (1984) teaching as a moral craft, wherein prospective teachers are encouraged to be aware of and reflect upon "the ethical decisions implicit in ordinary classroom instruction" and to analyze "the purposes of schooling and the political and moral choices implicit in routine teaching decisions" (Kleinfeld & Noordhoff, 1988, p. 10).

At the most general level, those who view teacher preparation from a deliberative ethic are concerned about the rightness of conduct, general questions of valuation, and the pursuit of desirable ends. One key moral dimension of teaching is the student/teacher relationship, especially since schools are compulsory and students have less power than teachers. Another moral dimension is the curriculum. The moral argument is that the selection of content should not be random but should be based on the identification of a worthwhile direction for learning (Tom,

1984). From this moral perspective, reflective teachers consistently monitor the rightness of their conduct in relation to students and develop curricula with a conception of the most worthy end. The determination of what is moral is left up to the individual teacher's judgment as it is shaped and constrained by community consensus. In many cases, the moral is intuited or guided by tacit conceptions of value.

A set of questions, cases, or problems typically focus moral deliberation. Tom (1987), for instance, has proposed replacing pedagogical knowledge with pedagogical questions, arguing that teaching improvement efforts should "begin with the reality of teaching and . . . address both the moral and craft elements of teaching" (p. 14), that pedagogical questions should revolve around the classic problems of teaching and should address our obligations as teachers. Examples of questions with moral implications are "How can I develop learning environments which entice youngsters to want to learn a particular topic or skill? . . . "Is a particular topic significant enough for me to compel a youngster to learn it?" (p. 14) and "Is the proper role of the school to conserve the best of our heritage, yet also to challenge elements of that heritage?" (pp. 15–16).

These types of questions are used to guide moral deliberation or decision making in a number of teacher education programs. For example, the Teachers for Rural Alaska program asks moral and goal-oriented questions of those preparing to teach in a setting culturally different from their own, questions such as "If I teach science by using the local environment, am I contributing to the maintenance of cultural traditions or am I likely to violate these traditions? What should be my goals in teaching science anyway . . . ?" (Kleinfeld & Noordhoff, 1988, p. 12).

At the Catholic University of America, faculty use such concepts as "wait time" to encourage students to reflect not only on technical proficiency ("Have I waited three seconds before calling on a student?") but on moral aspects as well: "Is it wise to extend wait-time in this situation? What will it do to a child's self-esteem? Do I unconsciously give certain types of students (e.g., lower SES) less wait time than others? Is that fair?" (Valli & Taylor, 1987, p. 10).

Like some other approaches to reflective teaching (Posner, 1985; Zeichner & Liston, 1987), the CUA program uses a conceptual framework constructed from Schwab's (1973) four commonplaces of education, Van Manen's (1977) three levels of reflectivity, and Berlak and Berlak's (1981) dilemmas of schooling. The framework serves as a formal way of representing dimensions of reflection (foci, process, and issues), as a way to ensure broad preparation of teachers, and as a means of designing instructional strategies to promote a reflective orientation.

Each dimension of the framework encourages reflection on both moral and technical aspects of teaching. Van Manen's highest level of reflective rationality, the critical-dialectical, includes deliberation on norms and the worthiness of social goals. It focuses on questions of the desirable, of "what ought to be" in terms of justice, equality, and human freedom. A person who is critically reflecting does not ask how to do something but, rather, if it is worthwhile, if it is good, and for whom it is good.

Schwab's four commonplaces (teacher, learner, subject matter, and context) facilitate this critical level of reflection by forcing preservice students to consider all aspects of a teaching situation before arriving at a moral decision: "Is this decision good for this particular student? In this context?" The Berlaks' dilemmas of schooling similarly broaden the range of information included in moral decision making and enable students to see that educational decisions frequently involve a tradeoff between competing goals. They are designed to facilitate a more conscious examination of alternative positions and courses of action.

This framework is used to guide questions, journal writing, field observations, and supervision; to help students analyze curriculum approaches and case studies of teaching; and to structure student teachers' action research projects. Heath's (1982) "Questioning at Home and at School" is an example of a case study frequently used in the program. It is presented as a situation in which teachers engage in moral deliberation in order to understand and overcome classroom problems of cultural conflict.

The conceptual framework guides the analysis of this case. Students learn from the commonplaces the importance of teachers' looking beyond the context of the classroom, not to lay blame on local communities but to understand their students' interaction patterns. They learn from the dilemmas the problem of treating students as though they come from a common culture, the importance of tapping into students' private knowledge, and the value of using a holistic rather than a fragmented instructional design. And finally, they learn the necessity of using all three levels of reflection. The teachers in the case study had a technical problem of communicating with their culturally different students. To understand how to adjust instruction to help these students learn, they had to think interpretively, to discover why their classroom questions made no sense to these students. When the teachers decided to adjust their questioning to a cultural style familiar to the students, they implicitly engaged in critical reflection. They had a sense of the common good and of moral responsibility. This was not merely a technical problem for them, but a relational and ethical one as well.

Supervisors also use this conceptual framework to structure observations and conferences with student teachers. The commonplaces and
levels of reflection create a grid for their questions and comments. The
grid serves as a reminder to consider all levels of questions across all
commonplaces. The student teachers' action research projects contain
similar written reminders to use the conceptual framework in their
problem-solving activities. They are asked to explain why the problem is
worthy of being addressed, to explore multiple ways of viewing the
problem, to ask all persons involved their perception of the problem, to
examine conflicting explanations, to envision an ideal situation, to consider the role of commonplaces and dilemmas in the problem and potential solutions, and so forth.

Recently, Liston and Zeichner (1987) have asserted that a deliberative approach is problematic because it is not grounded in any ethical
theory. They argue that reflective practice should teach students how to
make decisions deductively by examining an educational issue from two
different systems of ethics. They call this an "ethic of duty," which "utilizes abstract principles to assess day-to-day situations" (p. 4). Their
assumption is that moral decision making demands choice and that
choice should be based on clearly delineated and distinctive principles.
They see this model as a corrective to the moral craft orientation of the
programs described here, which have no explicit ethical theory to
ground them.

The Relational Approach

Ethic-of-caring programs, based on Noddings's philosophical work
Caring: A Feminine Approach to Ethics and Moral Education (1984), are
prime examples of a relational approach to reflective practice. Argued
within the discourse of moral philosophy, this ethic is rooted in the
natural relation of mothering, subjective experience, and the uniqueness of human encounters. While this approach does involve moral
deliberation, its rootedness in receptivity, relatedness, and responsiveness rather than in moral reasoning precludes its being subsumed under the category of moral deliberation. As in other personalistic approaches to teacher education (Combs, 1972, 1978; Zeichner, 1983),
relationships are more important than rationality, empathetic understanding more important than abstract principles.

The primary goal of teacher-preparation programs based on this
relational ethic is to help new teachers become caretakers, to enable
them to care for their students. According to Noddings, this requires
that teachers apprehend the reality of each student and give primacy to

their affective growth. A caring teacher would be less concerned that students do well on achievement tests and more that they "support worthy institutions, live compassionately, work productively but not obsessively, care for older and younger generations, be admired, trusted, and respected" (1987, p. 10).

Situated within feminist and humanist traditions, this focus on affective ends and the whole person is a deliberate attempt to return the aims of schooling to the education of a moral populace. Noddings (1987) regards a "relational ethic rooted in and dependent upon natural caring" (p. 6) as the best means of accomplishing that end. She explicitly contrasts this ethic with a Kantian ethic of duty and argues that affective growth occurs through the creation of an ethical ideal and a caring community, which must be mutually constructed. A caring teacher cannot impose an ethical ideal on an unwilling student. For this mutual construction to occur, the voice of the cared-for must be invited and heard. Since voice can only be created by reflection on experience, reflection becomes a necessary condition for the caring relation and community (Richert, 1987).

To accomplish the educational goal of producing moral, caring persons, Noddings argues that we must live "with those whom we teach in a caring community" (1986, p. 502). It is as important to create this community in teacher education programs as it is in elementary and secondary schools. Those who will be expected to care about children must themselves experience a caring community through modeling, dialogue, practice, and confirmation. A caring teacher educator would model such desirable qualities as meticulous preparation and constructive evaluation, encourage autonomous decision making through dialogue, provide practice in caring for and fidelity to persons, and confirm worthy motives and attainable images of moral educators.

Noddings (1984) provides a case study of a mathematics teacher's caring dilemma, which can be used in teacher education to model the caring teacher. The reader is invited to enter into the reality of a teacher who loves mathematics. A student who is doing poorly tells her he hates mathematics. Rather than attempting to understand what this experience is like, the teacher sets a goal of helping the student to love math. At this point, Noddings writes, the "student becomes an object of study and manipulation" (p. 15). He is not being cared for. Helping a student to love a subject is not necessarily a noble aim in this ethic. What matters is that a student find his or her own reason to learn a subject or "reject it boldly and honestly" (p. 15). In contrast to the teacher described here, the caring teacher would continue to model love of mathematics but would also try to understand what it feels like to hate math, to find it bleak, scary, and boring. From this vantage point, teacher and student mutually explore the rewards of mathematics. The student, however, remains free to hate math.

Henderson (1988) describes a secondary school teaching seminar in which he attempted to apply a relational ethic to reflective professional development. For Henderson, like Noddings, students' growth needs are the central concern. Using a process called affirmation inquiry, wherein students reflect on their own professional growth, the class relates prior experience to "the variety of interpretations of professional development which they were studying" (1988, p. 92). This affirmation inquiry process, through which students identify their own strengths and weaknesses, results in intentional learning plans. Students individually select projects important to their professional growth. One student worked on improving her Spanish through a translation project, another worked on resolving a shyness problem, a third studied critical theory so that, as a teacher, he could better uphold democratic values. These reflective projects are in keeping with an ethic of caring since "each one represents distinct hermeneutics of growth. Each one emerges from a unique autobiographical context" (1988, p. 94).

Reflective teacher education programs based on a caring ethic would use modeling, dialogue, practice, and confirmation to develop the relational capacities needed by "one-caring" as teacher. These relational capacities include listening and responding to the cared-for, being engrossed in the other's reality, identifying individuals' growth needs, helping students find their own reasons for what they choose to do, and mutually struggling toward competence and ethical ideals. Though prospective teachers in these programs would learn how to teach reading, mathematics, and social studies, they would primarily learn how to live a caring ethic in the classroom "to induce an enhanced moral sense in the student" (Noddings, 1984, p. 179).

The Critical Approach

The critical approach to reflective practice described below is derived from political philosophy, with the primary influence coming from variants of Marxist thought. It is the only one of the three approaches that explicitly treats schools and school knowledge as political, rather than neutral, constructions that impede social justice and equality. Feminism has also contributed to this approach, but in a way quite different from its contribution to a relational ethic.

Rather than using images of the teacher as caretaker or as moral decision maker, reflective teacher education programs based on a critical ethic prepare teachers to be "critical pedagogues" or "transformative intellectuals" (Giroux & McLaren, 1986). Proponents of this approach to teacher education argue that schools, as social institutions, help reproduce a society based on unjust class, race, and gender relations and that teachers have a moral obligation to reflect on and change their own practices and school structures when these perpetuate such arrangements. For critical theorists, the primary goal of teacher preparation is to assist prospective teachers in understanding ways in which schools might be contributing to an unjust society for the purpose of engaging in emancipatory action.

Critical theorists argue that conventional knowledge, insititutions, and social relations are socially constructed and should not be taken for granted. Reflective teacher education programs based on a critical ethic typically challenge students to examine their own assumptions and biases and to break through the parameters of conventional thought (Zeichner, 1981–82). These goals stem from the notion that dominant ideologies maintain an unjust and repressive social order; thus programs should "strive to prepare students with analytic and reflective abilities, teachers who would not accept 'unthinking submergence in the social reality that prevails'" (Adler & Goodman, 1986, p. 4).

Critical approaches have been developed for field experiences and seminars, methods courses, and social foundations courses. In contrast to traditional field experiences, which socialize prospective teachers to commonly accepted practice, the goals of field experiences in this reflective orientation are to help students question the moral basis of these practices and understand how schools reproduce and legitimate social inequality (Beyer, 1984; Zeichner, 1981–82). Students receive assignments that help them critically analyze conventional wisdom, reject technocratic approaches to teaching, and view schools from the perspective of those who benefit from them the least.

For example, in the University of Wisconsin–Madison seminar for elementary student teachers, students are encouraged to critique dominant resolutions to educational problems. From multiple perspectives, they read about and discuss such issues as ability grouping, alternatives to objective-based planning, and possible consequences of labeling students EMR or LD (Zeichner, 1981–82). A goal of field experiences at Knox College is that students use critical theory to transform commonsense perceptions, observations, and attitudes into problem situations. Two instructional activities are classroom ethnographies, which focus on the experience of "students of color, students from working class backgrounds, girls/young women and the like" (Beyer, 1984, p. 39), and the analysis of curricula for examples of such elements as gender discrimination and technical control. The overriding concern is that students take "seriously the ideological and ethical question of 'who benefits'" from a given curriculum approach (Beyer 1984, p. 39).

Adler and Goodman (1986) describe a social studies methods course with a critical approach. One of the course goals is "strengthening the link between critical viewpoints of education and teaching practice" (p. 4). The authors address this goal through class sessions in which students reflect on whose history is taught in schools and the notion of social (versus military or diplomatic) history. The course introduces students to the idea that "traditional history tends to reflect the power structure of a given society" (p. 5) and demystifies the discipline by having students *do* rather than *learn about* history. Students in programs based on a critical ethic inquire into the schooling implications of unequal and historically conditioned race, class, and gender relations.

Helping students develop critical perspectives about multicultural education is also a major goal for social foundations courses at Santa Clara University. These courses encourage prospective teachers "to exercise a moral commitment to education that is democratic and respectful of student diversity in their philosophy and practice" (King & Ladson-Billings, 1988, p. 7). In the undergraduate course, the authors employ a threefold strategy of having students confront their own belief systems about other races and cultures; helping students expand their understanding of historical and sociopolitical events while examining culturally diverse learning types; and requiring an action research project assessing the commitment of teachers, schools, or school districts to multicultural education. In a graduate-level course, the social goals of schooling are made problematic by exposing students to information that causes them to reexamine their beliefs about concepts like social mobility and the American Dream. Students are challenged to "choose the social purposes they want to bring about through their philosophy and practice" and "to envision possibilities for changing schools and society through their own thought and action" (King & Ladson-Billings, 1988, p. 21).

In her analysis of feminist efforts at curricular change in teacher education, Lather (1984) discovered several courses with critical and emancipatory orientations which expose the political and subjective nature of knowledge production and view "curriculum as a site of ideological struggle" (p. 4). These courses are interdisciplinary; analyze race, class, and gender dynamics; integrate cognitive, affective, and behavioral objectives; and make knowledge problematic. Some of the specific strategies used in the courses are small-group discussions that connect the personal and the political; journals that give voice to students' personal reactions; nonsexist curriculum development; case study analysis of women's class-based educational experiences; and inquiry into the political nature of theories about women's nature and abilities, the sexual division of labor, and feminist teaching.

Each program based on a critical ethic promotes a vision of schools as sites for personal empowerment and social transformation. Each argues that for society to be just it must contribute most to the least advantaged. For this to happen, the social order must cease to promote the accumulation of goods, profits, and credentials and, instead, maximize economic, social, and educational equality (Apple, 1979). Critical theorists believe that teacher education programs should prepare teachers to question social arrangements and premises, to have a preferential concern for the oppressed and disadvantaged, and to engage in pedagogical practices "based on and cultivating a deep respect for a democratic and ethically-based community" (Giroux & McLaren, 1986, p. 223).

CONTRASTING DIMENSIONS OF MORAL APPROACHES

These three approaches to reflective practice—deliberative, relational, and critical—all emphasize moral aspects of teaching, claim some relation to Dewey, link reflection to action, use similar instructional strategies, and include the same issues or topics in coursework (e.g. tracking, multiculturalism, learning environments). However, the three approaches are distinguishable from one another on several important dimensions, chief among them being the role of reflection in the approach, the content of reflection, and criteria for judging ethical teaching. A comparative analysis of these dimensions exposes the conflicting views of social reality upon which they rest, so that although incorporating all three ethics into teacher preparation might seem desirable, the result would be riddled with contradiction.

The Role of Reflection

While reflection is essential to each approach, its purpose and function vary. In the deliberative ethic, reflection is pedagogically necessary to make students consider moral aspects of their craft. Reflective assignments give them experience in moral reasoning and encourage an orientation toward practice that subsumes technical decisions to ethical considerations or embeds technical decision making within moral deliberation. With the exception of Liston and Zeichner's (1987) ethic-of-duty model, the emphasis in the deliberative ethic is on asking questions that will elicit moral judgments, not on providing theories or principles from which to answer those questions.

In a relational approach, reflection seems to have two purposes. The first purpose is to provide the grounds for caring relations and communities. The prospective teacher must be given the opportunity to reflect so that the supervisor or teacher educator can enter into his or her reality. Prospective teachers must allow themselves to be cared for by sharing their reflective experiences. The second purpose for reflection in this approach is to model the type of caring relations and communities prospective teachers would be expected to create in their own classrooms—relations that are dependent on reflection, dialogue, and mutual construction of the ethical ideal. Overall, reflection serves the humanistic goal of moral development.

Reflection in a critical approach also serves two purposes, which are quite different from the above. The first is epistemological. For critical theorists, breaking through dominant ideologies and hegemonic control is a primary goal. Reflection is thus used as a way to make knowledge problematic through deconstruction. This is often done by introducing students to radical social theory. The second purpose is pedagogical and has been most forcefully articulated in feminist strands of the critical ethic. Feminist pedagogy necessitates reflection, necessitates the voicing of personal experience. As Lather (1984) argues:

> Counter-hegemonic consciousness is not produced by emancipatory content alone. Feminist pedagogy is seen as central if we are to provide the powerful images and experiences that can shake us out of the mutually confirming aspects of hegemony, especially our sense of the limits of possibilities. (p. 15)

In its pedagogical function, reflection in a critical ethic resembles its use in caring relations. It seeks to empower the voiceless. In an ethic of caring, however, the individual or, at most, the small community is the beneficiary of this power. In critical theory, the aim is far broader: to expose the race-, class-, and gender-biased construction of present society in order to radically transform it. No such broad social goals are evident in a caring ethic, which is situated within a traditional liberal democratic framework wherein social improvement occurs by improving the quality of personal relations. If we only care more, society will be perfected. There is no structural critique in this essentially humanistic and developmental approach.

The Content of Reflection

A second dimension on which the approaches differ is in what they consider important objects of reflection. Tom's (1985) concept of the arenas of the problematic is useful in distinguishing the approaches. An arena is an aspect of teaching that is the object of problematic thinking. Tom proposes four arenas, ranging from the small to the large: the teaching-learning process; subject-matter knowledge; political and ethical principles underlying teaching; and, most broadly, the nature of educational institutions and society itself. The arenas of the problematic in the three approaches discussed here have a similar range. The primary object of inquiry in a relational ethic is the teacher's responsibility to individual students, whereas in a critical ethic, the primary object is the teacher's responsibility to society. The object in a deliberative ethic is diffuse, potentially covering all arenas, but with an emphasis on ethical principles underlying teaching.

In a relational approach to reflective practice, prospective teachers reflect on, engage in dialogue about, and practice creating caring relations and communities. All issues covered in their professional preparation are filtered through the lens of the caring relationship. These issues could be the school organization, size, rules, and penalties. Or they could be issues like testing, labeling, sorting, and credentialing. Students are taught to analyze and resolve these issues by reflecting on relational questions: What effect will a given practice have on the cared-for? On nurturing the ethical ideals of meeting the other morally and creating caring communities?

The moral issues on which programs with a critical ethic focus are those with broad social implications, issues of social justice, equity, emancipation. Critical theorists analyze these issues from a radical political perspective, which they teach so students will have a broader frame of reference from which to make moral and political decisions. In this respect, there is a tension, albeit constructive, between a critical approach and reflection. This tension is acknowledged by Zeichner's statement that:

> The commitment of a student teacher to a position on an issue is a matter to be decided by the student. Student teachers should not be manipulated or coerced into taking particular stances or adjusting particular education practices. Instead, the emphasis should be on

having the students consider an issue seriously—i.e., in terms of its educational, ethical, social, and political implications before taking a stance. (1981–82, p. 19)

Unlike the two other approaches, the problematic objects in a deliberative ethic do not fall into one arena. Prospective teachers in these programs might be asked to reflect on moral aspects of student/teacher or student/student relationships, of curriculum choice, or of instructional or management decisions. They might also be asked to reflect on the social implications of particular educational practices. The objects for reflection in moral decision making are not circumscribed by the approach.

Labeling, for example, is often an object used for problematic thinking in each of the approaches. But the way it is treated would still vary across the arenas. Relational programs focus on the impact of a label on the quality of the caring relation between student and teacher. Critical programs focus on the historical context of labeling and its role in justifying and maintaining social inequality. Deliberative programs might include both the personal and social consequences of labeling but would not necessarily use the theoretical frameworks of the other two approaches to analyze the practice. In addition, students in deliberative programs might be asked to reflect on additional aspects of labeling, such as whether labeling can have beneficial effects or how one can tell when the effects are adverse or beneficial.

Similarly, many of the same instructional strategies are used across approaches, such as journal keeping and action research projects. But the way in which they are used is clearly different. For example, in a deliberative approach the object for journal reflections varies across arenas or is left open to student choice. In a relational approach, the object is the examination of the self in relation to others; journals are autobiographical. In a critical approach, the object is the perception of injustice in the social context of schooling. These differences are logical outcomes of their theoretical orientations.

Judging Moral Practice

A third dimension on which the three approaches differ is their basis for judging moral practice. The question here is how each approach teaches students to evaluate ethical decisions. The two bases for judging moral practice in most deliberative approaches are the long-range benefit to the student and the importance of the knowledge taught. However, few guidelines are offered for determining important knowledge or student benefit. In the Catholic University of America program, for example, only procedural criteria for moral decision making are explicit. Students are required to respond to questions at Van Manen's (1977) critical level of reflection, to look at a situation from the students' perspective as well as their own, to consider broad social implications, and to explain their decisions persuasively. An exception is Liston and Zeichner's (1987) ethic-of-duty model, wherein decisions are evaluated against different ethical principles.

A relational approach to reflective practice evaluates moral choice according to its benefit to the cared-for. The individual's talents, aspirations, and personal desire supersede broad societal needs (Noddings, 1984). Caring teachers assess ethical practice by asking themselves what effect their choices are having on particular students, on the development of good persons, and on the caring community they are trying to build (Noddings, 1986). Those who teach from a critical ethic, on the other hand, judge their practice to be moral if its purpose is to resist repressive hegemonic control, assist the least advantaged, or transform unjust structures.

In each case, then, the moral criteria are found within the approach itself. That is why each is referred to throughout this chapter as both an "approach" and an "ethic." Each embodies its own principles of good conduct. Moral deliberation, caring, and social criticism are in themselves the ethically correct practice of the reflective teacher in the respective approaches.

So although the approaches might address similar issues, they do so with different purposes, different problematic objects, and different evaluative criteria. A relational approach teaches students how to negotiate areas of interest with their pupils. Guidelines for moral teaching focus on the quality of the negotiation or the caring relationship. In a deliberative approach, prospective teachers satisfy criteria for moral reflection if they ask a question of curricular worth and offer a reasonable answer. In a program using a critical ethic, students are expected to emphasize school knowledge that promotes emancipatory social change rather than individual upward mobility or individualistic personal development.

CONCLUSIONS

In some respects, these three ethics can be viewed as complementary. Conceivably, morally reflective teachers could integrate the three ethics into their practice. They could use a relational ethic when considering student/teacher relations, a deliberative ethic for curricular and instructional issues, and a critical ethic for social implications of teaching.

But this solution is problematic. The student/teacher, curricular, and societal arenas are connected, not discrete. The perceptions people form about the world and the moral perspectives they develop are not easily compartmentalized. It is difficult to imagine one teacher consciously or unconsciously shifting perspectives from relational to deliberative to critical.

The very notion of caring, for example, is different for a critical theorist from the concept Noddings has described. For a critically oriented teacher, caring would be impossible apart from a political struggle to change oppressive structures that harm individuals who are already disadvantaged by society. Without that political engagement, caring would be a race-, class-, and gender-biased activity reproducing an unequal society wherein the privileged continue to receive more of everything, including care. Without a critical analysis, little within this relational ethic itself, beyond its vision of a caring community, would prompt the social transformation critical theory requires.

By reducing reality to personal relations, structural analysis becomes irrelevant. Human beings become free agents unaffected by social conditions. Even though a generous reading of Noddings finds implications for changing unjust structures that limit viable caring, the implication is illusive. As Diller (1988) has stated, this ethic leaves "no recourse but to go on caring as best we can under a set of antithetical conditions while the larger structures remain beyond our power to change." (p. 338).

Those who function within a relational ethic would, in turn, object to the formalized principles and analyses that critical theory and some deliberative approaches promote. These are considered overrationalized and opposed to basic ontology (Noddings, 1984). Similarly, critical theorists fault moral decision makers for not providing a systematic basis for deciding what is moral. The question of what and whose knowledge is regarded as important enough for the official school curriculum, they would argue, is not only a matter of relative values within a pluralistic society but also a problem of dominant groups maintaining and legitimizing their own power. Conversely, those who uphold a deliberative ethic argue that critical theorists do not promote reflection over competing, viable decisions but tend to promote dogmatically held views. Liston and Zeichner (1987) argue that the critical ethic is "an inadequate basis for the moral education of future teachers as it unduly limits the possible moral perspectives" (p. 3).

Ultimately then, because they have different views of social reality, the three ethics give different answers to the question of what is the right thing for the reflective teacher to do. In a relational ethic, society is a community of individuals; in a deliberative ethic, of pluralistic interest groups; and in a critical ethic, of dominating and subordinated groups (Tom, 1988). For a deliberative teacher, the morally right thing is making sound judgments while acknowledging legitimate differences; for a relational teacher, it is becoming involved in the reality of the other; and for a critical teacher, it is exposing and transforming social ills.

These conflicting perspectives suggest that the use of the term *reflective practice* is deceptive. Reflective practice is not singular. Different approaches do not lead to the same reflective practice, even when those approaches are all grounded in moral considerations. Only by unreflectively incorporating conflicting perspectives into daily practice could one teacher be caring, critical, and deliberative. This is an unlikely (and surely undesirable) option for those who prepare reflective teachers.

REFERENCES

Adler, S., & Goodman, J. (1986). Critical theory as a foundation for methods courses. *Journal of Teacher Education, 37*(4), 2–8.

Apple, M. W. (1979). *Ideology and Curriculum.* London: Routledge & Kegan Paul.

Berlak, A., & Berlak, H. (1981). *Dilemmas of schooling: Teaching and social change.* London & New York: Methuen.

Beyer, L. (1984). Field experience, ideology, and the development of critical reflectivity. *Journal of Teacher Education, 35*(3), 36–41.

Combs, A. W. (1972). Some basic concepts for teacher education. *Journal of Teacher Education, 23*(3), 286–290.

Combs, A. W. (1978). Teacher education: The person in the process. *Educational Leadership, 35*(7), 558–561.

Dewey, J. (1964). The relation of theory to practice in education. In R. D. Archambault (Ed.), *John Dewey on Education* (pp. 313–338). Chicago: University of Chicago Press.

Diller, A. (1988). The ethics of care and education: A new paradigm, its critics, and its educational significance. *Curriculum Inquiry, 18*(3), 325–342.

Giroux, H., & McLaren, P. (1986). Teacher education and the politics of engagement: The case for democratic schooling. *Harvard Educational Review, 56*(3), 213–238.

Heath, S. B. (1982). Questioning at home and at school: A comparative study. In G. Spindler (Ed.), *Doing the ethnography of schooling: Educational anthropology in action* (pp. 103–127). New York: Holt.

Henderson, J. G. (1988). An ethic of caring applied to reflective professional development. *Teaching Education, 2*(1), 91–95.

Henderson, S. G. (1987, April). *Case knowledge of hermeneutical elegance: Rationale and phenomenological quest.* Paper presented to the annual meeting of the American Educational Research Association, Washington, DC.

King, J. E., & Ladson-Billings, G. (1988, February). *The teacher education challenge in elite university settings: Developing critical perspectives for teaching in a democratic and multicultural society.* Paper presented at the annual meeting of the American Association of Colleges of Teacher Education, New Orleans, LA.

Kleinfeld, J., & Noordhoff, K. (1988). *Re-thinking teacher education programs: What are the right questions?* Paper presented at the western meeting of the Holmes Group, Boulder, CO.

Lather, P. (1984, April). *Women's studies as counter-hegemonic work: The case of teacher education.* Paper presented at the annual meeting of the American Educational Research Association, New Orleans, LA.

Liston, D., & Zeichner K. (1987). Reflective teacher education and moral deliberation. *Journal of Teacher Education, 38*(6), 2–8.

Noddings, N. (1984). *Caring: A feminine approach to ethics and moral education.* Berkeley: University of California Press.

Noddings, N. (1986). Fidelity in teaching, teacher education, and research for teaching. *Harvard Educational Review, 56*(4), 496–510.

Noddings, N. (1987, April). *An ethic of caring and its implications for instructional arrangements.* Paper presented at the annual meeting of the American Educational Research Association, Washington, DC.

Posner, G. (1985). *Field experience: A guide to reflective teaching.* New York: Longman.

Richert, A. E. (1987, April). *Reflection and pedagogical caring: Unsilencing the teacher's voice.* Paper presented at the annual meeting of the American Educational Research Association, Washington, DC.

Schwab, J. J. (1973). The practical 3: Translation into curriculum. *School Review, 81*(4), 501–522.

Shulman, L. (1986). Those who understand: Knowledge growth in teaching. *Educational Research, 15*(2), 4–14.

Tom, A. R. (1984). *Teaching as a moral craft.* New York: Longman.

Tom, A. R. (1985). Inquiry into inquiry-oriented teacher education. *Journal of Teacher Education, 36*(5), 35–44.

Tom, A. R. (1987). Replacing pedagogical knowledge with pedagogical questions. In J. Smyth (Ed.), *Educating teachers: Changing the nature of pedagogical knowledge* (pp. 9–17). London: Falmer.

Tom, A. R. (1988, August 22). Personal communication.

Valli, L., & Taylor, N. (1987, October). *Reflective teacher education: Preferred characteristics for a content and process model.* Paper prepared for the University of Houston/OERI Conference on Reflection in Teaching and Teacher Education, Houston, Texas.

Van Manen, M. (1977). Linking ways of knowing with ways of being practical. *Curriculum Inquiry, 6*(3), 205–228.

Zeichner, K. (1981–82). Reflective teaching and field-based experience in teacher education. *Interchange, 12*(4), 1–22.

Zeichner, K. (1983). Alternative paradigms of teacher education. *Journal of Teacher Education, 34*(3), 3–9.

Zeichner, K., & Liston, D. (1987). Teaching student teachers to reflect. *Harvard Educational Review, 57*(1), 23–48.

4 Reflectivity as a Function of Community

JEFFREY H. CINNAMOND
Indiana University of Pennsylvania

NANCY L. ZIMPHER
The Ohio State University

Dewey's (1904) classic distinction between apprenticeship and laboratory experience cautions against the misguided view that the process
of becoming a teacher is strictly concerned with the acquisition of the
necessary tools of the profession, control of classroom technique, and
skill and proficiency in making teaching an instrument of "real and vital
theoretical instruction" (p. 9). We have come to understand this latter
orientation as "the bases upon which the habits of a teacher as a teacher
may be built up" (p. 15). Thus the clarion call for teacher educators has
become, "Can we teach teachers to be reflective?" (for example, Gore,
1987; Korthagen, 1985; Zeichner & Liston, 1987). Focusing on the preparation of teachers as inquiring professionals, some (Howey, 1988) have
drawn from original applications of action research (Corey, 1953; Lewin, 1949) to establish processes for inquiry and reflective action. Others have viewed reflection as a cyclical phenomenon (Bagenstos, 1975;
Feiman, 1979; Kemmis & McTaggart, 1982). Sergiovanni (1987) relates
reflectivity to a process of forming "mindscapes"—"implicit mental images and frameworks through which administrative and schooling reality and one's place within these realities is envisioned" (p. xi).

TEACHING AND COMMUNITY

These are helpful images for fostering a vision of teaching that acknowledges the complex and interactive process of learning to teach. As we
struggle with a concept that appears to have great potential for grounding our programs of teacher preparation in more theoretical and
thoughtful understanding, reflection and inquiry-based activities seem
a powerful conduit. Our challenge in this chapter is to modify the notion of reflectivity in yet another direction. We draw in this analysis on

the work of George H. Mead (1932, 1934), a proponent of the notion of reflective action as a fundamental process in attaining a sense of self and a sense of community. For Mead, a sense of self arises out of social behavior, which involves the dynamics of communication within a social structure (or community). Since others have portrayed the process of becoming a teacher as one of socialization into the profession, we will attempt to present Mead's view of community as a way of thinking more clearly about this socialization process. The socialization framework focuses on how beginning teachers adapt to the role of teacher, give meaning to their own beliefs, and adapt to the beliefs of others (Zeichner, 1979; Zeichner & Grant, 1981; Zeichner & Tabachnick, 1982). This process also incorporates Lacey's (1977) identification of social strategies used to conform to instructional demands.

Clearly, however, the process of socialization is more complex than simply acquiring knowledge about teaching. The student teacher, while still a member of the community of college students, comes into contact with the communities of teachers, administrators, students, parents of students, university professors, and student-teaching supervisors. Not only must teaching candidates gain access to the communities of the school, they must also learn to function well within these multiple communities. Interaction connotes exchange, discourse, and change for both the social group and the individual. The question of how such change occurs is important for all concerned.

One aspect of this socialization process (that is, coming to grips with multiple communities) is encouraged among novice teachers through a process of reflectivity: Teachers acquire the ability to move students, the schools, and themselves toward change and growth through reflective or inquiry-oriented teacher education programs. To a large extent, literature on this topic grounds itself in the work of Dewey (1909/1933). By examining his distinction between routine and reflective action, teacher educators have created an orientation that would make teaching less of a technical and authoritarian enterprise. Within this orientation, Dewey's phases of reflective thought have been detailed to the point of making of them a highly structured, almost instrumental model for action (Beyer, 1984). More fundamental than the propensity of some to rationalize the process of reflectivity is the general omission of any acknowledgment of the interactive nature of the reflective process. Dewey's work, and, more importantly, the work of teacher educators based upon Dewey, is grounded in the idea that the individual student teacher learns to reflect on a particular experience individually. As such, the growth and development of student teachers appears to take place outside the very communities we propose as teacher educators to be socializing them into—those of veteran teachers and other school personnel.

What appears to be missing from a discussion of reflective practice is an account of the individual student teacher's active dialogue with the various groups that exist within the context of the school as a social system. In much of the literature, the school is seen as a single community, not a collection of interacting communities (Beyer, 1984; Ross & Hannay, 1986; Zeichner & Liston, 1987). Through language and other significant gestures, teachers must learn how to interact with many groups, not a homogeneous community labeled "X school." When dissonance occurs in this interaction, or an action is impeded, self-reflection is stimulated. Dialogue with the other participants is necessary for appropriate understanding and reflection. The continual interest by educators in reflection as a significant resource for the improvement of the teacher, the environment, and student/teacher interaction requires an examination of some initial constructions of social interaction and the role that reflection plays in these interactions.

MEAD'S SOCIAL THEORY

Although a contemporary of Dewey's, Mead has been cited much less frequently in the teacher education literature. However, Mead's social theory as related to the processes of community and discourse deserves a closer reading by teacher educators. This somewhat abbreviated presentation of Mead's notion of the development of self and society, which focuses on language and community, is intended to inform the conception of reflection discussed in this chapter. As Mead's principles are enunciated, we will relate them to general conditions of student teacher socialization. Then contemporary articles by teacher educators dealing with reflection and/or self-reflection will be analyzed to discover the degree to which they affirm or counter Mead's social theory. Although this chapter presents Mead's theory rather linearly, the process of becoming a "self" within a social group or community is not linear at all. The highly developmental and interactive character of the process will be highlighted in the following discussion.

Mead belonged to a circle of scholars whose works are generally perceived as a major turning point in social-psychological thought. Mead came, at John Dewey's request (Joas, 1985), to the University of Chicago, where he taught courses in the university and at the Laboratory School, edited a journal called the *Elementary School Teacher*, and developed a nonreductionist orientation to social psychology. Though he published only thirteen works, scholars have used student notes from his classes to reconstruct the principles that relate to his conceptions of the mind, self, and society as a continuing and reflexive process of constant interaction with others.

We propose that Mead's view of reflective action as a function of community will inform our understanding of the process of becoming a teacher. To orient our thinking, it is helpful to understand that for both Mead and Dewey, social psychology was, in essence, "a devastating critique of a psychology that believes it has found its goal in the apprehension of causal, law-like relations between stimuli and response" (Joas, 1985, p. 66). Rather, for Mead particularly, the concept of meaning is grounded in the transformation of reflection "not [as] something that as such has a value in and of itself. It is, rather, embedded in action-nexuses [linkages or connections]" (Joas, 1985, p. 79). Thus Mead tried to explain communication not as an isolated mental act, but as a set of actions directed at natural problems and the cooperative mastering of problems. This calls for a "consciousness of the relation between one's own actions and the responses of others to them" (Joas, 1985, p. 105).

SELF-DEVELOPMENT AND COMMUNITY

Mead (1934) described the development of the individual's relationship with mind, the self, and society as a continual process of construction and an internalization of the social environment and knowledge into the self. The self, for Mead, is constructed of two parts: the *I* and the *me*. It is significant that the *self*, and its parts, are not considered to be a static moment or substance. The self is constructed through an ongoing process that will continue throughout the life of the person and the community. It is not merely the process of being aware of one's self that is social—the self one becomes aware of in this manner is itself social. One is aware of one's self as a social object, or as a part of a dynamic social process, or as an agent. The self is an individual who organizes his or her own responses in accordance with the tendencies on the part of others to respond to his or her actions. The self is always preceded by the other. This other is generalized. Thus, the *generalized other* is a part of every self. It is only because of the generalized other that thinking or creative reflection can occur. The key component of this process is the dialogue that occurs between the *I* and the organized attitudes of others. The self becomes unified through social activity, and as a result it does not maintain itself as an individuated self. It is always linked to the social communities that help give it definition. Consequently, when individuals act, they take into account the behaviors, values, and orientations of their community.

Role-Taking and Communication

The ability of an individual to take the role of the other is accomplished through communication. Communication always implies the conveyance of meaning (Mead, 1932), typically through language and significant gestures. Mead defines gestures as "an affective expression" (quoted in Joas, 1985, p. 96). Language, which expresses conventions and practices, is a complex alignment of meanings that is adopted by a community through consensus. It is only because of language that a community can develop meanings that become known as common sense. Language is part of a cooperative process that leads to an adjustment of the response of others so that the entire interaction can continue. For Mead, language is the medium for all social processes. Gestures and significant symbols have common or shared meanings among social groups and are universal by definition because language is social. Thoughts and ideas cannot be subjective or private because of this shared quality of language and gestures. The widest community is the rational community of universal discourse (Mead, 1934). Rationality and modes of interaction are learned through language and universal discourse from the community and develop within the self. Because of this, rational conduct includes a self-reference that is always reflexive (Mead, 1934). The function of language, then, is to evoke action, not to describe it. This ties language to the doing of reflection as both a function and a necessary condition of social development.

An Illustration of Self and Community

Since Mead's abstractions are difficult to translate specifically, we can draw on his notion of child development to think more clearly about the development of self and community among students of teaching. In the formation of self, Mead posited two constructions of children's activities, which he called *play* and *game*.

In play, the child interacts with an imaginary partner and through this activity gains practice at anticipating the behaviors of the imaginary other. This stage is followed by the development of the capacity to engage in real group play (or, in Mead's language, the generalized other). As Joas observes, "the behavioral expectations of this 'generalized other' are, in the case of group play, the rules of the game, and more generally the norms and values of a group." (1985, pp. 119–120).

This illustration provides a vehicle for viewing the development of the self as first an almost imaginary, fantasy, or personal dialectic, followed ultimately by the ability to anticipate both the responses of others as well as the norms and values of the community into which one is attempting entrance. Now we can look more closely at these concepts in relationship to the student teacher's development or that of students of teaching at any level.

THE STUDENT TEACHER'S DEVELOPMENT OF ROLE IN COMMUNITY

Student teachers must consult and cognitively organize the generalized other of the supervising teacher, university professors and supervisors, and pupils, as well as their own knowledge of what a teacher is based on their own experiences as students. As such, this process allows student teachers to become objects to themselves and invoke self-reflection, which is ultimately the process of role-taking. The self can exist for an individual only if that person can learn to assume the roles of others. Student teachers must organize their interactions through cognitive representation of the multiple communities with which they interact and through attempts to assume the roles they believe others want them to acquire. Student teachers learn to anticipate the response of others to their gestures and actions and to develop the most appropriate interaction. Becoming professional, then, depends on the degree to which the novice can assume the attitudes of the others in the teacher-training program. As a result, role-taking becomes an important mode of self-reflection and self-criticism (Mead, 1934).

Obviously, one is both a subject and an object to one's self during this process. Further, one validates one's behavior by the response of the others through interactions. Student teachers may begin to feel like full-fledged teachers when their students respond to them in the same way they respond to certified teachers. Ultimately novice teachers reach the point where they can predict the response of the other to their own behavior even before they have begun the act. This ability legitimates their membership in the community of professionals.

The Evolution of Community through Reflection

"All reflective thought arises out of real problems present in immediate experience" (Mead, 1934, p. 7). In this construction of the social world, reflective thinking occurs when action has been impeded. For

Mead, reflection does not have a value in and of itself; its value lies in the potential for dealing with the next action or interaction. Reflection does not occupy a separate place in social processes but is already embedded in them. As a result, Mead does not have to rely on a separate theory to explain the process or reason for reflection; it is inherent in lived experience.

By entering a community, in this instance the multiple communities of teachers, students, administrators, and university supervisors, an individual (the student teacher) takes on the values that belong to the other members of the community (Mead, 1934). One is not, however, bound by the community to static or absolute values or meanings (Mead, 1934). Discourse is the process by which changes are made within the community. To listen and then respond to the dialogue of others, and in the process to generate new universals for the community, is how change occurs. Mead states that it is the consciousness of change that is the essential part of the reflective process (1934). Individuals have not only the right but the duty to engage in dialogue with the community of which they are a part and to bring about change through their intervention (Mead, 1934).

In this sense, the individual members of each community have the obligation to use discourse to present any new meaning(s) constructed by them as individuals to the community for possible incorporation into universals. This is the key concept that will be examined later in the discussion of Mead's ideas as they relate to the teacher education literature. This process of change identified by Mead has a striking similarity to the notions of critical theory articulated by Horkheimer (1972), who views the entire society as engaged in a practice of discourse that transcends individuals for the transformation of the society.

Within this notion of community, the process of reflection emerges. It involves self-reflection upon the meanings and practices for the purpose of generating a consensus to create new meanings or to take away obstructions to appropriate action. An impediment to action or the dissonance occasioned by a prior action can serve as a stimulus for reflection. Reflection may also be stimulated by a desire to understand the necessary conditions for maintaining the current social order (Blum & McHugh, 1984). Self-reflection is reflection upon its source: that is, the social and community meanings that are held in common. To this end, Blum and McHugh (1984) state: "If the self reflective actor is a language user and if language is social there is no essential difference between self reflection and [other actions]" (p. 56).

Language and social interaction already incorporate and accommodate self-reflection as a part of the commonly shared experience of the life-world. The implicit assumptions and the meanings of metaphors are carried within the language. As such, reflection is not to be seen as a separate action to be used instrumentally in particular circumstances. It cannot be a skill taught for use in certain instances; rather, it is an ongoing process of the everyday life-world that needs to be emphasized explicitly through dialogue. Reflection is inherently and explicitly a linguistic event.

Reflection and Experience

Reflection on meanings, that is, the meanings of one's experience, would appear to be of two sorts. There is the immediate knowledge of meaning that occurs through perception, and then there is the second-ary meaning, achieved through the reflective processes. It is this latter level that attracts our interest in teacher education. Blum and McHugh (1984) detail an interactional theory of reflection, noting that the inter-actions in which one becomes engaged are limits to reflections—not limits in doing reflection, but limits in the knowledge and histories used to construct the interpretation and reflection.

Hall (1976) notes that what appears in the perceptual field or con-text is changed in significance by embedded factors. He goes on to note five factors in this context: the subject or activity, the situation, one's status in a social system, past experiences, and culture (Hall, 1976). Other authors point toward the inability to achieve absolute knowledge of an interaction through reflection as well as absolute ability to be reflective. "Contextual meaning is potentially infinite" (Bakhtin, 1968, p. 145). Self-reflective actors will limit the multiplicity—that is, the actuali-ty—of the interaction through the cognitive selection process. They will choose which particular items, events, and symbols are subjects for reflection. The contextual meaning can be actualized only by the ac-companiment of the student teacher's meaning and the meanings of the others involved in the interaction. So reflectivity is enhanced to the degree that a student teacher has knowledge of the professional commu-nity adequate for insightful reasoning about appropriate actions. This necessitates discourse with others regarding events in order to develop the most principled and appropriate reflective experience, that is, a social experience of reflection.

In *Mind, Self, and Society* (1934), Mead describes the human social ideal. The ideal community requires that each individual be a partici-pant in the society. All of the members' roles should be so coordinated that each interrelationship more fully develops the necessary system of communication. Each participant should be able to take the role of every other participant whom she or he will affect, and new meanings/ creations must include shared values.

This is what generates the problems that occur when one moves across social communities. Teachers assume shared values and understood meanings of students and student teachers. Student teachers assume the same of teachers, students, and supervising faculty. This matrix is played out across all social groups that interact through the members' activities.

The ability to communicate is the crucial issue for the development of, in this case, professionalism. First there is the doing of something, and then comes the interpretation. As a result of reflection, one must continually communicate with others to unify the principles of the communities involved. This implies that teachers cannot be spectators in an "objective" world called "school." Rather, they are caught up in the interaction between communities within the school. As a result, they are always participants in the social interplay. Thus the question is whether the teacher education literature calls for dialogue with all the social groups in the school as a part of the reflective process or whether it limits reflection to the individuated student teacher?

REFLECTION AS REPRESENTED IN CONTEMPORARY TEACHER EDUCATION LITERATURE

Mead's theory of experience and community represents a perspective on reflectivity that is both interactive and multifaceted. The theory opposes the Deweyan construction of the reflective process as essentially an individualized phenomenon. For purposes of drawing relationships between the contrasting approaches to reflectivity represented by these two theoreticians, several contemporary articles in teacher education will be examined. The concern in this analysis will be to discuss ways in which authors use language to describe the reflective process and to examine whether these interpretations are congruent with or distinct from Mead's theory. As a touchstone for this analysis, we refer first to Beyer's (1984) observation that many teacher education programs do not go much beyond a notion of reflection as a highly structured skill to be added to the preservice teacher's repertoire. The following review suggests that there is considerable variation in the degrees to which teacher educators incorporate Mead's notion of reflective action.

Korthagen's (1985) experience with teacher education in the Netherlands leads him to conclude that "prospective teachers can be trained to reflect" (p. 15). Although Korthagen does not ground his work in

Dewey, he draws from Zeichner and Liston's (1987) use of Dewey for distinguishing between routine and reflective activity. Accordingly, he describes a teacher education program that combines the use of a reflective log book and interviews to focus on the relationship between the learning effects reported by the teacher candidates and aspects of the preparation program. He cites several excerpts from log books, and although they are generally insightful, they are the remarks of isolated individuals struggling to develop a self within the social group of certified and experienced teachers. The reflections in the log books are not used as catalysts to further reflection and discourse with the teachers, students, or administrators within the particular school; nor are they used to generate dialogue with the university supervisor in order to discuss notions of role-taking or the communities of interaction. Korthagen does not make any distinction between self-reporting and self-reflection. Therefore, this effort does not lie within the framework outlined by Mead as a process of adjustment and emergence, since the potential of the reflective experience is not brought to fruition. Two other works offer approaches to reflective analysis that also operate outside of Mead's framework.

Adler and Goodman (1986) claim that reflective analysis is an integral part of teaching and learning and is one of the goals in a course they describe. In this course, the authors developed a procedure to increase the historical awareness of student teachers, give them practice in instructional techniques, and develop the process of reflection. Reflection, they note, is a procedure that occurs after prescribed moments in the curriculum. The analysis/reflection does not involve only members of a social community who may have immediate experience about the historical themes under study, but the artifacts selected and detailed in the classroom as well. Instrumental self-reflection relies heavily on facts and does not allow for other possible interpretations. Although artifacts are used in the course, multiple interpretations of them do not appear to occur. The mutual efforts of teacher and students in constructing a social history of the classroom or school would be a suggested alternative. In this instance, the students could exchange roles with the teacher and allow for dialogue regarding the construction of interactions. This course, in its present form, does not fit with the perspective on reflection that Adler and Goodman espouse. The habitual part of the self is not being creatively stimulated by new understandings.

Relatedly, Boud, Keogh, and Walker (1985) identify reflection as "intellectual activities used to lead to new understandings and appreciations" (p. 19). They move toward Dewey as their grounding but acknowledge that they attended more closely to "the affective aspects of learning" (p. 21). They note that reflection is used to recapture experience in order to evaluate it. But they do not acknowledge the problems of reconstruction of a particular event from experience. The limits of language and the particular perspective of the individual are not addressed. Although the assistance of others involved in the interactions might enhance the reconstructions, they do not include communication with others in any form, except as a process of debriefing to identify feelings surrounding the experience. The emphasis is on good and bad feelings generated by particular experiences and on the use of these feelings as the starting point for reflection. They constrain reflection by turning it into a mental activity that excludes both the behavioral element and dialogue with others involved in the process. While the attention to feelings cannot be dismissed out of hand, questions arise as to the origin of these feelings and the identification of those particular feelings as important. The nonacknowledgment in these works of the interactive, emergent, and social nature of reflection suggests that these views are still considerably distanced from that of Mead.

We turn now to several other approaches that appear to incorporate Mead's perspective to some degree. Britzman (1986) begins with the statement that "understanding the complex process of learning to become a teacher requires a qualitatively different perspective on the context with which learning to teach occurs" (p. 442). To this end, Britzman identifies one of the generalized others that the preservice teacher will have to organize and consult. This is the *other* that preservice teachers constructed through interactions when they themselves were students. Britzman also directs attention to the manner in which the students of the preservice teacher will coach the student teacher into the appropriate behaviors in that particular school or classroom. If this should deviate from the generalized other of the preservice teacher, he or she will adjust the teaching role accordingly. For Britzman, reflection is an exploration of one's biography as a condition for individual transformation. While the article calls attention to the potentially destructive power of such individualized learning in the process of learning to teach, Britzman does not move to a model of constructive power. A model of this type would include discourse with all the social groups—that is, teachers, students, and administrators at the particular school of the preservice teacher—in order to identify the appropriate behaviors that can be practiced and transformed through role-taking.

A more constructive or participatory approach is presented by Ross and Hannay (1986), who elaborate upon reflective inquiry as a process of decision making in the social studies. Decisions concern the social problems of the participants. Beginning with Dewey's (1916/1961, p.

150) five aspects of reflective thought, Ross and Hannay outline the history of reflective thinking in social studies education, concluding by saying that Dewey has been "proceduralized" and reduced to a "technical" approach (p. 11). They propose combining a critical-theoretical perspective with Dewey's ideas. As critical theorists, they subscribe to the socially constructed nature of human activity. Although Ross and Hannay do not cite Mead, they seem to advocate his notions. In one case they mention that reflection must be an acknowledged and internalized activity of the preservice teacher if it is to become practice. There is a connection here to the power of the generalized other and to the incorporation into the self that comes from the social. They speak to the need for university instructors to model reflective inquiry. Again, in an apparent reference to the generalized other, they are aware of how the self first organizes the attitudes of others in its development and then how others develop self through the process of role-taking and anticipating the responses of others.

At the conclusion of their article, Ross and Hannay place hope in Dewey's notion of the attitudes of openmindedness, responsibility, and wholeheartedness; yet they do not give direction as to how student teachers can understand or achieve these attitudes. The modeling of university instructors in classes can assist, but the twelve to fourteen years of history built up through the personal experience of schooling must be accommodated as well.

Zeichner and Liston (1987) also reflect an awareness of Mead through their reference to his use of the word *action* (p. 23) and their explanation of the interconnection of the cognitive and the behavioral aspects of action. It is significant to compare the language used by Zeichner and Liston to that of Korthagen (1985), who wants to train preservice teachers. Zeichner and Liston want to stimulate reflection, which is an acknowledgment of the importance of internalization that occurs in the process of role-taking. Stimulating reflection provides yet another way to extend the socialization process in university classrooms. Among the necessary components of Zeichner and Liston's program are school and university-based teachers who can be "living models of the moral craftsperson teachers" (p. 26). This view supports Mead's inclusion of significant gestures agreed upon by the social group as another contributor to the attitude of the other.

A closer look, though, at the elements of the program described by Zeichner and Liston suggests that inquiry is limited to observation and analysis. There is no role-taking, no interaction with the people or groups being observed. Dialogue is not initiated to discover shared meanings or new conceptions of interaction, except with the university supervisor. While substantial dialogue occurs with other student teachers and the supervisor from the school and the university, it does not appear that the student teacher interacts with his or her own students in any manner other than that which the novice teacher would have come to expect from his or her own sense of the community of schools. The question remains of how to generate a new community, a more enlightened and reflective community, and to allow for transformative role-taking by student teachers in their preservice experience.

In this cluster of reviews, varying degrees of reference to a sense of self and community as advocated by Mead appear in the selected program descriptions. Claims of reflective analysis as integral to these approaches to teacher preparation appear at times far too instrumental and individuated. Others acknowledge the desirability of the self's interaction with others but appear unable to accomplish this goal as they describe program activity. Rarely are multiple levels of interaction among students and in school communities reflected in these descriptions. Without discourse regarding reflection and subsequent action, the reflective action becomes instrumental and controlling in application. If student teachers' actions in the classroom are to move beyond an apprenticeship model, they must explore their actions with the communities and individuals at the school site—that is, students, teachers, and administrators—and with teacher educators on campus and in the field. Without such communication across these interacting communities, teacher education programs will be less than effective in building up a disposition toward reflection among students of teaching.

CONCLUSIONS

A summary of these contemporary works in teacher education suggests a rather uneven application of Deweyan reflectivity, with only minimal reference to the social theory of Mead. Beyond the specific application of either theory, it would appear as well that the teacher education community has not attained consensus in either its construction of the reflective process or its perception of the relevance of reflection to the socialization of teachers. Relatedly, the goals that teacher educators appear to subscribe to cannot be met by the technical, linear, and highly individualized reflective processes proposed in the writings reviewed in this chapter. The interactions among all groups in the teaching community must be considered in designing programs to prepare prospective teachers.

When the educational community adopted Dewey's reflective inquiry (1909/1933) as an organizing theme for change, it limited itself to instrumentalism and individuation of the teacher. The normative conceptions of self-reflective preservice teachers do not allow the necessary conditions for understanding the interactional processes of reflectivity. Blum and McHugh note that self-reflection is a way to orient one's self to the normative order of the practitioner (1984). Reflectivity without discourse maintains the relationship of a teacher-dominated social interaction. The approach called for in this chapter advocates a type of interaction that values the meanings of all participants. This interactive model will open the control of the knowledge and practices of teaching to the students, student teachers, teachers, and all other communities involved in the school. A closer reading of Mead provides the teacher educator with a different approach to the processes of change and reflectivity. By using the generalized other of all the groups with which the student teacher comes into contact in the school system, and by placing the student teacher in the position of sustaining dialogue with each of the separate generalized others, a community could emerge that would be close to Mead's ideal human society (1934).

In this community, communication would create change for all the individuals and social groups involved in the institution of the school. The isolated individual student teacher who reflects on a particular experience and then makes changes, as described in the articles reviewed, is no less authoritarian than an unreflective student teacher. The commitment to discourse and processes of adjustment is a significant contribution of Mead to the goal of the reflective student teacher. This attention to the total social experience of the student teacher allows for dialogue and communication with all participating social groups and does not permit the growth of authority in one source only. The source of the authority, instead, becomes the social groups that work together through dialogue to construct shared values and expectations. Significantly, this has to include the one group that is missing from all teacher educator literature examined here, that is, students in elementary and secondary classrooms.

The professional development of teachers must incorporate a fuller dialogue with all participants in the system(s) of schools because it must focus on the lived experience of the members of the system(s). Individuated reflective teachers are unable to grasp fully the power of any reflections without discourse because they are distanced from those they are reflecting about. The power of reflection is that it is an instance of social action, and it must be understood as being grounded in the everyday life-world. For the fullest potential of community, discourse, and reflection to be realized, these conceptions cannot be separated or made into technical procedures. The crux of Mead's theory is communication in dialogue between the self and the generalized other of community. Language is the central feature of this public discourse. It is the way in which meaning is given to the everyday life-world and the self. To achieve a richer self-understanding and a fuller knowledge of social groups, discussion must be a feature of teacher-preparation programs. Teacher educators cannot compartmentalize community(ies), discourse, and reflection; rather, these perspectives must be unified to support each other in a more complete development of the individual student teacher and the communities of schools.

An approach such as Mead's attends to the community(ies) and the processes of interaction in such a manner that the means and process of reflection are already incorporated in the development of self and community. The student teacher is not precluded from becoming a reflective and active participant in the different social groups that inhabit the institution of the school. By attending to Mead's idea of community and the process of emergence through language, as well as Hall's conception of context, we educators could capture the empowerment and enhancement of teacher education we seek.

REFERENCES

Adler, S., & Goodman, J. (1986). Critical theory as a foundation for methods courses. *Journal of Teacher Education, 37*(4), 2–8.

Bagenstos, N. (1975). The teacher as an inquirer. *The Educational Forum, 39,* 231–237.

Bakhtin, M. (1968). *Speech genres and other late essays.* Austin, TX: University of Texas Press.

Beyer, L. (1984). Field experience, ideology and the development of critical reflectivity. *Journal of Teacher Education, 35*(3), 36–41.

Blum, A., & McHugh, P. (1984). *Self reflection in the arts and sciences.* Atlantic Highlands, NJ: Humanities Press.

Boud, D., Keogh, R., & Walker, D. (1985). Promoting reflection in learning: A model. In D. Boud, R. Keogh, & D. Walker (Eds.), *Reflection: Turning experience into learning* (pp. 18–40). London: Kogan Page.

Britzman, D. (1986). Cultural myths in the making of a teacher: Biography and social structure in teacher education. *Harvard Educational Review, 56*(4), 442–456.

Corey, S. (1953). *Action research to improve school practice.* New York: Teachers College, Columbia University.

Dewey, J. (1904). The relation of theory to practice in education. In C. A. McMurry (Ed.), *Third yearbook of the National Society for the Scientific Study of Education* (pp. 9–30). Chicago: University of Chicago Press.

Dewey, J. (1933). *How we think*. Lexington, MA: D. C. Heath & Co. (Original work published 1909).

Dewey, J. (1961). *Democracy and Education*. New York: Macmillan. (Original work published 1916)

Feiman, S. (1979). Technique and inquiry in teacher education: A curricular case study. *Curriculum Inquiry, 9*(1), 63-79.

Gore, J. (1987). Reflecting on reflective teaching. *Journal of Teacher Education, 38*(2), 33-39.

Hall, E. (1976). *Beyond culture*. New York: Anchor.

Horkheimer, M. (1972). *Critical theory*. New York: Continuum.

Howey, K. (1988). Mentor teachers as inquiring professionals. *Theory into Practice, 27*(3), 209-213.

Joas, H. (1985). *G. H. Mead*. Cambridge, MA: MIT Press.

Kemmis, S., & McTaggart, R. (1982). *The action research planner*. Victoria, Australia: Deakin University Press.

Korthagen, F. (1985). Reflective teaching and preservice teacher education in the Netherlands. *Journal of Teacher Education, 36*(5), 11-15.

Lacey, C. (1977). *The socialization of teachers*. London: Methnea.

Lewin, K. (1949). *Resolving social conflict*. New York: Teachers College Press.

Mead, G. (1932). *The philosophy of the present*. Chicago: University of Chicago Press.

Mead, G. (1934). *Mind, self, and society*. Chicago: University of Chicago Press.

Ross, W., & Hannay, L. (1986). Towards a critical theory of reflective inquiry. *Journal of Teacher Education, 37*(4), 9-15.

Schön, D. A. (1987). *Educating the reflective practitioner*. San Francisco: Jossey-Bass.

Sergiovanni, T. (1987). *The principalship: A reflective practice perspective*. Newton, MA: Allyn & Bacon.

Zeichner, K. (1979, February). *The dialectics of teacher socialization*. Paper presented at the annual meeting of the Association of Teacher Educators, Orlando, FL.

Zeichner, K., & Grant, C. (1981). Biography and social structure in the socialization of student teachers: A reexamination of pupil control ideologies of student teachers. *Journal of Education for Teaching, 7*(3), 298-314.

Zeichner, K., & Liston, D. (1987). Teaching student teachers to reflect. *Harvard Educational Review, 57*(1), 23-48.

Zeichner, K., & Tabachnick, B. (1982). The belief system of university supervisors in the elementary student teaching program. *Journal of Education for Teaching, 8*(1), 34-54.

5 The Conversation of Practice

ROBERT J. YINGER
University of Cincinnati

CUTTING UP AN OX*

Prince Wen Hui's cook
Was cutting up an ox.
Out went a hand,
Down went a shoulder,
He planted a foot,
He pressed with a knee,
The ox fell apart
With a whisper,
The bright cleaver murmured
Like a gentle wind.
Rhythm! Timing!
Like a sacred dance,
Like "The Mulberry Grove,"
Like ancient harmonies!

"Good work!"
The Prince exclaimed,
"Your method is faultless!"
"Method?" said the cook
Laying aside his cleaver,
"What I follow is Tao
Beyond all methods!

"When I first began
To cut up oxen
I would see before me
The whole ox
All in one mass.
After three years
I no longer saw this mass.
I saw the distinctions.

"But now, I see nothing
With the eye. My whole being
Apprehends.
My senses are idle. The spirit
Free to work without plan
Follows its own instinct

Guided by natural line
By the secret opening, the hidden space,
My cleaver finds its own way
I cut through no joint, chop no bone.

"A good cook, needs a new chopper
Once a year—he cuts.
A poor cook needs a new one
Every month—he hacks.

"I have used this same cleaver
Nineteen years.
It has cut up
A thousand oxen.
Its edge is as keen
As if newly sharpened.

"There are spaces in the joints:
The blade is thin and keen:
When this thinness
Finds that space
There is all the room you need!
It goes like a breeze!
Hence I have this cleaver nineteen years
As if newly sharpened!

*Thomas Merton, *The Way of Chuang Tzu.* Copyright 1965 by The Abbey of Gethsemani. Reprinted by permission of New Directions Publishing Corporation.

"True, there are sometimes
Tough joints. I feel them coming,
I slow down, I watch closely,
Hold back, barely move the blade,
And whump! the part falls away
Landing like a clod of earth.

"Then I withdraw the blade,
I stand still
And let the joy of the work
Sink in.
I clean the blade
And put it away."

Prince Wen Hui said,
"This is it! My cook has shown me
How I ought to live
My own life!"

THE CONCEPT OF PRACTICE

The world of practice is a world in crisis. The conversation of practice has degenerated into monologue, self-talk, or silence. Specialization and institutionalization have cut off the practitioner from a sense of place, a sense of participation, and a sense of community. The thoughtless present tense of technology has replaced the thoughtful growth of tradition. As a result, persons are searching for meaning in isolation, disconnected from essential relationships of life.

Such is the thoroughly modern milieu of practice. Anguished analyses like this are heard across the domains of skilled practice, craft, and art. They can be heard in the prestigious professions of law, medicine, architecture, and engineering and in the "lesser" worlds of teaching and farming. They are even a part of the "other" worlds of theater, music, and poetry. My purpose in this chapter is to try to capture these cries and to reformulate them as a problem of communication and relationship. The metaphor I have chosen to represent practical action is that of a conversation. A healthy conversation of practice is my goal.

Bootstrapping on similarities with status professions like medicine, law, and architecture is a popular method for those practices "on the way up." Mingling with folks like artists and farmers is not the fast track to professionalism. This promised land, however, is populated by institutions and specialists and may be a poor model of healthy practice. By looking to the practical arts and fine arts one can still find practice resisting these modern trends. This is practice in a more natural state or, at least, on a more human scale.

Farmers and Practice

As a field of practice, agriculture has come under close scrutiny in recent years. Criticism of it, though strong, has been mostly unheard and unheeded by society at large. Whereas a practice like education touches nearly every family directly through their children, experience with agriculture is removed by a long chain of processing, packaging, advertising, and marketing. As a result, few Americans consider more than the price and availability of food products. Even fewer understand the real costs associated with modern agriculture. Those who do are concerned that we are quickly losing the means by which to feed ourselves.

The crisis in agriculture results from a complex array of technological, economic, biological, and social causes (Berry, 1977, 1981; Fox, 1986; Fukuoka, 1978; Jackson, 1980; Jackson, Berry, & Colman, 1984; MacFadyen, 1984; Paddock, Paddock, & Bly, 1986). A few examples highlight the depth of this problem.

At the biological level, we are faced with a progressive loss of soil, the source of fertility. Each year farms in the United States lose approximately 4 billion tons of topsoil to wind and water erosion. This averages out to approximately nine tons per acre (Jackson, 1980). To put it more graphically, for every bushel of corn grown in Iowa two bushels of topsoil are lost (Berry, 1977). Estimates suggest that after only one century of agricultural activity, the topsoil in Iowa is half gone (Paddock, Paddock, & Bly, 1986).

Most of the soil that remains has lost its natural fertility. The miraculous yields reported in recent decades, the so-called green revolution, is almost entirely due to the application of millions of tons of petrochemical-based fertilizers, herbicides, and pesticides. The modern practice of monoculture, single-crop farming focusing primarily on the growth of cereal grains for animals, has all but eliminated crop rotation as a means of fertility restoration.

In 1935 the United States had well over 600 million acres of actual or potential cropland. Since then, approximately 100 million acres of potential cropland have been destroyed by erosion or development. Half the topsoil has disappeared on an additional million acres (Jackson, 1980). Pressed by increased debt, farmers have brought into use millions of acres of marginal land even more susceptible to erosion and overgrazing.

Waterways and aquifers are so polluted in parts of the country that some farmers are forced to drink bottled water. In the West, irrigation of dry lands has drawn down aquifers to crisis levels. Water is being used in amounts far exceeding replenishment rates; and heavy irrigation, using more salty, deep water, has led to the abandonment of thousands of acres of soil too salty to support any crops.

The news is no better in technical and economic areas. Energy dependence on U.S. farms has skyrocketed. Agricultural economies that were traditionally solar and biologically based have become petrochemically based. On many large farms inputs in the form of fuel, technology, fertilizer, pesticides, and herbicides account for 90 cents of every earned dollar (MacFadyen, 1984). Larger operations and compacted soils require increasingly larger and prohibitively expensive machinery. Agribusiness and its government supporters rally under the cry of "get big or get out." American corporations, attracted by profits from controlling multiple stages of food production, have entered and remained in farming by subsidizing costly, inefficient agricultural operations with nonfarming profits.

The social costs of modern agriculture may prove to be the most serious and most difficult to remedy. Agribusiness proponents boast that fewer than 5 percent of Americans produce all of the food for our country, with enough left over for export (Berry, 1977). This statement obscures the fact that practices and policies encouraging the reduction of small family farms in favor of large industrial agriculture have, over the past forty years, displaced millions of farm families and destroyed thousands of rural communities. The collapse of inflated land prices and easy credit in the last decade have further removed people from the land. Farmers possessing cultural knowledge and forms of practice developed over thousands of years have been reduced to unskilled labor and now add to the economic pressure on urban areas and social services.

Critical voices in agriculture are slowly gaining strength. Pre-agribusiness government policy and heavy agribusiness funding of the land-grant universities have made serious study of small-farming practices difficult. Research and advocacy have resided in independent institutes and such practitioner-based groups as the Rodale Institute of Ammaus, Pennsylvania; the New Alchemy Institute of Falmouth, Massachusetts; the Land Institute in Salinas, Kansas; and the Agroecology Program at the University of California, Santa Cruz. The increasing evidence of the costs of industrial agriculture has only recently motivated mainstream agricultural researchers to look closely at agricultural alternatives.

Ideas such as organic farming, bioregionalism, and "appropriate technology," which originated and were nurtured outside of mainstream technological optimism, are at the forefront of the reform movement. Advocates of sustainable agriculture, the practice of farming in such a manner as to sustain and regenerate fertility and health, are beginning to address the crucial questions facing the future of farming in the Western world. What is the proper scale for farming? What mixes of crops and animals are most productive and healthful? What new or traditional practices can be used to restore depleted cropland? What practices can reduce the economic and material inputs required for farming and make agricultural practice more independent and vigorous? How many and what kind of people are needed for proper husbandry and stewardship? What social forms and cultural practices need to be restored to enliven rural life? What role should farming and farmers play in the nation's priorities and values? How is the health of the land and its produce related to the health of society?

Advocates of sustainable and regenerative agriculture point to three main areas in which practice has broken down. The first is the relationship between the farmer and the land. The increasing size of farms and the resulting loss of farmworkers have reduced greatly the "eyes to acres" ratio in farming. Fewer farmers and bigger farms mean there is less time and energy available to pay attention to detail, uniqueness, and change in complex biological agricultural systems. Intimate knowledge and care is rarely possible. The scale of large farms exceeds that needed for a reasonable and careful application of human intelligence. Technological optimism hoped to solve this problem with larger machines, automated care, and information systems. Critics see the answer only in a return to small, family-run farms.

Specialization is a second area of concern to critics. One aspect of this problem is the increasing influence of nonfarmer specialists, such as chemical industry representatives and professors of agriculture. Many practitioners complain about misinformation and unsuitable techniques fostered by specialists who are not currently farming and who seem to be primarily driven by specialized motives, such as sales profits or career advancement. Such specialists have advocated the simplification and streamlining of farm operations by narrowing the range of farm activities, causing, in effect, the specialization of farmers. By putting all their eggs into one basket, so to speak, farmers have become more susceptible to fluctuation in commodity markets and more dependent on nonfarm inputs. (It is ironic, for instance, that agricultural specialists have convinced many farmers that they cannot afford to raise their own food.) The remedy to this problem, say reformers, is to reestablish diversification in farming. This would foster independence and greater resilience in the farm sector. It would also increase the labor intensity of farming, requiring smaller operations and more farm employment.

The recommendations surrounding a return to small, diversified family farms is linked to a third criticism—that the agriculture crisis is also due to a disregard for traditional forms of work, family, neighborhood, and community. Research is finding that traditional forms common to agricultural practice and rural communities prior to the Second

World War are highly efficient and ecologically sophisticated. The promise of technology and the resulting efficiencies of scale are proving to have been oversold. Unanticipated technological side effects, such as increased soil erosion, aquifer and waterway pollution, loss of fertility, reduced genetic diversity of plant strains, and soil compaction, are forcing farmers to consider anew the wisdom of traditional practices. The importance of healthy farm communities is causing farmers to realize the value of having a farmer as a neighbor instead of buying the neighbor's farm.

Reforms of this type constitute a direct challenge to the cult of efficiency in agriculture. Economics is being redefined from its narrow production and monetary meaning in favor of its traditional meaning, the stewardship of households. A healthy farm economy (earth household) is being defined as one including a close relationship and "conversation" between a farmer and the land; a diversified, ecologically sound set of practice; and the embedding of work, family, and community in a rich cultural tradition.

Poets and Practice

One initially does not associate poets with farmers, though traditionally the farmer, like all other community members, contributed fully to a community's poetry and song. Recently, criticisms of current practice in poetry and accompanying calls for change parallel those made regarding agriculture. Relationships between the practitioner and his or her place have broken down. Practice has become too specialized, and technique is being misapplied. There is a growing disregard for forms and tradition. Modern voices of criticism include such poets as Wendell Berry (1983), Denise Levertov (1973), and Gary Snyder (1980). These voices echo older criticisms by Edwin Muir (1962), John Crowe Ransom (1968), and Ezra Pound (Eliot, 1954).

The loudest lament heard among contemporary poets is concern about the loss of an audience for poetry. Once a central form of expression and understanding in everyday life, poetry is now rarely read by people other than students of literature or other poets. The effective range and influence, the "estate of poetry," has dwindled to the point that "the public has become one of the subjects of poetry, but is no longer its audience" (Muir, 1962, p. 7).

The poet's lost audience, according to Wendell Berry (1983), is due to the specialization of modern poetry and the focus by the specialists-poets on language and words. Whereas the traditional subject of poetry has been the world that poets have in common with other people, for the specialists-poets it is a "seeking of self in words." Berry continues: "For poets who believe this way, a poem is not a point of clarification between themselves and the world on one hand and between themselves and their readers on the other, nor is it an adventure into any reality or mystery outside themselves" (1983, p. 7). As Denise Levertov says, great writing must move beyond mere expression or transmission to translation. *Translation* here refers not only to interpretation but also to the older meaning of being conveyed from one place to another—"putting the receiver in the place of the event—alive" (Levertov, 1973, p. 94). To the degree that this place is only the words or the ego of the writer, it becomes less accessible to the reader.

The conversation between poets and society in general has broken down because of this specialization and isolation. Too few poets are writing out of a place in the world held in common by their readers. The poet stands removed. The audience, if it exists, is not likely to be the poet's neighbors.

The focus on one's own words and the expression of one's own inner world has also contributed to a disregard for technique and traditional form. Literary discussions today are often characterized by a distinct lack of interest in form or tradition. Wendell Berry recognizes this as a reason for the weakness of the poet's voice. Literary tradition, he says, is a common ground "that joins all the sharers of literature, writers and readers, living and dead" (1983, p. 10). The preoccupation of many poets with the present and the new cuts off both writer and reader from the longevity of human experience: what is possible, what is practicable, and what is imaginable.

> Our past is not merely something to depart from: it is to commune with, to speak with: "Day unto day uttereth speech and night unto night showeth knowledge" [Psalm 19:2]. Remove this sense of continuity, and we are left with the thoughtless present tense of machines. If we fail to see that we live in the same world that Homer lived in, then we not only misunderstand Homer; we misunderstand ourselves. The past is our definition. We may strive, with good reason, to escape it, or to escape what is bad in it, but we will escape it only by adding something better to it.
>
> If, as I believe, one of the functions of tradition is to convey a sense of our perennial nature and of the necessities and values that are the foundation of our life, then it follows that, without a live tradition, we are necessarily the prey of fashion: we have no choice but to emulate in the arts the "practical men" of commerce and indus-

try whose mode of life is distraction of spirit and whose livelihood is
the outdating of fads. (Berry, 1983, p. 14)

Being bound to form for expression binds the practitioner to discipline as well as tradition. The art of poetry has traditionally involved the
ability to create image and meaning by skillfully arranging words and
phrases within the constraints of pattern provided by rhyme, meter, and
stanza. Though many contemporary poets reject these patterns as being
mechanical, poets such as Berry say this is based on a misperception of
the organic nature of working within a form. Denise Levertov, testifying
to this organic relationship, argues that content determines form and,
moreover, that content is discovered in form (1973).

These critiques of farming and poetry portray a convergent view of
effective and responsible practice. Practice is grounded in a close relationship, a conversation, between the practitioner and his or her place
(farmer and soil, poet and audience). This conversation is carried out in
a cultural context defined by a rich tradition of practice (diversified,
locally adapted small farms; the narrative and form of poetry). The
means and technique of practice are holistic and nonspecialized, growing out of local knowledge and attending to basic relationships (biological and communal).

Practice breaks down, according to these critiques, when it becomes specialized and isolated, when the practitioner is no longer able
or no longer cares to respond to the particulars of place and context.
When appropriate scale of practice is exceeded, intelligent application
of technique is no longer possible—the farm becomes too big or the
audience too vague. Specialization is based on limiting practice. Narrowing of concern cuts off the practitioner from essential relationships
and responsibilities to the wider community. Specialization leads to
generalization; and, once rootless, practice becomes essentially self-
serving and exploitive (economics narrowly defined). The specialized
practitioner tends to see specialized problems and offer specialized
solutions. Too often the focus is on the cure itself rather than on health
in general.

Teachers and Practice

Education has gotten a lot of press lately, some bad and some good.
Governors, legislators, corporate executives, state school officers, union
leaders, and many others have lamented the state of American education. Test scores, curriculum content, quality of personnel, working
conditions, and professional training have become the focus of concern.

As a result, many reform efforts have been launched by states, corporations, and professional organizations. Some have been backed by substantial financial resources.

Lengthening the school day, increasing requirements in core school subjects, raising teachers' salaries, instituting more distinct career tracks, and increasing the rigor of teacher education programs are all areas receiving attention and action. These are easy targets for policy makers and ones with quick political payoffs.

Not yet adequately addressed is the nature of healthy teaching practice and the conditions necessary for its existence. Like other professional practices, teaching is grounded in specialized practice in generalized and somewhat isolated institutions. Are the criticisms leveled by critics of agricultural and literary practice applicable to teaching in our educational system? Is isolation, specialization, and disregard for tradition responsible for the disintegration of practice? For example, has centralization and standardization cut off the teacher and learner from a sense of place and community? Has the "basics-only" curriculum and the emphasis on standardized tests homogenized schools and isolated them from local needs, issues, and involvement? Do large class sizes preclude the kinds of interaction needed for effective teaching and effective learning? Have industrialized models of productivity and efficiency been misapplied to learning settings? In what ways are technology, command and control models, and social science methods dehumanizing educational endeavors? These are all questions about the nature of the practice of teaching, its goals, its methods, and its outcomes. Until we look more closely at the nature and conditions of practice, the achievement of healthy, effective teaching may continue to elude us.

THE CONVERSATION OF PRACTICE

We often regard conversation as a uniquely human enterprise. As such, conversation has been used to represent the central goal of education—"participation in the great conversation"—and even the central activity of life—"the conversation of mankind" (see Oakeshott, 1959). Using conversation as a metaphor for practice allows the examination of three important aspects of practical action. First, conversation refers to the means by which social practices are conducted. Language as utterance or text frames social interaction, and evidence suggests that a practitioner's interaction with materials and places is framed by a "language of practice" as well (Yinger, 1987a, 1987b).

Second, the conversational metaphor expresses the multifaceted, give-and-take nature of human thought. Thinking is responsive interchange between thought and action, between the organism and the environment. This is the meaning Schön (1983) assigns when he describes the work of the practitioner as a "reflective conversation" with the situation at hand. Conversation even captures the basic interchange between operations and tests represented by Miller, Galanter, and Pribram's (1960) test-operate-test-exit model of cognition: Thought is composed of action and information flowing responsively within a general goal framework.

A third aspect, one possibly fundamental to practice, is alluded to in the etymology of the word *conversation*. One of the Latin roots for the word is *conversari*, meaning "to dwell with." This suggests that conversation involves an entering into and living with a context and its participants. As such, conversation is not only a means of interaction and a way of thinking but also a type of relationship with one's surroundings.

The conversation of practice involves three central partners: a practitioner, his or her collaborators, and a place. A practitioner is one who possesses particular knowledge and skill that are employed to produce specific yields or outcomes for participants (including oneself). These aims are accomplished by interacting in a participatory mode with another set of actors, variously referred to as partners, clients, audience, and so forth, depending on the nature of the interaction. This interaction always takes place in a particular place—an identifiable world made up of specific patterns, structures, substance, and meanings. This practical world is physical, cultural, and communal and possesses a tradition grounded in history, knowledge, and belief. To practice a particular occupation, craft, or art one must enter into a relationship with participants and place. Neither of these partners can be safely ignored.

The conversation of farming involves a farmer interacting (co-laboring) with soil, plants, animals, and other persons in a particular place defined by a field, a farm, a bioregion, a family, and a community. The farmer's intelligence and effectiveness are based on situated knowledge and skill—how to interact with particular crops and soil, for instance, given the particular farming context. A good farmer will consider a complex set of patterns, forms, and information related to a particular place. This may range from considerations of climate and geography, to the effects of various means of cultivation or husbandry, to the traditional forms of work and produce desired in a particular community and culture. Farming can be considered effective when it yields healthy produce and practices benefiting all the participants and the place: good food, sustained fertility, and enriched community.

The conversation of poetry, likewise, should be judged by its ability to generate health and well-being. The forms this takes include increased understanding and meaning, personal enjoyment and satisfaction, and enriched communal life. The poet's experience with fellow inhabitants and their jointly constructed world yields particular oral or written products to be shared with audiences and readers. The place of poetry includes both a particular living community and also the traditions, forms, and knowledge connecting conversational partners to the past. To the degree that a poet, or any other writer for that matter, loses touch with or disregards audience and place, the conversation of practice degenerates into monologue or self-talk.

In the same manner, the conversation of teaching must include all three partners to be effective and healthy. A good teacher must co-labor with students (and with parents and other educators) in a particular place with its particular patterns, traditions, and forms. This place, like other practical worlds, is organized at a number of levels, such as community, school, classroom, curriculum, activity, problem, story. Knowledge and skill must be artfully adapted to the particular participants and context. The teacher's intelligence and action, like the farmer's and poet's, must be situated and responsive. Understanding, meaning, satisfaction, enjoyment—healthy learning—result when this is accomplished.

THE INTELLIGENCE OF PRACTICE

The intelligence of practice is based on an ability to fit tool and method to specific needs of specific people and places. The essence of practice is work-in-place. Practical action can be most simply divided into aspects of performance and aspects of consideration. Performance refers to the doing, the enacting, the accomplishment of practical action. Consideration is the careful thought and attention directed toward past and future performance conducted apart from the immediacy and demands of actual performance. To consider is to observe, to examine, and to think about in order to understand or decide. Part of the Latin root for *consider*, *sideris*, meaning "star," suggests that consideration, like astronomy, is conducted at a distance from the phenomenon of interest. In teaching, consideration is often labeled *planning* and *reflection*, while *performance* is the actual teaching, or implementation, of plans. Such labels, however, cannot be construed as rigid categorizations. In the practice of teaching, performance and consideration are meshed in an ongoing conversation.

Planning, Implementation, and Reflection

The methods of practice embodied in the prescriptive language of modern practice—planning, implementation, and reflection—describe a framework of sound practice. This involves the careful alignment of goals and means in a design, action conforming to the design, and thoughtful analysis and evaluation of the outcomes. To the degree that practice follows this framework, it is "rational"; failures and departures from this framework are considered undesirable or even unreasonable.

Planning, implementation, and reflection have each been identified closely with an analytic, means-ends formulation of thought. Early in this century, thinking in general was portrayed in this process framework. John Dewey in *How We Think* (1909/1933) went so far as to state that worthwhile thought is reflective thought, thereby identifying thinking with an analytic process guided by a hypothesis-testing mode of problem solving. For Dewey, thinking dealt necessarily with the problematic and proceeded by means of analysis and testing.

As an outgrowth of general formulations like Dewey's, planning and reflection were described according to similar rational frameworks. The rational-planning model developed in economics and adopted widely by professionals, researchers, and educators incorporated four basic steps: careful specification of goals (usually in operational terms); the generation of possible alternatives; the assignment of outcomes to each alternative; and the selection of the best alternative in light of outcomes and goals (see Yinger, 1977, 1980, for a description and critique of the use of this model in education).

Reflection as a process has been described in a similar manner. A reflective experience, according to Dewey, includes the following general features:

> (i) perplexity, confusion, doubt, due to the fact that one is implicated in an incomplete situation whose character is not yet fully determined; (ii) a conjectural anticipation—a tentative interpretation of the given elements, attributing to them a tendency to effect certain consequences; (iii) a careful survey (examination, inspection, exploration, analysis) of all attainable consideration[s] which will define and clarify the problem at hand; (iv) a consequent elaboration of the tentative hypothesis to make it more precise and more consistent, because [of its] squaring with a wider range of facts; (v) taking one['s] stand upon the projected hypothesis as a plan of action which is applied to the existing state of affairs: doing something overtly to bring about the anticipated result, and thereby testing the hypothesis. (Dewey, 1916/1944, p. 150)

The third component of rational practice, implementation, has been considered mainly in terms of fidelity. Implementation is thought effective to the degree it adheres to the plan and accomplishes the goal. Reflection is the process by which planning and action are tracked and assessed. Reflection links past and future action by supplying information about operations and outcomes. By viewing practice through these three processes, every action becomes problematic and thus amenable to rational attack.

Improvisation, Contemplation, and Preparation

An alternative language of performance and consideration to that of planning, implementation, and reflection is the language of practice used by Prince Wen Hui's cook in the poem at the beginning of this chapter. There is certainly skill in his performance and a type of reasonableness in his explanations, but it appears to be quite different from typical notions of rationality. Analysis gives way to holistic comprehension; planfulness gives way to instinct; the work itself seems to carry the practitioner along. This is the language of preparation, improvisation, and contemplation.

Improvisation. Improvisation is skilled performance that is especially sensitive to moment and place. The impromptu, responsive nature of improvisation has generated connotations of being unprepared and off guard. The reality of improvisational performance is quite different. It is highly patterned, intelligently composed, and quite complex to learn. In a review of improvisation in music, oral poetry, theater, conversation, and traditional work (Yinger, 1987b), I generated the following propositions regarding improvisational performance.

1. Improvisation is a form of action especially suited to situations that discourage or prevent deliberative processes such as planning, analysis, and reflection.
2. Improvisation is a compositional process using as building blocks a set of situationally (contextually) grounded patterns for thought and action.
3. These patterns are holistic configurations of "embodied thought," called upon to be composed and enacted (lived) within the special constraints of the context.
4. The working method of improvisation is primarily "retrospective," using patterns from past action to other future action.
5. Skillful improvisation is based on the incorporation of patterns and

pathways in a way that is continually responsive to changing exigencies and purposes.

6. Improvisational patterns are structured by action and include constellations of knowledge, beliefs, and goals.
7. Improvisational skill is synthetic and compositional, not analytic.
8. Improvisation is primarily directed toward the establishment and maintenance of relationship: between actor and material, between actor and instrument (tool), between actor and other participants.

Descriptions of improvisation as a performance language for practice have been most fully developed in the performance arts of music, theater, and oral poetry. As an example of improvisation in a practical art, I have been studying the classroom interaction of an eighth-grade algebra teacher, Bob Knight (see Yinger, 1987b, for a fuller account of this research).

Mr. Knight's method of teaching involves the use of patterns within patterns. Math problems provide the basic patterns of meaning and action. Problems are embedded in the larger patterns of lesson activity cycles and unit lesson cycles. Working the other direction, problems provide the contexts for teaching and learning, the academic task structure (Erickson, 1982), and the focus of the instructional conversation. Like all conversations, action in these instructional frameworks is accomplished by local improvisation. The performances of the participants are compared on the spot by using knowledge and interaction patterns bounded by social participation structures, such as working together, demonstration, and working alone.

The teacher is cast as an actor in a three-way conversation between teacher, students, and problems. The teacher's action along the teacher-problem pathway is composed of calling up knowledge and procedures holistically associated with particular problem types. These patterns manifest themselves in the written production of the solution steps and the teacher's talk associated with them.

Action along the teacher-student conversation pathway is composed of a number of recurring patterns. Thinking aloud, explicating knowledge, and debugging mistakes are ways of making the teacher's interaction with the problem more public. Getting to specifics and decomposing/rebuilding problems are patterns used to work from the basis of the students' previous interaction with the problem.

For any one problem, for any specific instructional conversation, these patterns are composed on the spot as part of the teacher's performance. At times demonstration is the form of conversation in a lesson presentation or homework check, at other times it is working together;

sometimes they appear in the same lesson. Within these conversational types, various teaching patterns are used. Composing lessons while doing them seems to build on the same kind of mechanism of situational similarity recognition that directs the interaction with specific problems.

To the extent that action is improvisational, the instructional conversations and the strategy patterns of teaching can be described only generally. They constitute action pathways with a general orientation and purpose. Interaction within the patterns is reactive and responsive; thought and action are adapted to the dynamics of social interaction and conversation.

Contemplation. Whereas improvisation provides an alternative performance language for practice, the notions of contemplation and preparation supply an alternative language for consideration. Reflection and planning, as described earlier, are focused by goals and driven by analysis and evaluation. Contemplation and preparation describe a different relation to the work.

To contemplate something is to look at and think about it attentively and intently. While reflection implies a focused consideration of the past without a particular stance or orientation, contemplation suggests thought-in-place. The root of *contemplate* is *templum*, meaning *temple* or *sanctuary*. More specifically, *templum* refers to a space marked out for observation by an augur. Contemplation thus implies observation and thinking in a separate, protected, or holy place—a place occupying a particular relationship to a larger community and cultural order.

Contemplation bears a close relationship to practice. It is a way of being in the work even when the work is not being performed. Reflection is vision looking down from without. Contemplation is looking up and out from traditional familiarity and use, out of "a place marked out." The reflective mind, in modern terms, is focused and coolly analytic. The contemplative mind, to paraphrase Denise Levertov (1973), uses the heat of feelings to warm the intellect. Contemplation, in contrast to focused deliberation, allows the mind to roam widely over the terrain of practice. Current states of affairs are considered for their possibilities. Possibilities are considered in light of practice in place.

Reflection, according to Dewey, allows the practitioner to rise above tradition, authority, and circumstance by analysis and evaluation (the criteria under consideration being pragmatic, utilitarian, and instrumental). Contemplation suggests that tradition, authority, and circumstance should be the starting point for consideration, though not the complete definition. Considering common ground becomes the basis for considering new ground. Contemplation is a generalist's stance—considering holistically in terms of order, balance, harmony, and symmetry and resisting the lure of autonomy and control. Contemplation is a language of conversation and stewardship.

Preparation. Preparation, like planning, addresses the conversation of practice with the future. The nature of this conversation, however, is quite different. Planning, on the one hand, results in some framework for future action, a plan. The range of possibility is prescribed, choices are made about parameters for action, the future is narrowed. Planning seeks to deal with uncertainty by controlling action and outcomes. The goal is to constrain the unpredictable, the random, and the wild.

On the other hand, preparation acknowledges our limited ability to predict and the constructive nature of life. Preparation expects diversity, surprise, the random, and the wild. To prepare is to get ready, to become equipped, and to become receptive. The focus of preparation is on oneself, not on a framework to constrain possibility. In a sense, preparation enlarges the future.

In traditional cultures, one sometimes finds a concerted effort to avoid planning as we know it. A plan is seen as an unwarranted attempt at control, an effort that by limiting one's concept of the future implies an arrogant belief that one fully understands the present. For example, in their work with Athabaskan languages, Ron and Suzanne Scollon (1985) found that native speakers are very careful about using future word forms, even though their language includes abundant grammatical means for coding future statements. The Scollons believe interpretations suggesting that the Athabaskan people do not concern themselves with the future but live in a "simple present that looks nostalgically back on the past" are in error.

> We think that this is not what is happening at all. An Athabaskan man going out to check his traps will be very careful not to say that he is going to get his furs, or even that he hoped to find anything. He will simply say he is going out for a few hours or days. But in his packs will be all the preparations for the animals he might find in his traps, a fishbone for the mink, or fat to rub on the nose of another. It is the concern not to limit the future that leads to this great care in speaking of it. (Scollon & Scollon, 1985, p. 31)

To reject planning in favor of preparation is not to reject the future or a consideration of it. It is a stance, an attitude, toward one's relation to the work and to the world. Planning takes the side of rationality and control. Preparation leans toward participation and responsiveness. Every practitioner will both plan and prepare, implement and improvise, reflect and contemplate. The differential stock put in these activities reflects one's relational stance. Planning, implementation, and analytic reflection, in the conversation of practice, pull away from thought-in-place; improvisation, contemplation, and preparation draw toward it.

LEARNING TO PRACTICE

Learning to practice involves learning to think and behave in ways appropriate to the demands of practice. This goes beyond booklearning and other forms of schooling. Good farming and good poetry are not ensured by agriculture or English degrees. A teaching certificate falls short of certifying good teaching. As work-in-place, these practices rely on an ability to participate in the conversation of practice. A central task to learning a practice, therefore, is learning the language of practice: those patterned ways of meaning and acting that are uniquely suitable and effective for accomplishing specific practical activities (Yinger, 1987a). Included in this learning task are the tasks of learning place and learning past (Scollon & Scollon, 1985).

Learning Language

The foundation of learning practice is to learn to think and act in appropriate ways, that is, to learn the language of effective practice. When I use the term *language* I use it broadly. It includes words and sayings practitioners use within a profession. More importantly, language of practice refers to modes of thinking and acting. A spoken language includes a syntax, a semantics, and a pragmatics. Likewise, a language of practice includes a logic or grammar for thought and action, a system of meaning, and criteria and guidelines for effective practice.

A language of practice is not primarily a verbal matter; it also includes embodied structures of meaning that are a part of orientation, movement, and manipulation (Johnson, 1987). It is not limited to speaking about or representing practice to oneself or others. Rather, a language of practice is a set of integrated patterns of thought and action. These patterns themselves constitute a kind of syntax and semantics for action. The words and phrases in this language are behavior, activities, and routines. As such, a language of practice is found in the practitioner's action rather than speech. It is rarely heard, but it is seen and felt.

A language of practice consists of patterns of thought and action useful for both contemplation and performance. For instance, when one faces a problem, one does not usually try to solve it from scratch. The problem activates stored patterns, which become the foundation for creative thought. The use of a pattern language, then, is responsive and sensitive to context. Goals and means are intimately connected. Standard processes are adapted to produce unique forms. The use of a pattern language builds upon the existing state of affairs to make it more whole, more unified, more complete. Problem solving becomes a process of differentiation, beginning with the whole and proceeding through a step-by-step unfolding of the parts.

Likewise, when one performs a practice, the components of action are not invented on the spot. Performance involves the practitioner in the compositional orchestration of patterns of action suitable for the task at hand. Whereas implementation activates patterns within a framework prescribed by planning, improvisation activates patterns elicited by the demands of the moment. To the degree that patterns are organized in repeated ways, the action is called routine or scripted. When patterns are organized newly each time, the action is improvisational or creative. Regardless of the form taken by the conversation of practice, it is grounded in a basic repertoire, a language of practice.

Some aspects of a language of practice are more general and thus applicable in different places. Others are more local, more of a dialect. Conversation, however, is always local; particular partners converse in a particular place. For this reason, learning practice involves learning place.

A failure of practice mentioned earlier is the failure of specialization. As practice specializes, local practice degenerates into generalized and abstract action. To the degree that the learning of practice resides in institutions removed from places of practice, the learning will be abstract and placeless. To learn practice one must be engaged in local practice. Without a place, there is no practice. Without a practitioner interacting with particular collaborators in a particular place, there is no conversation.

Learning Place

Learning place means learning how the practitioner fits into surrounding life. It involves learning in detail about the other participants in practice, their lives, their histories, and their relations to one another. It includes learning the characteristics that define a place: family, neighborhood, community, culture. It also includes learning aspects of the physical world defining a place. How is place defined in terms of land, bioregion, plant and animal life? Learning place involves learning about any aspect of life bearing on the meanings, beliefs, and actions of its inhabitants.

Learning place implies a commitment to place. The specialist practitioner too often is passing through on a "career path." The conversation of practice is rooted, grounded, and locally committed. If place is important to the conversation of practice, then practice must become liberated from the industrial doctrine of interchangeable parts, interchangeable places, and interchangeable people (Berry, 1987).

Learning Past

Learning place requires learning past. A present place is linked to past places; current practice is linked to past practice. Learning past can be both broadly and narrowly construed. Broadly speaking, learning past includes the full range of the cultural heritage: history, literature, science, music, art, philosophy. How does past thought and action influence that of the present? More narrowly, learning past means learning the traditional means and traditional forms of effective practice in a particular place. What has worked when and with whom? What forms bind and what forms liberate? As Wendell Berry says, it is tradition that protects us from falling prey to fashion. Unfortunately, fashion has had too much say in modern practice.

Learning by Participating

Conversation is learned through participation. Instruction can sensitize a beginner to aspects of practice, but the real learning is in the doing. Too often the language of schooling, including schooling for practice, is specialized, generalized, and abstract. When practitioners' schooling includes experiences with practice-in-place, like co-ops, internships, and practica, learners attribute more learning to these experiences than to those in the classroom. Schooling allows one to *study* practice, but learning *to* practice must be done in place.

As long as the intelligence of practice is defined by the techniques of planning, implementation, and reflection, learning can comfortably remain indoors. These activities can be taught abstractly and rehearsed in such artificial or limited settings as laboratories. However, once the intelligence of practice is defined by activities such as contemplation, preparation, and improvisation, learning is forced to move outdoors into the real world of practice. These latter activities are so tied to and dependent upon time and place that they have no meaning abstractly. This is why traditional means for learning these techniques have been tied closely to forms such as apprenticeship, discipleship, and mentoring. In a sense, the conversation of practice can be learned but not taught.

CONCLUSIONS

In this chapter, I have used the conversation of practice as a metaphor to describe a particular form of practice that I and others consider to be desirable. The goal of this practice is the healthy interaction between participants and place that yields outcomes benefiting all those involved. The means for this practice has been described as participation and conversation. Its intelligence is portrayed as sensitive and responsive consideration and performance. Improvisation, contemplation, and preparation are its techniques.

This description of practice embodies a particular set of values. Place is set before "word." Participation is placed before analysis. Conversation is valued above isolated thought. Community is valued above the isolated individual. Practice is healthy when it is participatory, unifying, and resonant. Work, song, story, and ritual are important forms for practice to take. These forms of human interaction are healthy because they are focused on action and, more importantly, on right action. Morality and ethics are too often held at arm's length by specialization and technology. The conversation of practice is either moral and healthy or immoral and diseased. Practice is either an instrument of good or an instrument of evil.

Practice is healthy and life-giving when it embodies the goals, intelligence, and values of the conversation of practice. Certain forms of practice seem to capture the conversation more easily. Those pursuing sustainable and regenerative agriculture are advocating a return to the small, family-run farm. The "poet in residence" responds to critics' concerns that poetry again take a vital role in community life.

In teaching, the desired form is less clear. The current focus on the teacher as a professional may encourage more harm than benefit, unless this image is detached from the professions as currently practiced and rekindled by the original meaning of professional: one who vows or professes a core value (health, truth, and justice were the original core value of medicine, teaching, and law) and seeks to pursue these values in practice. The image of the career teacher treads the same dangerous ground as that of the professional teacher. The teacher as manager, executive, diagnoser, or information processor all suffer the error of narrowed emphasis. Master teacher, though somewhat redundant, implies a meaning much closer to that which we need. *Master* is a traditional term that in practice described one who was highly skilled and able but also one who was qualified to instruct others.

It may be that the most desirable image for teaching lies in the word *teaching* alone. In its base sense, *teaching* means "to show, or to demonstrate," both of which are face-to-face, interactive, communal, and conversational activities. In our search for a correct modifier, we may be too distracted by the lure of other places and other practices. The real meaning of teaching and learning and the real work is closer to home and within ourselves.

REFERENCES

Berry, W. (1977). *The unsettling of America: Culture and agriculture.* New York: Avon.

Berry, W. (1981). *The gift of good land: Further essays cultural and agricultural.* San Francisco: North Point.

Berry, W. (1983). *Standing by words.* San Francisco: North Point.

Berry, W. (1987). *Home economics.* San Francisco: North Point.

Dewey, J. (1933). *How we think.* New York: Heath. (Original work published 1909)

Dewey, J. (1944). *Democracy and education.* New York: Free Press. (Original work published 1916)

Eliot, T. S. (Ed.). (1954). *Literary essays of Ezra Pound.* New York: New Directions.

Erickson, F. (1982). Classroom discourse as improvisation: Relationships between academic task structure and social participation structure. In L. C. Wilkinson (Ed.), *Communicating in the classroom* (pp. 153–181). New York: Academic.

Fox, M. (1986). *Agricide.* New York: Schocken.

Fukuoka, M. (1978). *The one-straw revolution.* New York: Bantam.

Jackson, W. (1980). *New roots for agriculture.* Lincoln: University of Nebraska Press.

Jackson, W., Berry, W., & Colman, B. (Eds.). (1984). *Meeting the expectations of the land: Essays in sustainable agriculture and stewardship.* San Francisco: North Point.

Johnson, M. (1987). *The body in the mind.* Chicago: University of Chicago Press.

Levertov, D. (1973). *The poet in the world.* New York: New Directions.

MacFadyen, J. T. (1984). *Gaining ground: The renewal of America's small farms.* New York: Ballantine.

Merton, T. (1965). *The way of Chuang Tzu.* New York: New Directions.

Miller, G. A., Galanter, E., & Pribram, K. H. (1960). *Plans and the structure of behavior*. New York: Holt, Rinehart & Winston.

Muir, E. (1962). *The estate of poetry*. Cambridge, MA: Harvard University Press.

Oakeshott, M. (1959). *The voice of poetry in the conversation of mankind*. London: Bowes & Bowes.

Paddock, J., Paddock, N., & Bly, C. (1986). *Soil and survival*. San Francisco: Sierra Club.

Ransom, J. C. (1968). *The world's body*. Baton Rouge: Louisiana State University Press.

Schön, D. (1983). *The reflective practitioner: How professionals think in action*. New York: Basic Books.

Scollon, R., & Scollon, S. (1985). *The problem of power*. Haines, AK: The Gutenberg Dump.

Snyder, G. (1980). *The real work: Interviews and talks 1964–1979*. New York: New Directions.

Yinger, R. J. (1977). *A study of teacher planning: Description and theory development using ethnographic and information processing methods*. Unpublished doctoral dissertation, Michigan State University.

Yinger, R. J. (1980). A study of teacher planning. *Elementary School Journal, 80*, 107–127.

Yinger, R. J. (1987a). Learning the language of practice. *Curriculum Inquiry, 17*(3), 293–318.

Yinger, R. J. (1987b, April). *By the seat of your pants: An inquiry into improvisation and teaching*. Paper presented at the annual meeting of the American Educational Research Association, Washington, DC.

PART II

IMPROVING PROFESSIONAL PRACTICE
THROUGH REFLECTIVE INQUIRY

6 Programmatic Structures for the Preparation of Reflective Teachers

DORENE D. ROSS
University of Florida

The ability to reflect about practice does not develop in one course or even in a few courses. Enabling preservice students to be reflective requires the development of a clearly articulated program of study. Therefore, helping students develop this ability must be viewed as the task of a teacher education program, not of individual faculty members. While most efforts at developing the reflective abilities of teachers have occurred within specific courses or program components, faculty at a few institutions have attempted to evolve a programmatic commitment to the development of reflection.

The purpose of this chapter is to identify and discuss six issues critical in the development of programs emphasizing reflective teaching. These six issues include:

1. developing a common definition of reflection;
2. developing awareness of strategies that support reflection;
3. building a coherent, integrated, and logically sequenced program;
4. developing collaborative relationships with schools;
5. developing ways to provide ongoing support for graduates;
6. developing means for evaluating the impact of programs.

Examples of the ways teacher educators are dealing with each issue are drawn from descriptions of teacher education programs, courses, and program components, as well as from the experiences of faculty at the University of Florida.

DEVELOPING A COMMON DEFINITION OF REFLECTION

Barnes (1987) notes that any teacher education program with a strong thematic focus should present a clear view of teaching that is well grounded in current research. In most teacher education programs, however, the images of effective teaching that shape educators' decisions about the educational opportunities provided to students and their evaluation of the impact of their efforts are individually constructed and "only implicitly held in each person's mind" (Simmons & Sparks, 1987, p. 2). Consequently, articulation of the meaning of reflection is a critical first step for teacher educators.

Multiple definitions of reflection exist. In Chapter 2 of this volume, Grimmett and colleagues suggest three potential conceptions of reflection: (1) instrumental mediation of actions; (2) deliberation among competing views; and (3) reconstruction of experience.

Alternative descriptions or definitions of reflection have been offered by Tom (1985) and Valli (Chapter 3, this volume). The nature of these differences clarifies the importance of developing a common definition for reflection. As Zeichner (1987) notes, educators who target reflective teaching as a goal are "not necessarily committed to the same ends beyond their general agreement on the importance of providing some vehicle for structuring the analysis of teaching" (p. 566). When such differences exist within programs, the messages sent to students may be confusing, and the effectiveness of the program may be undermined.

A brief description of the definition used at the University of Florida will provide a basis for understanding the description of our program components throughout this chapter. In developing our definition we have drawn on the work of Schön (1983); on the work of Kitchener and King (1981), who have developed and validated a seven-stage model of the development of reflective judgment; and on the works of teacher educators.

We define reflection as a way of thinking about educational matters that involves the ability to make rational choices and to assume responsibility for those choices (Goodman, 1984; Ross, 1987a; Zeichner & Liston, 1987). The elements of the reflective process include (not necessarily in this order):

- recognizing educational dilemmas;
- responding to a dilemma by recognizing both the similarities to other situations and the unique qualities of the particular situation;
- framing and reframing the dilemma;
- experimenting with the dilemma to discover the implications of various solutions;
- examining the intended and unintended consequences of an implemented solution and evaluating it by determining whether the consequences are desirable.

Schön (1983) stresses that reflective practice is grounded in the practitioner's appreciation system (i.e., repertoire of values, knowledge, theories, and practices). The appreciation system of the teacher influences the types of dilemmas that will be recognized, the way teachers frame and reframe dilemmas, and the judgments teachers make about the desirability of various solutions. For example, Liston and Zeichner (1987) note that teachers must use moral as well as educational criteria in examining the consequences of implemented solutions. Consequently, the preparation of reflective practitioners requires not only teaching the elements of the reflective process but also increasing the range and depth of knowledge in each student's appreciation system.

Our definition also requires the development of several attitudes and abilities. Requisite attitudes include introspection, open-mindedness, and willingness to accept responsibility for decisions and actions (Dewey, 1909/1933). The introspective teacher engages in thoughtful reconsideration of all that happens in a classroom with an eye toward improvement. The open-minded teacher is willing to consider new evidence (such as unexpected occurrences in a classroom or new theoretical or research-based knowledge) and willing to admit the possibility of error. The characteristics of mature reflective judgment (Kitchener & King, 1981) indicate that students must also develop the ability to view situations from multiple perspectives, the ability to search for alternative explanations of classroom events, and the ability to use evidence (such as events occurring in a classroom, the characteristics of an individual child or group of children, the characteristics of an educational setting, and theoretical or research knowledge) in supporting or evaluating a decision or position. A willingness to accept responsibility implies that students recognize the decisions they make, evaluate the impact of those decisions for children, and appropriately accept responsibility for the consequences of their actions. Therefore, reflection within the PROTEACH program at the University of Florida is defined as a way of thinking about educational matters that involves the ability to recognize dilemmas; make rational choices; assess the intended and unintended consequences of those choices using practical, pedagogical, and ethical criteria; and accept responsibility for those consequences.

This definition of reflection provides a framework for helping students become more reflective and for evaluating their progress toward that goal. Additionally, Noordhoff and Kleinfeld (1987) stress that the language used in the definition must be carefully considered. For example, they note that defining reflection as problem solving creates difficulties, because *problem* has negative meanings for students and practitioners and because a focus on *solving* underemphasizes the important process of problem setting. They found that defining reflection as a design process (from Schön, 1983) is more productive.

DEVELOPING AWARENESS OF STRATEGIES
THAT SUPPORT THE DEVELOPMENT OF REFLECTION

In a program with a thematic focus, all program courses and practices should support the philosophy of the program and help students develop conceptions of teaching that are consistent with the thematic focus (Barnes, 1987). While the development of a coherent and consistent programmatic focus is clearly desirable, it is not easily accomplished. Programs are composed of individual faculty members, not all of whom have the commitment to or knowledge about reflection necessary for a thematic focus. Several researchers have noted that instructors fail to encourage the connection of theory to practice (Erdman, 1983; Goodman, 1986a) and fail to encourage serious reflection about practice. In fact, Tabachnick, Popkewitz, and Zeichner (1979–80) found that many instructors actually discourage reflection by reinforcing the students' idea that the most important part of student teaching is to fit in, get along, and get good recommendations. Clearly then, the development of faculty awareness of appropriate strategies to support reflection is essential.

While many strategies supporting the development of reflection exist in the literature, Zeichner (1987) identifies six major ones: "reflective teaching" (Cruickshank, 1985), action research, ethnography, writing, curriculum analysis and development, and supervisory approaches. In this section, each of these strategies is explained, although action research, ethnography, and curriculum analysis and development have been clustered and labeled inquiry activities. Two additional strategies, faculty modeling and questioning and dialogue, are also described. The strategies discussed in this section are drawn from published literature on the development of reflection and from descriptions of teacher education programs emphasizing reflection. It is important to note that inquiry into the effectiveness of these strategies is in its infancy. To date, there is little evidence of the impact of the strategies on the development of reflective ability in students (Zeichner, 1987).

Reflective Teaching

Tom (1985) argues that some inquiry-oriented programs view knowledge as lawlike, while others view it as socially constructed. This distinction has implications for the identification of strategies that support the development of reflection. Programs that view knowledge as lawlike accept a technical definition of reflection and adopt strategies that help students master and appropriately apply teaching skills, such as direct instruction, cooperative grouping, lesson planning, and classroom management.

Reflective teaching, a procedure developed at Ohio State University, is the best-known example of this approach (Cruickshank, 1985). Reflective teaching provides student teachers with repeated opportunities to teach and analyze brief lessons developed by the program designers. Analysis helps students identify and develop increased control over variables that influence learners' achievement and satisfaction with learning. Taking a slightly different approach to helping students master and selectively apply technical skills, the faculty at Iowa State University teach students to assess the effectiveness of various teaching behaviors using interactive videotapes. In addition, students apply their knowledge by critiquing lessons from a live videotape of classroom instruction (Volker, 1987).

Inquiry Activities

Although most programs stressing reflection use strategies designed to help students acquire technical competence, many teacher educators who target reflection as a goal believe that knowledge is socially constructed. For example, Calderhead (1988) argues that preservice teachers enter their programs with images and commonsense knowledge about learning, teaching, and students. Teacher education, then, requires that faculty identify strategies that encourage continuous inquiry about the relationship between entering (and primarily intuitive) knowledge and knowledge derived from theories and research (Valli & Taylor, 1987). By helping students see curricula as negotiated between teacher and student and as guided by educational and ethical values, educators help students assume a more active role in curriculum evaluation and construction (Beyer, 1984; Feiman, 1979). Action research, case studies, ethnographies, and curriculum analysis and design are examples of inquiry activities used by teacher educators to accomplish this purpose.

Action research, case study, and ethnography provide preservice teachers with disciplined ways to evaluate both their intuitive beliefs about teaching and the effectiveness of instructional approaches derived from theories and research. Action research is defined as "research undertaken by practitioners in order that they may improve their practices" (Corey, 1954, p. 375). Action research includes three essential characteristics: (1) It is conducted in a field setting by participants in the field who often, but not always, have the assistance of an outsider; (2) the problems studied are problems of practice, selected by the practitioner (i.e., inservice or preservice teacher); and (3) much of the data collection and analysis are done by the practitioner (Noffke & Zeichner, 1987).

At the University of Florida and the University of Virginia, preservice teachers return to the classroom in which they completed their final student teaching experience to investigate questions arising from that experience (Moore, Mintz, & Bierman, 1987; Ross, 1989b). At the University of Wisconsin, preservice teachers' action research projects encourage them to become "students of teaching" as they complete their final internship (Noffke & Brennan, 1988). Ross (1989a) argues that action research contributes to the development of reflection in teachers by helping teachers improve their instructional effectiveness (Hanna, 1986), become better decision makers (Cohen & Alroi, 1981), and view teaching as a form of experimentation or inquiry (Biott, 1983; Cohen & Alroi, 1981).

Similar arguments are made about the benefits of case study and ethnography. Using these methods, students become sensitive to the multiple factors that influence teachers' and children's perspectives on school situations, learn to assess critically their ideas about the nature of good teaching (McCarthy & Clift, 1987), and learn "to explore the ideological nature of curriculum, pedagogy and evaluation and the interrelationships between these socially constructed practices within the school and the social, economic, and political contexts within which they are embedded" (Zeichner, 1987, p. 569).

For example, preservice teachers at the University of Houston conduct a study of a community in which their students live. The students are directed to study a community that is least like the community in which they were reared to increase their sensitivity to factors that influence how children make sense of and respond to the school and to help them understand how such factors influence and are influenced by school life (McCarthy & Clift, 1987). At the University of Wisconsin, students' ethnography projects have focused on topics such as the allocation of classroom resources among students of various ability levels and examination of the types of questions asked within different classrooms (Zeichner & Liston, 1987).

A final inquiry activity used in programs stressing reflection is curriculum analysis and development. Curriculum analysis can be directed toward curriculum developed by others or by the teachers themselves. Zeichner and Liston (1987) and Gillette (1988) describe curriculum analysis projects at the University of Wisconsin in which teachers analyze materials to ascertain their implicit assumptions and values. Students also examine the social and historical context of curriculum development in their schools to determine how and by whom curriculum decisions were made, why certain decisions were made, and what factors influenced those decisions.

Most reflective teacher education programs also involve preservice teachers in the development and analysis of personally developed curricula. Goodman (1986b) describes one approach to such a project. Within a methods course students develop, implement, and analyze the impact of an interdisciplinary unit. Goodman (1986b) notes that involvement in such a project encourages students to take an active role in curriculum construction rather than perceiving themselves as passive technicians teaching prepackaged lessons. Additionally, the requirement that students actively develop a curriculum helps students link theory and practice and emphasizes that they have a personal responsibility for the education of children.

Using a similar requirement, faculty at the University of Florida ask their students to analyze the development and impact of their teaching units in terms of their beliefs about the social and educational purposes of teaching (Ross, 1987b). Similarly, at the University of Alaska students analyze units they have developed in terms of their broader goals for children. This program is designed to prepare teachers to work with culturally diverse children in rural Alaska. Consequently, faculty place especially strong emphasis on preservice teachers' justification of goals, methods, and materials for the particular children involved in each lesson (Noordhoff & Kleinfeld, Chapter 9, this volume). This analysis requires knowledge of educational goals and of the cultural and social environment in which they teach.

At the University of Virginia, faculty emphasize the importance of the analysis of teaching plans by requiring students to defend their plans to university and field-based faculty (Moore et al., 1987). Although the collection of evidence for curriculum analysis projects is not as disciplined as that required in action research projects, this activity provides a focus on teaching as inquiry and emphasizes the necessity of self-evaluation of teaching in terms of the educational and social implications of one's practices.

Reflective Writing

Writing is an important component of programs stressing reflection for two reasons. First, reflective writing provides a way for preservice teachers to practice critical analysis and reasoning (Copeland,

1986). Second, writing provides faculty with a way to challenge and support each student's reflective thinking. Schmidt and Davidson (1983) stress that a faculty member must understand each student's current level of understanding (or reflection) in order to present appropriate challenges. They note that progress in the development of reflective judgment is facilitated by providing students with examples of reasoning that are slightly different from their current level of reasoning. Students' writing provides a faculty member with examples of student thinking and provides a means for the faculty member to interact individually with each student.

Although several types of writing may stimulate reflection, journal writing is the most common (Copeland, 1986; Zeichner, 1987). Copeland (1986) stresses that journal writing contributes to the development of reflection only when (1) students are directly taught techniques (such as what questions to ask) that will encourage thoughtful journal writing and (2) students receive thoughtful, meaningful feedback about the content of their entries. All of the programs reviewed for this chapter provide a structure for students to use as they write in journals. For example, at the University of Florida, journal entries (called reflective reports) must begin with the identification and explanation of a dilemma that the students have experienced in their internship. Then students are required to share their thinking as they resolve the dilemma or report their lack of resolution and why. Specific questions guide students in the identification of dilemmas and in sharing their thinking (Weade, Shea, & Seraphin, 1988).

Supervisory Approaches

The development of reflection requires a different orientation to supervision than is provided in traditional clinical supervision. In clinical supervision, the supervisor and student engage in the rational analysis of instructional behavior. Simmons and Sparks (1987) state that reflective supervision builds on clinical supervision by focusing on the "inter-connections among the cognition, behaviors and beliefs involved in the act of effective teaching" (p. 10). Zeichner and Liston (1987) note that inquiry-oriented supervision differs from clinical supervision by:

1. including analysis of the intentions and beliefs of students;
2. viewing institutional form and social context of teaching as topics of analysis;
3. analyzing the content as well as the behaviors of instruction;
4. analyzing unintended as well as intended outcomes of instruction.

Simmons and Sparks (1987) provide a detailed description of the characteristics of the reflective supervision model used at Michigan State University and at Eastern Michigan University. Key questions are used to focus student attention on their initial intentions, their thoughts and feelings during teaching, related pedagogical concepts, cause-and-effect relationships, contextual interpretations of events, potential solutions to problems, advantages and disadvantages of various solutions within the particular instructional context, and development of a plan to monitor the effects of any solution attempted. Simmons and Sparks stress that interaction during the conference should provide students with informal guidance to help them think aloud about their teaching. As students gain experience in the classroom and with reflective thinking processes, the supervisor's role within the conference should become minimal, because the ultimate goal is for the student to develop the ability to reflect about his or her teaching practices independently.

Faculty Modeling

While many educators stress the importance of modeling as an instructional strategy, it has most frequently been suggested in relation to the learning of technical or factual knowledge. Collins, Brown, and Newman (in press) note that modeling can also play an important role in helping students learn complex conceptual knowledge, such as reflection.

At the programmatic level, Zeichner and Liston (1987) note that students must see their teacher education program as inquiry oriented because this provides an important model of the process of self-directed growth. One of the most striking features of all programs reviewed for this chapter is that the faculty are actively engaged in self-study at a programmatic level (e.g., Kleinfeld & Noordhoff, 1988; Zeichner & Liston, 1987) and at an individual level through action research of their own teaching (e.g., Hoover, 1987; Noffke & Brennan, 1988; Ross, 1989b). This type of modeling provides students with a generalized role model of the reflective practitioner. More specific modeling focusing on developing competence as a reflective practitioner is also important.

University faculty can provide appropriate modeling of reflection in several ways, including:

- publicly sharing their line of reasoning in making decisions about significant issues (Schmidt & Davidson, 1983)
- communicating to students that knowledge is at times uncertain (Kitchener, 1977)

- allowing students to question the instructors' sources of knowledge and decisions (Schön, 1983)
- demonstrating the strategies used in the skilled performance of a reflective practitioner (Schön, 1987)

Questioning and Dialogue

Teacher educators stress questioning and dialogue as strategies that facilitate the development of common meaning between the teacher educator and preservice teacher. Only by listening effectively to students and determining how a student is interpreting the communication of the teacher educator and other students can common meaning be pursued. For example, Simmons and Schuette (1988) state that language provides teachers with precise labels for concepts and the relationships among concepts. Language enables teachers to "capture an event" so that they can make thoughtful decisions or "store an event" so they can think about it after the teaching day ends. Simmons and Schuette advocate the use of questions to stimulate students to use newly acquired language (concepts), to discuss relationships among concepts and teaching experiences, and to pose their own questions. Simmons and Schuette stress that the purpose of questioning is not to assess but to encourage dialogue and to stimulate students to view situations from multiple perspectives.

BUILDING A COHERENT, INTEGRATED, AND LOGICALLY SEQUENCED PROGRAM

Each teacher education program reviewed is struggling with the development of a coherent, integrated program. For most, this is the most difficult issue they confront (Clift & Houston, 1988).

With the exception of the reflective teaching strategy (Cruickshank, 1985), all of the strategies discussed as important in the development of reflection emphasize the social construction of knowledge. Using these strategies, teacher educators work collaboratively with students to construct knowledge about such things as the nature of learning, the relative importance of various school goals, and the criteria that might be used to select and evaluate instructional strategies. As a part of this collaborative process, teacher educators gain information about students' perspectives, understandings, and misunderstandings in order to challenge student thinking and to encourage students to reanalyze their entering perspectives about teaching.

The theme of reflection should pervade all program courses and field experiences and should be sequentially developed over the course of the program (Barnes, 1987). However, such integration is not the norm within higher education for several reasons. First, Zeichner and Liston (1987) note that most large universities are characterized by "ideological eclecticism and structural fragmentation," which makes coordinated action by faculty from different programs or disciplinary areas difficult. The norm of autonomy undercuts our efforts at collaboration and makes it difficult to develop a "program" as opposed to a collection of courses.

Second, most universities rely on graduate students to assist with the supervision of student teachers. Zeichner and Liston (1987) note that the heavy workload of graduate students and the transitory nature of this assignment make it difficult to ensure continuity between university coursework and supervision of field work. Third, Clift and Houston (1988) report that the actions of policy makers can constrain faculty efforts at program development and coherence. As the University of Houston faculty developed and initiated their revised teacher education program, the Texas legislature passed a law limiting teacher education students to eighteen hours of education courses. This law, which is inconsistent with the faculty's ideas about the importance of extensive pedagogical preparation, has necessitated revision of the program for the third time in four years.

The actions of the Texas legislature relate to another constraint teacher educators confront as they struggle for program coherence. If students take fewer education courses, they take more courses within the liberal arts and sciences. Teaching within these courses should, but frequently does not, model socratic teaching, reflection, experimentation, and writing (Moore et al., 1987). A coherent program requires commitment from faculty outside as well as inside colleges of education. While none of the programs have solved the problems associated with developing a coherent, unitary focus, each has taken steps to make certain the emphasis on reflection is a recurring theme in the program. A few examples may be useful to others interested in developing greater programmatic coherence.

Several programs have taken steps to encourage faculty dialogue about reflection, about teaching that fosters reflection, and about program development. Faculty at the University of Houston meet regularly in interdepartmental teams to review curriculum, to discuss student responses to the program and the instructional formats they have developed, and to reflect on their own experiences as teachers (Clift & Houston, 1988). University of Florida faculty pursue similar goals during informal, interdepartmental brown-bag lunches. At these lunches, both faculty and graduate students have felt comfortable sharing the successes and failures of their emergent attempts to foster reflection in students (Krogh, 1987). Through group discussion, many suggestions for modification or extension of teaching practices have been offered and faculty and graduate students have developed a stronger knowledge of the "program" and connections among the courses students take.

Another strategy is the development of structural supports that foster integration. At the University of Alaska the program director or assistant director attends all meetings of student seminars and helps guide discussions in order to ensure integration of coursework into discussions of field experiences (Kleinfeld & Noordhoff, 1987). Obviously, this strategy is only practical within small programs. In a slightly larger program, the faculty at Catholic University use their conceptual framework to foster coherence throughout the program. This framework, based on the commonplaces of teaching (Schwab, 1973), the dilemmas of schooling (Berlak & Berlak, 1981), and levels of reflection (Van Manan, 1977), provides a structure that enables each faculty member to relate his or her discipline to the reflective focus of the program (Valli & Taylor, 1987).

At the University of Florida, a course taken by all field advisors provides structural support that helps faculty and graduate assistants develop a shared understanding about the purposes of the program and the teaching strategies that are useful in achieving those purposes. In developing this course, several steps were taken to foster program coherence. First, all faculty working in the field provided suggestions about appropriate course content. Second, these same faculty members were invited to assist in teaching the course or to attend the course (and most did). Third, the instructor modeled the instructional practices suggested as appropriate for the development of reflection. And finally, the field advisors continued to meet throughout the year during biweekly seminars to discuss practical concerns and necessary modifications and extensions of the ideas developed in the course. Thus the course provides a vehicle for faculty and graduate assistants to work collaboratively in revising their understandings about the meaning of reflection and the strategies most likely to help students become more reflective about teaching.

The last strategy to be discussed here is course review. Faculty at the University of Virginia review all required liberal arts and sciences courses and all education courses (Moore et al., 1987). The purpose of this review is to increase communication about the purposes of the teacher education program and to stimulate discussion about how each course can contribute to program goals. Given the recommendations of the Holmes report (1986), this strategy may be of vital importance to any thematically organized teacher education program, because in the future a greater proportion of a preservice teacher's education may be provided outside of a college of education.

DEVELOPING COLLABORATIVE RELATIONSHIPS WITH SCHOOLS

If students are to develop the ability to teach reflectively, field settings must provide a supportive and challenging environment. Goodman (1985) stresses that teacher educators should select sites that provide student teachers with freedom from constraints. While this seems logical and essential, it is often very difficult to implement.

The school context is mentioned by most teacher educators as a problem that limits students' reflective abilities. McCaleb (1979) and Erdman (1983) note that students often experience difficulty because of discrepancies between ideas developed in university coursework and the practices encountered and expected in the field. The structure of the school day, the use of predetermined curriculum materials, and the typical school emphasis on order and control frequently limit the ability of students to experiment with new ideas and methods or to reflect about the consequences of their actions (Tabachnick et al., 1979–80).

As Bagenstos (1975) notes, schools are bureaucracies and teachers must therefore function within the constraints of a bureaucracy, which means that they are not necessarily free to act on the results of their inquiry. These limitations are even more powerful for student teachers because of their desire to fulfill the expectations of the practicum site (Goodman, 1984) coupled with the fact that students have little or no control over decisions about what is taught and how it is taught (Tabachnick et al., 1979–80). Careful selection of field sites is clearly a necessity. Additionally, constant communication with cooperating teachers is essential.

What are some of the strategies used to foster improved collaboration between universities and schools? The University of Virginia has a unique (but very expensive) program. Teachers apply to the university for positions as clinical faculty (Moore, Comfort, & Reese, 1988). If selected, they are paid $500 per intern supervised and $200 for a weeklong orientation session. They also receive faculty perks (e.g., parking, access to faculty tickets to sports events). The selection system ensures that cooperating teachers are highly qualified and encourages their commitment to program goals. A computerized communication system between the university and participating schools facilitates an ongoing dialogue about student progress, university requirements, and program goals (Moore, 1988).

In a pilot program at the University of Wisconsin–Madison, students are supervised by clinical teacher supervisors working in professional development schools (Gillette, 1988). The professional development schools were selected because they exemplify excellent teaching practice. Clinical teacher supervisors teach half-time and supervise student teachers for the rest of the day. In addition, the clinical teacher supervisors are active project participants who meet with university personnel to discuss project goals, strategies suggested in methods courses, and school-based concerns. Gillette (1988) notes that a strength of this model is that university and school faculty work as partners in the education of preservice teachers. That is, teachers are aware of and help students implement strategies suggested within methods courses. Faculty at the University of Houston also involve teachers (called school-based teacher educators) in collaborative planning of the experiences of preservice teachers (McCarthy & Clift, 1987). University and school faculty develop field assignments together, and both try to model effective and reflective teaching strategies for students.

PROVIDING ONGOING SUPPORT FOR GRADUATES

Wildman and Niles (1987) note that schools are busy places in which little time or support is provided for reflection. They stress that even experienced teachers need structural and personal support in order to think reflectively about teaching. The need for this type of support is even greater for beginning teachers than for experienced ones. This suggests that teacher educators who wish to prepare reflective teachers must extend their efforts beyond the years of academic preparation. While most teacher education programs recognize that graduates need support from teacher education faculty during their first years of teaching, faculty are just beginning to develop ideas about the nature of effective support and how to provide it (Clift & Houston, 1988; Moore et al., 1987; Ross, 1987a).

Two strategies at the University of Florida are being implemented to provide ongoing support. The first strategy is to help graduates identify and select initial teaching positions within schools that are likely to

support their professional growth. The faculty have identified characteristics of supportive contexts by drawing on research in the areas of
teacher efficacy, teacher commitment, teacher empowerment, induction, school effectiveness, and school improvement.

Supportive schools are characterized by norms of collegiality and
continuous improvement. In these schools teachers have significant influence over decisions related to instruction and curriculum (e.g.,
Ashton & Webb, 1986; Borko, 1986; Frymier, 1987; Goodman, 1987;
Wildman & Niles, 1987). Teachers spend time planning together (Ashton
& Webb, 1986; Klausmeier, 1982), talking about teaching and observing
and critiquing each other (Borko, 1986; Little, 1982), and providing emotional and technical support for one another (Goodman, 1987; Wildman
& Niles, 1987). Providing time and structural support for these activities
encourages teachers to engage in activities that are essential for reflective teaching. Such activities include taking risks (Wildman & Niles,
1987), viewing their own learning as important (Borko, 1986), engaging
in group planning (Ashton & Webb, 1986), and proposing alternative
instructional ideas (Goodman, 1987). An additional characteristic of
supportive schools is the presence of a strong, supportive administrator
(Hall, 1987; Mortimore & Sammons, 1987). Wildman and Niles (1987)
note that administrators who lack knowledge about or commitment to
reflective teaching may create obstacles that limit teachers' reflective
abilities. Additionally, they note that many teachers will be unwilling to
take the risks involved in reflective teaching if they lack appropriate
administrative support.

Based on this review, the faculty at the University of Florida have
designed a series of sample questions to help beginning teachers assess
the nature of a school context in interviews with principals. In the
future, we hope to work collaboratively with our graduates and with the
department of educational administration to identify school systems
and individual schools likely to support the professional development of
beginning teachers.

A second strategy used to support the development of program
graduates is the development of a series of conferences for beginning
teachers. Each February, all program graduates from the past three
years are invited to campus for a weekend conference focusing on the
beginning years of teaching. Based on information provided by graduates in questionnaires and interviews, workshops are designed to assist
them with the problems they are encountering. In addition, they have
the opportunity to share their experiences with faculty and peers, enabling them to maintain their identification with the program. If stu-

dents are to maintain a commitment to the development of reflection, the maintenance of their identification with fellow students and with program faculty is considered vital.

DEVELOPING MEANS FOR EVALUATING THE IMPACT OF PROGRAMS

There has been little systematic evaluation of teacher educators' efforts to facilitate the development of reflective teachers. Zeichner (1987) notes that most studies are self-reports and/or isolated examples of success and that the Wisconsin Study of Teacher Socialization (Zeichner & Liston, 1987) is the only example of a longitudinal study to determine whether teachers continue to use inquiry-oriented approaches to teaching after the preservice years. One of the reasons for the lack of systematic evaluation undoubtedly is that reflection is a complex mental process that is difficult to assess. Teacher educators working in programs that target reflective teaching as a goal have not resolved the problems associated with evaluation of progress. However, they are interested in documenting the effects of their efforts and are working to develop useful assessment strategies.

In assessing their programs, teacher educators are conducting both formative and summative evaluation studies. Programs are collecting formative evaluation data to help them make decisions about how to improve their programs and provide coherent, integrated programs. In conducting summative evaluations, program developers are interested in the evaluation of program outcomes rather than the achievement of program objectives. Eisner (1985) notes that evaluating outcomes includes evaluation on achievement of objectives (i.e., the development of reflective teachers) but also enables the evaluator to identify unintended and tangential outcomes. Although all of the programs reviewed here specify the development of reflective teachers as their goal, their real and ultimate goal is improved teaching and learning within classrooms. This means that evaluation efforts move beyond asking whether the program fosters the development of reflective teachers to asking broader questions about what happens to preservice teachers as they move through a teacher education program and how their experiences influence their interactions with students in classrooms.

Most evaluation efforts have used qualitative methods of data collection and analysis (e.g., ethnography, case study, simulation, analysis of students' work in journals and other assignments) to study the impact of preservice teacher education on the perspectives and practices of preservice teachers (e.g., Goodman, 1983, 1985; Hursh, 1988; Ross, 1989b; Tabachnick et al., 1979–80). One reason for this is that program developers recognize that teaching practice is situated within and influenced by the social context in which the preservice teacher is educated and subsequently the social context in which he or she teaches (Popkewitz, Tabachnick, & Zeichner, 1979). Thus a qualitative evaluation that describes the development of reflection within particular contexts is required.

A second reason why teacher educators have turned to qualitative methods is that reflective practice has yet to be defined clearly, and therefore quantitative assessment is precluded. In fact, because reflection is a mental process, as opposed to an observable behavior or set of behaviors, it may never be possible to develop a definition with enough behavioral specificity to measure it quantitatively. Consequently, several teacher educators are concerned with the development of ways to analyze and code writing assignments in which students attempt to communicate their ability to reflect about teaching practice (Ross, 1989b; Simmons & Sparks, 1987).

Although writing assignments are commonly used, there are questions about whether they are a sufficient measure of reflective ability. Clearly, written assignments provide a record of student thoughts and their ability to articulate attitudes and abilities associated with reflection. However, reflective action is the ultimate goal, and we do not yet know whether and how action is related to reflective ability as revealed on paper. Several researchers are attempting to devise more structured assessment strategies focusing on reflection in action. For example, Noordhoff and Kleinfeld (Chapter 9, this volume), combine videotaped examples of students' teaching with interviews designed to evoke their reflections about their teaching purposes and the instructional strategies they selected to achieve those purposes.

Kleinfeld and Noordhoff (1988) note that a major advantage of their procedure is that it provides information about both teaching behavior and the judgments that underlie that behavior. An obvious weakness is that students are not teaching real lessons, in real classrooms, to real children. The methodology clearly could be adapted so that students plan, videotape, and analyze lessons taught in classrooms. However, Kleinfeld and Noordhoff (1988) stress that analysis of the data requires that the researcher be familiar with each student's classroom context in order to determine whether the student is considering appropriate issues in making instructional decisions. One additional issue of importance is the time involved in collecting and analyzing videotaped data. Clearly, it would be desirable to collect data about all students in a teacher education program, and, in fact, the procedure described by Kleinfeld and Noordhoff would have tremendous educational benefit for students. However, the time necessary to collect and analyze this data in a large teacher education program would be prohibitive. Though samples of students can be used to assess the impact of the program, these students will have experienced a different program simply because they had the opportunity to participate in the study and review videotaped examples of their teaching behavior. The fact that this assessment strategy may, in fact, be a treatment should be considered as evaluators design studies investigating the impact of reflective teacher education programs.

CONCLUSIONS

Although teacher educators have demonstrated increased commitment to the preparation of reflective practitioners, we have not yet resolved the practical problems involved in reaching a goal that is complex, difficult to teach, and difficult to assess. Resolution of these problems requires that faculty work collaboratively in ways that are not necessarily rewarded within higher education. This chapter has shown that the development of a program emphasizing reflection requires all faculty members to work to develop collaborative relationships with public school colleagues, to alter their instructional strategies, to increase collaborative efforts among college faculty, to investigate the outcomes of the teacher education program, to make and assess the outcome of program revisions, and to provide support for students after graduation. Although these are things that should happen continuously in every teacher education program, the reality is that they do not because there are few institutional rewards for these extremely time-consuming tasks. It seems significant that every program described in this chapter engaged in program development efforts with the support of external funding. This funding enabled one or more faculty members to devote extensive time to program development and evaluation.

Essentially, this chapter indicates that the development of reflective preservice teachers requires the commitment and efforts of reflective teacher educators. For this to occur, teacher educators, like their public school colleagues, must teach in supportive contexts. That is, we need time, significant influence over programmatic and instructional decisions, administrative support, colleges characterized by norms of collegiality and continuous improvement, and support for risk-taking (Wildman & Niles, 1987). Without this institutional support, reflective teaching will never be more than a slogan in the majority of our teacher education institutions.

REFERENCES

Ashton, P. T., & Webb, R. B. (1986). *Making a difference: Teachers' sense of efficacy and student achievement.* New York: Longman.

Bagenstos, N. T. (1975). The teacher as an inquirer. *The Educational Forum, 39,* 231–237.

Barnes, H. L. (1987). The conceptual basis for thematic teacher education programs. *Journal of Teacher Education, 38*(4), 13–18.

Berlak, A., & Berlak, H. (1981). *Dilemmas of schooling: Teaching and social change.* New York: Methuen.

Beyer, L. (1984). Field experience, ideology, and the development of critical reflectivity. *Journal of Teacher Education, 35*(3), 36–41.

Biott, C. (1983). The foundations of classroom action research in initial teacher training. *Journal of Education for Teaching, 9*(2), 152–160.

Borko, H. (1986). Clinical teacher education and the professional teacher. In J. V. Hoffman & S. A. Edwards (Eds.), *Reality and reform in clinical teacher education* (pp. 45–64). New York: Random House.

Calderhead, J. (1988, April). *Reflective teaching and teacher education.* Paper presented at the annual meeting of the American Educational Research Association, New Orleans.

Clift, R. T., & Houston, W. R. (1988, February). *Making reflection a reality: Reflective practice begins at the university.* Paper presented at the annual meeting of the Association of Teacher Educators, San Diego.

Cohen, A., & Alroi, N. (1981). Diagnostic action research as an instrument in teacher education. *Journal of Education for Teaching, 7*(2). 176–186.

Collins, A., Brown, J. S., & Newman, S. E. (in press). Cognitive apprenticeship: Teaching the craft of reading, writing and mathematics. In L. B. Resnick (Ed.), *Cognition and instruction: Issues and agendas.* Hillsdale, NJ: Erlbaum.

Copeland, W. D. (1986). The RITE framework for teacher education: Preservice applications. In J. V. Hoffman & S. A. Edwards (Eds.), *Reality and reform in clinical teacher education* (pp. 25–44). New York: Random House.

Corey, S. M. (1954). Action research in education. *Journal of Educational Research, 47,* 375–380.

Cruickshank, D. R. (1985). Uses and benefits of reflective teaching. *Phi Delta Kappan, 66*(10), 704–706.

Dewey, J. (1933). *How we think.* Chicago: Henry Regnery Co. (Original work published 1909).

Eisner, E. W. (1985). *The educational imagination.* New York: Macmillan.

Erdman, J. (1983). Assessing the purposes of early field experience programs. *Journal of Teacher Education, 34*(4), 27–31.

Feiman, S. (1979). Technique and inquiry in teacher education: A curricular case study. *Curriculum Inquiry, 9*(1), 63–79.

Frymier, J. (1987). Bureaucracy and the neutering of teachers. *Educational Leadership, 69*(1), 9–14.

Gillette, M. (1988, February). *Reflective teaching and education that is multicultural.* Paper presented at the annual meeting of the Association of Teacher Educators, San Diego.

Goodman, J. (1983). The seminar's role in the education of student teachers: A case study. *Journal of Teacher Education, 34*(3), 44–49.

Goodman, J. (1984). Reflection and teacher education: A case study and theoretical analysis. *Interchange, 15*(3), 9–26.

Goodman, J. (1985). What students learn from early field experiences. A case study and curricular analysis. *Journal of Teacher Education, 26*(6), 42–48.

Goodman, J. (1986a). Making early field experience meaningful: A critical approach. *Journal of Education for Teaching, 1*(2), 109–125.

Goodman, J. (1986b). Teaching preservice teachers a critical approach to curriculum design: A descriptive account. *Curriculum Inquiry, 1*(2), 179–201.

Goodman, J. (1987, October). *The disenfranchisement of elementary teachers and strategies for resistance.* Paper presented at the annual meeting of the Bergamo Conference on Curriculum Theory and Practice, Dayton, OH.

Hall, G. E. (1987, April). *The principal as leader of the change facilitating team.* Paper presented at the annual meeting of the American Educational Research Association, Washington, DC.

Hanna, B. (1986). Improving student teaching effectiveness through action research projects. *Action in Teacher Education, 8*(3), 51–56.

Holmes Group. (1986). *Tomorrow's teachers.* East Lansing, MI: Author.

Hoover, N. (1987, April). *Complex role acquisition: Field advisor, teacher educator and graduate student.* Paper presented at the annual meeting of the American Educational Research Association, Washington, DC.

Hursh, D. (1988, April). *Reflecting on teaching teachers to become reflective: Proposals for reforming teacher education based on an ethnographic study of preservice teachers.* Paper presented at the annual meeting of the American Educational Research Association, New Orleans.

Kitchener, K. S. (1977). *Intellectual development in late adolescents and young adults: Reflective judgment and verbal reasoning.* Unpublished doctoral dissertation, University of Minnesota, Minneapolis–St. Paul.

Kitchener, K., & King, P. (1981). Reflective judgment concepts of justification and their relationship to age and education. *Journal of Applied Developmental Psychology, 2*, 89–116.

Klausmeier, H. (1982). A research strategy for educational improvement. *Educational Researcher, 11*(2), 8–13.

Kleinfeld, J., & Noordhoff, K. (1987). *Teachers for Alaska: A teacher-designed teacher education program.* Summary of presentation at the second annual conference of the Holmes Group, Washington, DC.

Kleinfeld, J., & Noordhoff, K. (1988, February). *Videotaped reflective teaching: A tool to assess teacher education programs.* Paper presented at the annual meeting of the Association of Teacher Educators, San Diego.

Krogh, S. L. (1987, April). *Reflecting on reflective thinking in methods classes. Where the buck finally stops.* Paper presented at the annual meeting of the American Educational Research Association, Washington, DC.

Liston, D. P., & Zeichner, K. M. (1987). Reflective teacher education and moral deliberation. *Journal of Teacher Education, 38*(6), 2–9.

Little, J. W. (1982). Norms of collegiality and experimentation: Workplace conditions of school success. *American Educational Research Journal, 19,* 325–340.

McCaleb, J. (1979). On reconciling dissonance between preparation and practice. *Journal of Teacher Education, 30*(4), 50–53.

McCarthy, J., & Clift, R. T. (1987, December). *Evaluating early field experiences: A report of curriculum development in the reflective inquiry teacher education program.* Paper presented to the Iowa State University Conference on the Evaluation of Teacher Education, Des Moines.

Moore, J. R. (1988). Restructured teacher education at the University of Virginia. Program document prepared by Committee to Restructure Teacher Education, Curry School of Education, Charlottesville, VA.

Moore, J. R., Comfort, R. E., & Reese, M. (1988, February). *The role of clinical instructor and the process of clinical supervision.* Paper presented at the annual meeting of the Association of Teacher Educators, San Diego.

Moore, J. R., Mintz, S. L., & Bierman, M. (1987, October). *Reflective inquiry: Teaching and thinking.* Paper prepared for the Houston/OERI Conference on Reflection in Teaching and Teacher Education, Houston, TX.

Mortimore, P., & Sammons, P. (1987). New evidence on effective elementary schools. *Educational Leadership, 45*(1), 4–8.

Noffke, S. E., & Brennan, M. (1988, February). *Action research and reflective teaching at UW–Madison: Issues and examples.* Paper presented at the annual meeting of the Association of Teacher Educators, San Diego.

Noffke, S. E., & Zeichner, K. M. (1987, April). *Action research and teacher thinking: The first phase of the action research on action research research project at the University of Wisconsin–Madison.* Paper presented at the annual meeting of the American Educational Research Association, Washington, DC.

Noordhoff, K., & Kleinfeld, J. (1987, October). *Rethinking the rhetoric of "reflective inquiry": What this language came to mean in a program to prepare rural teachers.* Paper prepared for the University of Houston/OERI Conference on Reflection in Teaching and Teacher Education, Houston, TX.

Popkewitz, T. S., Tabachnick, B. R., & Zeichner, K. M. (1979). Dulling the senses: Research in teacher education. *Journal of Teacher Education, 30*(5), 52–60.

Ross, D. D. (1987a, October). *Reflective teaching: Meaning and implications for preservice teacher educators.* Paper prepared for the University of Houston/OERI Conference on Reflection in Teaching and Teacher Education, Houston, TX.

Ross, D. D. (1987b, April). *Teaching teacher effectiveness research to students: First steps in developing a reflective approach to teaching.* Paper presented at the annual meeting of the American Educational Research Association, Washington, DC.

Ross, D. D. (1989a). Action research for preservice teachers: A description of why and how. *Peabody Journal of Education, 64*(3), 131–150.

Ross, D. D. (1989b). First steps in developing a reflective approach. *Journal of Teacher Education, 40*(2), 22–30.

Schmidt, J. A., & Davidson, M. L. (1983). Helping students think. *The Personnel and Guidance Journal, 61,* 563–569.

Schön, D. A. (1983). *The reflective practitioner.* New York: Basic Books.

Schön, D. A. (1987). *Educating the reflective practitioner.* San Francisco: Jossey-Bass.

Schwab, J. J. (1973). The practical three: Translation into curriculum. *School Review, 81*(4), 501–522.

Simmons, J. M., & Schuette, M. K. (1988). Strengthening teacher reflective decision-making. *Journal of Staff Development, 9*(3), 18–27.

Simmons, J. M., & Sparks, G. M. (1987, October). *The need for a new model of teacher supervision and evaluation: The implications of identifying reflection as an explicit goal of teacher education.* Paper prepared for the University of Houston/OERI Conference on Reflection in Teaching and Teacher Education, Houston, TX.

Tabachnick, B., Popkewitz, T., & Zeichner, K. (1979–80). Teacher education and the professional perspectives of student teachers. *Interchange, 10,* 12–29.

Tom, A. R. (1985). Inquiring into inquiry-oriented teacher education. *Journal of Teacher Education, 36*(5), 35–44.

Valli, L., & Taylor, N. E. (1987, October). *Reflective teacher education: Preferred characteristics for a content and process model.* Paper prepared for the University of Houston/OERI Conference on Reflection in Teaching and Teacher Education, Houston, TX.

Van Manan, M. (1977). Linking ways of knowing with ways of being practical. *Curriculum Inquiry, 6,* 205–228.

Volker, R. (1987, October). *Methods for fostering teacher education students' reflective analysis of research on teaching.* Paper prepared for the University of Houston/OERI Conference on Reflection in Teaching and Teacher Education, Houston, TX.

Weade, R., Shea, J., & Seraphin, A. (1988). *The Elementary Proteach Student handbook.* University of Florida, Gainesville.

Wildman, T. M., & Niles, J. A. (1987). Reflective teachers: Tensions between abstractions and realities. *Journal of Teacher Education, 3*(1), 25–31.

Zeichner, K. M. (1987). Preparing reflective teachers: An overview of instructional strategies which have been employed in preservice teacher education. *International Journal of Educational Research, 11*(5), 565–576.

Zeichner, K. M., & Liston, D. P. (1987). Teaching student teachers to reflect. *Harvard Educational Review, 57,* 23–48.

7 Reflection and the Acquisition of Technical Teaching Skills

H. JEROME FREIBERG
HERSHOLT C. WAXMAN
University of Houston

The reflective inquiry teacher education program (RITE) at the University of Houston provides ample opportunities for prospective teachers to speculate on their development as teachers as a way for them to improve their expertise. Students in the RITE program are taught to inquire about the nature of teaching and learning, the organization of schools, and the relationship between schooling and education. The students are encouraged to reflect on their reading, coursework, and experiences and to consider ways they could be more effective teachers. They are invited to try new ways, judge their effectiveness, and try again. The program blends the elements of technical skills with broader conceptual issues in the development of effective professionals (Waxman, Freiberg, Clift, & Houston, 1988). Critical to this development is the acquisition of technical skills that facilitate the students' professional maturation. Four such skills are discussed in this chapter:

1. systematic classroom observation of others;
2. self-assessment of student teaching;
3. journal writing;
4. simulated teaching.

The RITE program is organized in three phases, each equivalent to about one semester. Phase one is an exploration of the basic core concepts related to teaching. Students explore what it means to be a teacher, the influence of culture, and social-legal implications of education. Making systematic observations of communities and schools and re-

This work was funded in part by a contract from the United States Department of Education, Office of Educational Research and Improvement (Contract No. 400-85-1039). The opinions expressed in this chapter do not necessarily reflect the position, policy, or endorsement of that agency.

flecting on those observations are important to student development of reflective inquiry.

Phase two links learning theory with curricular methods, as students not only study the basic concepts of learning but also apply them as instructional principles in specific curricular fields. Audiotape analysis of micro-lessons helps students reflect on their instructional achievements.

Phase three is student teaching. Students are expected to demonstrate their ability to synthesize their previous studies into viable instruction of their students. Students are observed using a low-inference instrument, then dialogue with others about the meaning and implications of data. In the following sections of this chapter, the four technical skills listed above are discussed in terms of their use in the RITE program and to the development of reflective inquiry.

DEVELOPMENT OF TECHNICAL SKILLS

Although field experiences are designed to help the teaching candidate acquire knowledge about the functions of teaching through observations and limited participation, a number of studies have indicated that they are not helpful for the prospective teacher (Gibson, 1976; Hoy & Rees, 1977; Tabachnick, Popkewitz, & Zeichner, 1980). These studies have found that early field experiences contribute to the development of merely utilitarian teaching perspectives, as preservice teachers become less pupil-oriented and humanistic and more "custodial" in their approach to teaching (Becher & Ade, 1982). On the other hand, other studies have concluded that field experiences are necessary and useful components of teacher-preparation programs (Denton, 1982; Joyce, Yarger, & Howey, 1977; Sandefur, 1970). One explanation for these conflicting findings is that some field experiences are not sufficiently structured. As a result, preservice teachers often do not know what to focus on while observing.

Systematic Observation

One important instructional method for preservice teachers is systematic observation of teaching behaviors (Good & Brophy, 1987; Jackson, 1968; Posner, 1985; Waxman, Rodriguez, Padron, & Knight, 1988). This component is sometimes the first type of activity that prospective teachers encounter in their early field experiences (Henry, 1982). Systematic observations of classroom teachers provide prospective teachers with the opportunity to actually observe specific teaching behaviors that are emphasized in their teacher education courses. Furthermore, such focused observations allow prospective teachers to understand how these teaching behaviors can differentially influence student behavioral and affective outcomes.

Systematic classroom observation can provide a common language for describing effective teaching. Such observations enable prospective teachers to focus on specific teaching skills studied in their pedagogy courses. Unless prospective teachers actually observe the effectiveness of these behaviors in classroom settings, however, they may not acknowledge the value of these teaching skills.

Classroom observation requires some form of training for preservice teachers. There is a fundamental difference between observing teaching behaviors and student interactions in the classroom and just sitting in on a class. In the late 1960s and early 1970s (Ryan & Cooper, 1972), preservice students were taught fixed category observation systems, such as the Flanders Interaction Analysis System, to aid in identifying teacher/student interactions in the classroom. Flanders (1965) divided classroom interaction into ten categories. Seven of the categories were teacher-initiated behaviors (1, accepting feelings; 2, praise; 3, using student ideas; 4, asking questions; 5, lecturing; 6, giving directions; 7, criticizing), and two were student behaviors (8, responding to a question; 9, initiating a question). Category 10 represented silence or confusion in the classroom. Depending on the type of interaction in the classroom, the teacher would be categorized as either a direct (one who tells, 5-7) or indirect (one who facilitates, 1-4) teacher.

Providing tools for observing the rapid pace of classroom interactions is an important step in the development of student awareness of the context in which they will be teaching. Because the average classroom might consist of several hundred teacher/student interactions per hour, a system of identifying and coding the interactions is needed to allow a thorough and reflective analysis; simple, unstructured "watching" is insufficient. In addition to fixed category observational systems, preservice students have been trained to use verbatim and summary notetaking techniques to provide a record of the observed classroom that can be analyzed at a later date. Beginning education students have also been trained in the use of sociograms to identify friendship patterns in the classroom. These methods of observation provide data sources to preservice students about the intricacies and subtleties of teaching.

Student Teacher Self-Assessment Procedures

It is difficult or impossible for preservice teachers to become reflective if they are unaware of their own effectiveness during preservice teaching activities. Preservice teachers often lack basic information about the nature of their interactions with individual students. Consequently, they generally have inaccurate perceptions about their own performance. Student teachers' self-evaluations of their teaching tend to be significantly higher than their academic or field supervisors' ratings (Briggs, Richardson, & Sefzik, 1986; Wheeler & Knoop, 1982). Further, student teachers' perceptions of their instruction and classroom learning environment are often significantly different from those of their pupils and university supervisors (Waxman & Duschl, 1987). These differing perceptions underscore the problem of inaccurate self-assessment and thus the importance of preservice teachers' obtaining accurate feedback about their instruction.

Although several specific approaches, such as seminars (Hill, 1978), situational teaching experiences (Cohn, 1981), reflective teaching lessons (Korthagen, 1985), reflective peer-group teaching (Cruickshank, 1987), and collaborative conferencing (Hoover & O'Shea, 1987), have been designed to encourage preservice teachers to think critically about their own teaching, these methods often do not help preservice teachers become more reflective or link the knowledge acquired in teacher education courses to their classroom practice. These approaches may be less effective because they fail to provide preservice teachers with specific information about their teaching or the tools for accurately assessing their effectiveness with a class.

Teacher self-assessment procedures should be incorporated into inquiry-oriented teacher education programs, because studies have found that self-assessment procedures enhance the teachers' ability and willingness to be reflective about their classroom instruction (Koziol, Bohn, & Moss, 1983; Koziol & Burns, 1986). The key to effective self-assessment, however, lies in providing preservice teachers an accurate database for measuring their teaching.

Journal Writing

Journal writing is an instructional method that has been used in teacher education programs for many years, but it has only recently become an important component of many inquiry-oriented programs (Zeichner & Liston, 1987). Journal writing generally involves preservice teachers in keeping a daily or regular journal in which they record their experiences and raise questions about teaching.

Several studies have found that the use of journal writing helps preservice teachers progress through the cognitive-developmental stages and become more reflective (Bolin, 1988; Garman, 1982, 1987; Zeichner & Liston, 1987). Bolin (1988), for example, found that journals contribute to preservice teachers' growth toward critical analysis of their teaching. Benham (1979) found that student teachers who were involved in reflective writing showed less movement toward custodial attitudes about pupil control than those who were not. Yinger and Clark (1981) also found that preservice teachers thought that the use of a journal helped them relate what they learned in their introductory educational psychology course to their experiences outside of class.

Journals are sometimes used during the introductory phases of the preservice teacher education program (e.g., Waxman et al., 1988). In this context, the journal entries allow prospective teachers to raise questions and concerns about the course material from their teacher education courses as well as their field observations.

Dialogue journals are also used during student teaching. Here the student teacher writes regularly about what happens in the classroom and raises questions and concerns. The dialogue occurs when the university supervisor and/or the cooperative teacher reads the journal and responds to the student teacher either during a discussion or in writing. Sometimes the journals are shared with other student teachers in a small-group setting or seminar.

In both contexts, journals provide university supervisors or cooperating teachers with information on what prospective teachers think about teaching and how they are developing as teachers (Zeichner & Liston, 1987). The supervisors come to know the prospective teachers better and gain a clearer understanding of their concerns and problems. Similarly, journals provide prospective teachers "with a vehicle for systematic reflection on their development as teachers and on their actions in classroom and work contexts" (Zeichner & Liston, 1987, p. 33).

Simulated Teaching

Since the development of micro-teaching (Allen & Fortune, 1966; Bush & Allen, 1964), the use of simulated teaching has become a part of many teacher education programs. The usual micro-teaching format includes a preservice student's first learning and then employing a series of teaching behaviors, such as nonverbal cues, wait-time for questioning, motivating and facilitating set inductions, and higher-level questioning skills. These skills are usually demonstrated to preservice teachers during methods-related coursework. Later, the students are asked to teach a group of from five to six other preservice students for ten to twenty minutes.

The mini-lesson is videotaped, and the student receives feedback from the instructor or a graduate student. The feedback is provided while the student and instructor watch the videotape of the minilesson and, in many instances using a checklist, determine which previously identified behaviors are being exhibited. In some teacher education programs, the students are graded on their ability to perform a specific teaching behavior during the micro-teaching lesson. Both students and educators have questioned the appropriateness of this summative use of micro-teaching because of its differences from natural classroom settings (Good, Biddle, & Brophy, 1975). Although data are provided to the student teacher, reflection is not part of the specific teaching behaviors that determine a grade.

Reflection assumes some level of exploration. The summative environment of many micro-teaching situations, however, provides minimal opportunities for either exploration or reflection. Recent modifications of the micro-teaching process, however, have provided opportunities for using it as a reflective tool (Freiberg, 1986). Rather than making simulated teaching a summative occurrence, the opportunity exists for formative feedback, peer feedback, and self-assessment during micro-teaching experiences. Building in the opportunities and providing the encouragement and climate for reflection both individually and collectively in cohort groups increases the chance for professional growth. The combination of experience and reflection equals growth (Posner, 1985).

PHASE ONE:
WHAT IT MEANS TO BE A REFLECTIVE TEACHER

The RITE program introduces students both to research on teaching effectiveness and to those contextual factors that may affect the applications of that research. The image of the teacher as a reflective decision maker guides program development, since our objective is to have students develop both technical skills and the professional judgment needed to adapt or modify those skills in response to student needs and the curriculum goals.

Two projects help students understand schools and their contexts.

In the first project, students complete detailed studies of communities surrounding selected Houston-area schools. This firsthand knowledge provides the basis for subsequent discussions about community factors that might affect students' attitudes toward school itself and their performance there.

The second project focuses on school contexts and their influence on the practice of teaching. Students are introduced to research on effective schools, with a particular emphasis on the role of the principal (or other instructional leaders) in creating a climate conducive to learning. Additionally, they examine in depth at least four different classrooms and then compare the organizational patterns and the ways teachers organize instructional time. They are encouraged to raise questions, this time focusing on school-level factors that enhance or diminish a teacher's ability to work with children.

Once students have completed these projects, which focus on selected contextual factors that directly and indirectly affect the conduct of teaching, they are introduced to an overview of research on classroom management, direct instruction, cooperative learning, and the effective use of time. The technical skills of teaching are not taught until the environment in which those skills may be used is introduced. Throughout this process, systematic observation skills are taught and reinforced.

PHASE TWO: REINFORCING REFLECTION

This beginning level of awareness is reinforced in the six semester-hours following the introductory course. Once again, students are placed in a field site in which they become aware of contextual factors. Here they are also introduced to individual differences among students due to ability, development, social skills, and prior experiences with schooling. Research on learning and teaching effectiveness is emphasized as the prospective teachers practice their skills in micro-teaching assignments and in their field classrooms. These assignments include an analysis of lesson design prior to implementation and then an analysis of their actual teaching. The school-based teacher educator (SBTE), known historically as the cooperating or supervising teacher, encourages the prospective teacher to assume responsibility for teaching at least two lessons. Both the student and the SBTE review the lesson and analyze the presentation and content.

Journal entries and frequent meetings with teacher education instructors provide avenues for students and faculty to discuss the problems students face as they confront new material and work through instructional management issues. By the end of the second semester, the students have both declarative knowledge of and experience in working with time management, classroom management, lesson design, direct instruction, and three additional generic teaching strategies. They are aware that their teaching will need to be modified based on factors external to the classroom as well as ones operating within the classroom. They are aware of classrooms as social systems and the teacher's role in organizing the system to enable learning to take place. Developing such organizational skills—or sustaining routines that are already in place—occurs in student teaching.

Transfer

One of the long-term goals of the RITE program is for prospective teachers to provide opportunities for their own students to become problem solvers and reflective learners. Through observing and reflecting on both the successful and unsuccessful routines and structures of the SBTE, as well as their own initial plunge into actual teaching, students take a first step toward developing their own classroom organizational skills. If reflection and inquiry are to occur in the classroom, teachers must focus on their students rather than themselves. However, contextual problems may interfere with the ability of a new teacher to effectively implement problem-solving strategies in the classroom.

The issue of context goes beyond preservice education. Marks (1988) examines how problem solving is implemented in an algebra class from the perspective of an experienced teacher, identified as Sandy in the interview from the study. Sandy is discussing the impact student behavior has in deciding what types of instruction he will use in the algebra class.

> Their behavior is either going to limit or broaden the alternatives of types of instruction that I can use. . . . If I have to worry about discipline problems or students being able to sit next to each other or talk with each other, then I can't do the group work, or I can't do other techniques I might want to use. So let's say I decided to do it that way, the more nonteacher-centered. . . . It would probably be a two-day lesson . . . but in 50 minutes it's more difficult, with other housekeeping tasks and things to do. So that's a concern. (Marks, 1988, p. 21)

Classroom discipline is a very important issue for Sandy. Although he seems to have no trouble maintaining order, he dislikes unruly classes and takes some pains to ensure that disorderliness does not become a problem. Sandy's concern for discipline problems and time constraints limits his use of problem-solving strategies in the classroom. Sandy underscores this problem by stating: "Say I see a set of problems that I'd like the students to do. . . . The first thing I think of is behavior. . . . That's the first line I consider in everything I do. Is this going to create potential explosive situations?" (Marks, 1988, p. 22)

The need to blend a process of learning—reflective inquiry—with the skills of managing that learning is an absolute prerequisite for effective teaching. In the past, teacher education programs emphasized either skills or processes but ignored the interrelationship between the two.

PHASE THREE: REFLECTIVE STUDENT TEACHERS

The transfer of skills and processes to the classroom requires a merging of the knowledge and skills learned during the teacher education program. During student teaching several models are used to provide student teachers maximum contact with students and an opportunity to transfer the reflective experience to their own classrooms. Reflection continues during student teaching in several pilot projects which were designed to give student teachers instructional data upon which they could reflect. Student teachers are provided two additional data sources beyond the usual feedback from cooperating teachers and university supervisors: (1) instruction via audiotape analysis of low-inference self-assessment measure (LISAM), and (2) feedback from systematic classroom observation, e.g., Stallings Observation System (SOS) systems.

Feedback from Audiotape Analysis

One method for providing accurate feedback is to have student teachers audiotape their classrooms. Once the class is taped they can analyze six categories of teacher/student interaction using the low-inference self-assessment instruction (LISAM, see Figure 7.1) (Freiberg, 1987). The "low-inference" in the title reflects the ability of people to listen to the same tape and reach common agreement on the six categories.

Student teachers need accurate information about their interactions in the classroom before they can begin to identify strengths and weaknesses and formulate a strategy to facilitate change. The LISAM allows the neophyte teacher to systematically determine the types of interactions occurring in the classroom. Both elementary and second-

FIGURE 7.1 Audiotape Analysis Example

---

1. *Questioning Skills*
   Short answer: T̶H̶L̶ T̶H̶L̶ T̶H̶L̶   Total = 15 = 39.5%
   Comparison: 11   Total = 2 = 5.3%
   Opinions: 0   Total = 0 = 0%
   Yes/No: T̶H̶L̶ T̶H̶L̶ T̶H̶L̶ T̶H̶L̶   Total = 21 = 55.3%

2. *Teacher Talk/Student Talk*
   Teacher: Student:
   Total (T) = 335   Total (S) = 58   (T) + (S) = 393
   Teacher = 85%   Student = 15%   393/58 = 15%

3. *Identification of Motivating Set and Closure*
   Describe each from the tape:
       Set-induction: I used an Incan painting to develop descriptions from
           the students that would lead to a discussion of literary devices.
       Closure: The bell rang before I had time to bring closure to the lesson.

4. *Wait-Time*
   Time between teacher question and next teacher statement:
       1   3   2   2   2   4   3
       4   2   *2   2   3   *2
       1   3   4   2   *4   1

5. *Identify Number of Positive Statements Made by Teacher*   Total = 6
   Praise or encouragement
   1 to the class
   5 to individuals (used students' names twice)

6. *Identify the Number of Times Teacher Uses Student Ideas*   Total = 6

---

*Asterisks indicate higher order questions.
Source: Freiberg, H. J. (1987). Teacher self-evaluation and principal supervision. In NASSP *Bulletin*, p. 89.

ary student teachers have used the LISAM, and Hoover and Carroll (1987) also found that the use of audiotapes and self-assessment helps classroom teachers improve their elementary reading instruction.

Preservice teachers' reactions to analyzing their teaching have been very positive. Consistently, preservice teachers express relief at "knowing how well they are doing" and amazement at how their perceptions differ from reality.

During the last few years, students who have experienced simulated teaching combined with peer feedback and the LISAM audiotape analysis have expressed a very positive sense of having gained a new tool to reflect upon their teaching as they progress from student teaching into their first years of teaching. The following is a summary of one student teacher's assessment of the self-assessment process after listening to her tape.

> On the whole I was pleased with the data from the lesson. My wait-time seemed adequate for a discussion format. Although not entirely to my credit I improved the ratio of student to teacher talk from the previous teacher. Of course, I would like to have the students so enthralled with the subject and the discussion that my teacher talk was even less. One item not covered in the analysis was the use of personal phrases, e.g., "O.K.," "O.K., then," etc. I feel like I should attempt to limit my use of these as they will become monotonous. Also the discussion went a little quicker than I anticipated so that I had to ad lib a few questions toward the end to stretch the discussion. Therefore, if I taught this lesson again I would overprepare the questions in case of the variable time frame. Another improvement I would attempt would be more use of probing questions to delve into student responses. I think probing (not militaristically) might help the students to clarify and think through various answers.
>
> My only parting comment is this: as a novice teacher I want to thank you emphatically for this self analysis tool!

The technical tools for self-assessment provide opportunities for reflection that can be both introspective and interactive. Student teachers have the opportunity to reflect on the data from their teaching individually (introspective), with a mentor/cooperating teacher, and with a peer group (interactive). Combining the technical tools of providing accurate data about teaching with different contexts for reflection expands the universe of possibilities for professional growth.

Feedback from Classroom Observation Systems

The use of systematic observation instruments became prevalent in the mid-1960s with the use of the Flanders Interaction Analysis System (Flanders, 1965). The dissemination and use of the system for both preservice and inservice teachers peaked about ten years later (Freiberg, 1981).

In the 1980s, the Stallings Observation System (Stallings, 1986), which incorporates sixty-four teacher and student variables, built upon the earlier Flanders' system. Used primarily for inservice teachers, the Stallings system has recently been applied to observations of preservice teachers during student teaching (Freiberg, Waxman, & Houston, 1987). The Stallings Observation System consists of two independent observations, the snapshot, and the five-minute interaction. The snapshot (Figure 7.2) provides an overall picture of classroom activities, indicating the percentage of time that the teacher is involved in various activities, the materials being used, and with whom the teacher is working (Simons & Stallings, 1985).

The five-minute interaction (see Figure 7.3), as its name suggests, documents the interactions between teacher and student during five five-minute periods. The interactions are coded by type: academic, organizational, or behavioral (Simons & Stallings, 1985). Observations are made and averaged across a three-day period.

Snapshots are completed five times during one period, so that a total sample of fifteen are done during the three days of observation. Also, five five-minute interactions are coded each period, evenly distributed across the time. Approximately 300 interactions are coded during each fifty-minute period (Simons & Stallings, 1985).

The profiles that are generated from the snapshots and five-minute interactions provide systematic feedback to the student teachers. The criteria identified in the profiles were derived from the research on effective teaching. Preservice teachers would not be expected to achieve these levels during their initial teaching experiences. The profiles, however, do provide systematic feedback that helps students analyze their interactions from the beginning to the conclusion of student teaching.

Student teachers who received feedback via the Stallings system on their teaching and attended two three-hour seminars on the application of the profile findings to their classrooms improved their teaching effectiveness (Freiberg et al., 1987). The students also reported greater self-confidence and control over their instruction.

Data collected through the Stallings Observation System show that student teachers who received this type of support also had greater interactive instruction (71% vs. 60%) than a comparison control group, greater use of academic statements (85% vs. 77%), and fewer organizing statements (12% vs. 19%). Additionally, students in their classrooms were off-task less frequently than in the control classrooms (13% vs. 23%).

In another study (Freiberg, Waxman, & Blanchard, 1988), student teachers who had participated in the RITE program were compared with student teachers who entered prior to the implementation of the program. The RITE student teachers made more progress in areas of teaching effectiveness than non-RITE student teachers. Pupils of the RITE students were off-task less than those of pre-RITE students (10.3% vs. 15.8%) based on initial classroom observations. The time spent on classroom management for the non-RITE student teachers was 10.3%, while the RITE student teachers spent 5.3% in classroom management. The

(text continues on p. 135)

FIGURE 7.2 Observation Profile of Betty Brown's Classroom—Snapshot

Observation Variables	Criterion	Criterion	Betty's Class	Goal
			% of Time Spent	
Teacher Involved In				
Monitoring silent reading	X	15.0	.0	Monitoring 35% or less
Monitoring written work	X	20.0	36.0	
Reading aloud	X	6.0	.0	Interactive instruction 50% or more
Instruction/explanation	X	25.0	10.0	
Discussion/review assignments	X	10.0	13.0	
Practice drill	X	4.0	.0	
Taking test/quiz	X	5.0	.0	
Classroom management with students	X	2.5	.0	Organizing 15% or less
Making assignments	X	10.0	20.0	
Organizing-teacher alone	X	2.5	18.0	
Social interaction with students	X	.0	.0	
Students uninvolved	X	.0	.0	
Providing discipline	X	.0	3.0	

(continued)

FIGURE 7.2 (continued)

Observation Variables	Criterion	% of Time Spent		
		Criterion	Betty's Class	Goal
Students Involved In				
Reading silently	X	15.0	2.0	Seatwork 35%
Written assignments		20.0	55.0	or less
Reading aloud	X	6.0	0.0	Interactive
Receiving instruction/explanations	X	25.0	26.0	instruction 50%
Discussion/review	X	10.0	12.0	or more
Practice drill		4.0	7.0	
Taking test/quiz	X	5.0	6.0	
Social interaction		.0	14.0	Off-task 6%
Student uninvolved		.0	12.0	or less
Being disciplined	X	.0	3.0	
Classroom management	X	5.0	.0	Organizing 15%
Receiving assignments	X	10.0	10.0	or less

Source: Stallings, J. A. (1986). Using Time Effectively: A Self Analytical Approach. In K. Zumwalt (Ed.), Improving Teaching. 1986 ACSD Yearbook (pp. 24–25). Used by permission.

FIGURE 7.3 Interaction Profile of Betty Brown—Five-Minute Interaction

Variables	Percent	Percent	Recommended
001 All academic statements	80	65.28	Increase
002 All organizing or managing statements	15	30.76	Decrease
003 All behavior statements	3	3.83	OK
004 All social statements	2	.00	OK
005 Total for discrete variables	100	100.00	
006 Teacher instructs/explains	12	15.45	OK
007 Teacher asks direct questions or commands	10	4.00	Increase
008 Teacher asks clarifying questions	3	.13	Increase
009 Teacher asks open-ended questions	3	.79	Increase
010 Student asks academic questions	2	1.32	OK
011 Teacher calls upon new students (academic)	6	5.02	OK
012 Students respond academically	15	5.00	Increase
013 Student shouts-out/initiates remarks		7.39	Decrease
014 Student doesn't know answer	1	.13	OK
015 Student refuses to answer		.00	OK
016 All praise	8	2.00	Increase
017 Teacher praises or supports academic responses	6	2.00	Increase
018 Teacher praises behavior	2	.00	Increase
019 Teacher corrects academic responses	6	4.35	Increase
020 Teacher corrects with guidance	4	.00	Increase

(continued)

FIGURE 7.3 (continued)

Variables		Percent	Percent	Recommended
021 Teacher corrects behavior	X	2	3.03	Decrease
022 Teacher monitoring academic work	X	6	10.96	Decrease
023 All written work	X		.00	OK
024 Students read aloud	X	10	4.62	OK
025 Teacher reads aloud	X	1	2.24	OK
026 Teacher working alone	X	3	6.00	Decrease
027 Intrusions	X		3.14	Decrease
028 Teacher involved with visitor	X		2.20	Decrease
029 Positive interactions	X	4	.52	Increase
030 Negative interactions	X		1.50	Decrease
031 Teacher touching	X	5	.00	Increase
032 Teacher movement	X	3	1.12	Increase
033 All activity-related comments or actions	X	16	9.77	OK
034 Student organizing comments	X	1	.13	Ok
035 Student academic comments	X	3	.13	OK
036 Teacher organizing comments	X	5	1.98	OK
037 Students academic discussion	X	7	7.66	Increase
038 Students cooperative group academic	X	5	.00	Increase
Total Number of Interactions for Teacher 905				

Source: Stallings, J. A. (1986). Using Time Effectively: A Self Analytical Approach. In K. Zumwalt (Ed.), Improving Teaching. 1986 ACSD Yearbook (pp.24–25). Used by permission.

RITE student teachers had somewhat higher levels of academic statements (77.5% vs. 75.9%) and lower levels of organizing statements (19.6% vs. 20.1%) during their teaching.

The small sample for most of the studies precluded statistically significant changes in the comparisons. However, the differences were educationally significant. The gains made by the RITE student teachers indicate that a reflective program can have a positive impact on teaching effectiveness during student teaching.

IMPLICATIONS FOR TEACHER EDUCATION

Reflection, according to John Dewey, limits the impulsive nature of teaching and enables the educator to act with intention and deliberation (Dewey, 1909/1933). Reflectivity in teacher education may be viewed from a variety of perspectives, as evident from the range of positions taken in this book. The multiple data sources and methods of providing feedback to preservice teachers present a framework that could be readily adapted to many teacher education programs. The use of such sources as systematic feedback from classroom observation systems; systematic classroom observation; journal writing; and simulated teaching can be effective methods for raising the level of credible sources of data and feedback for preservice teachers. Overlapping data sources with different contexts for reflection (from introspective to interactive) enable teacher education programs to maximize the opportunities for students to learn about and be part of the teaching profession. They also allow prospective teachers to progress through cognitive-development stages that enable them to view teaching from a more interpretive and critical perspective.

REFERENCES

Allen, D., & Fortune, J. (1966). An analysis of micro-teaching: New procedures in teacher education. *Micro-teaching: A description.* Stanford University Press.

Becher, R. M., & Ade, W. E. (1982). The relationship of field placement characteristics and students' potential field performance abilities to clinical experience performance ratings. *Journal of Teacher Education, 33*(2), 24–30.

Benham, B. J. (1979, April). *The effect of reflective writing on identifying maintenance in student teachers.* Paper presented at the annual meeting of the American Educational Research Association, San Francisco.

Bolin, F. S. (1988). Helping student teachers think about teaching. *Journal of Teacher Education, 39*(2), 48–54.

Briggs, L. D., Richardson, W. D., & Sefzik, W. P. (1986). Comparing supervising teacher ratings and student teacher self-ratings of elementary student teaching. *Education, 106,* 150–159.

Bush, R., & Allen, D. (1964). *Controlled practice in the training of teachers.* Paper presented at the Santa Barbara Conference on Teacher Education sponsored by the Ford Foundation.

Cohn, M. (1981). A new supervision model for linking theory to practice. *Journal of Teacher Education, 32*(3), 26–29.

Cruickshank, D. R. (1987). *Reflective teaching: The preparation of students of teaching.* Reston, VA: Association of Teacher Educators.

Denton, J. J. (1982). Early field experiences influence performance in subsequent coursework. *Journal of Teacher Education, 33*(2), 19–23.

Dewey, J. (1933). *How we think: A restatement of the relation of reflective thinking to the educative process.* Boston: Heath. (Original work published 1909)

Flanders, N. (1965). *Teacher influence, pupil attitudes, and achievement* (Cooperative Research Monograph No. 12). Washington, DC: U.S. Office of Education.

Freiberg, H. J. (1981). Three decades of the Flanders Interaction Analysis System. *The Journal of Classroom Interaction, 16*(2), 1–7.

Freiberg, H. J. (1986). *Generic teaching strategies.* Unpublished course materials, University of Houston, Houston, TX.

Freiberg, H. J. (1987). Teacher self-evaluation and principal supervision. *NASSP Bulletin, 71*(498), 85–92.

Freiberg, H. J., Waxman, H. C., & Blanchard, K. (1988). *A comparison of teaching behaviors with RITE and non-RITE student teachers.* Part of the final report to the Office of Educational Research and Improvement, Washington, DC.

Freiberg, H. J., Waxman, H. C., & Houston, W. R. (1987). Enriching feedback to student teachers through small group discussion. *Teacher Education Quarterly, 14*(3), 71–82.

Garman, N. B. (1982). The clinical approach to supervision. In T. J. Sergiovanni (Ed.), *Supervision of teaching* (pp. 35–52). Alexandria, VA: Association of Supervision and Curriculum Development.

Garman, N. B. (1987). Reflection, the heart of clinical supervision: A modern rationale for professional practice. *Journal of Curriculum and Supervision, 2*(1), 1–24.

Gibson, R. (1976). The effect of school practice: The development of student perspectives. *British Journal of Teacher Education, 2,* 241–250.

Good, T., Biddle, B., & Brophy, J. (1975). *Teachers make a difference.* New York: Holt, Rinehart & Winston.

Good, T. L., & Brophy, J. E. (1987). *Looking in classrooms* (4th ed.). New York: Harper & Row.

Henry, M. A. (1982). Testing out the field. In D. E. Orlosky (Ed.), *Introduction to education* (pp. 495–518). Columbus, OH: Merrill.

Hill, S. (1978). Language education and field experiences. *Journal of Teacher Education, 37*(3), 56–59.

Hoover, N. L., & Carroll, R. G. (1987). Self-assessment of classroom instruction: An effective approach to inservice education. *Teaching and Teacher Education, 3,* 179–181.

Hoover, N. L., & O'Shea, L. J. (1987, April). *Effects of collaborative conferencing and feedback on student teachers' perceptions and performance.* Paper presented at the annual meeting of the American Educational Research Association, Washington, DC.

Hoy, W., & Rees, R. (1977). The bureaucratic socialization of student teachers. *Journal of Teacher Education, 28*(1), 23–26.

Jackson, P. W. (1968). *Life in classrooms.* New York: Holt, Rinehart & Winston.

Joyce, B. R., Yarger, S. J., & Howey, K. R. (1977). *Preservice teacher education.* Palo Alto, CA: Booksend Laboratory.

Korthagen, F. (1985). Reflective teaching and preservice teacher education in the Netherlands. *Journal of Teacher Education, 36*(5), 11–15.

Koziol, S. M., Jr., Bohn, S., & Moss, P. A. (1983, April). *Composition instruction in four suburban school districts: Grades 3-6.* Paper presented at the annual meeting of the American Educational Research Association, Montreal.

Koziol, S. M., Jr., & Burns, P. (1986). Teachers' accuracy in self-reporting about instructional practices using a focused self-report inventory. *Journal of Educational Research, 79,* 205–209.

Marks, R. (1988, April). *Problem solving with a small "p": A teacher's view.* Paper presented at the annual meeting of the American Educational Research Association, Washington, DC.

Posner, G. J. (1985). *Field experience: A guide to reflective teaching.* New York: Longman.

Ryan, K., & Cooper, J. M. (1972). *Those who can, teach.* Boston: Houghton Mifflin.

Sandefur, J. T. (1970). Kansas State Teachers College experimental study of professional education for secondary teachers. *Journal of Teacher Education, 21,* 386–395.

Simons, S., & Stallings, J. (1985, April). *Does the effective use of time program improve teaching practice of secondary content area teachers?* Paper presented at the annual meeting of the American Educational Research Association, Washington, DC.

Stallings, J. (1986). *The Stallings Observation System.* Training manual. Houston: University of Houston.

Tabachnick, B. R., Popkewitz, T. S., & Zeichner, K. M. (1980). Teacher education and the professional perspectives of student teachers. *Interchange, 10,* 12–29.

Waxman, H. C., & Duschl, R. (1987). Using student perception data to improve preservice teachers' instruction and classroom environment. In B. F. Fraser (Ed.), *Study of learning environments* (Vol. 2) (pp. 77–79). Bentley, Australia: Western Australian Institute of Technology.

Waxman, H. C., Freiberg, H. J., Clift, R. T., & Houston, W. R. (1988, February).

The development of reflective inquiry in teacher education. Paper presented at the annual meeting of the Association of Teacher Educators, San Diego.

Waxman, H. C., Rodriguez, J. A., Padron, Y. N., & Knight, S. L. (1988). The use of systematic classroom observations during field experience components of teacher education programs. College Student Journal, 22, 199–202.

Wheeler, A. E., & Knoop, H. R. (1982). Self, teacher, and faculty assessments of student teacher education. Journal of Educational Research, 75, 178–191.

Yinger, R., & Clark, C. (1981). Reflective journal writing: Theory and practice (Occasional Paper No. 50). East Lansing, MI: Institute for Research on Teaching.

Zeichner, K. M., & Liston, D. P. (1987). Teaching student teachers to reflect. Harvard Educational Review, 57, 23–48.

8 Promoting Reflective Practice among Beginning and Experienced Teachers

TERRY M. WILDMAN   SUSAN G. MAGLIARO
JEROME A. NILES   RUTH ANNE McLAUGHLIN
                Virginia Polytechnic Institute and State University

Teacher reflection is a difficult concept to pin down. In this chapter we attempt to construct a working view of reflection as it was revealed in the activities of beginning and experienced teachers (mentors) who collaborated in developing a large, systemwide induction program. During this program, reflection was encouraged through training activities that oriented mentors to ways of analyzing teaching and a small amount of release-time for mentors and beginners to work together. Beyond these inducements, what emerged was left to the teachers' own discretion, shaped by their needs and the contexts in which they worked.

As we followed the progress of mentors and beginning teachers through interviews and periodic reports of their collaborative activities, four questions emerged as important keys to understanding their reflection on teaching:

1. What forces stimulate reflective activity?
2. What are the activities and processes that define reflection?
3. What forces constrain reflection in school settings?
4. What is the impact of reflection on teachers?

These questions are important because they helped us organize a diverse and complex array of data. The first question, for example, acknowledges the fact that reflection does not just happen; rather, it is an active, effortful enterprise that arises when certain motivational forces are allowed to operate. The second question led us to understand that reflection can be a natural response to day-to-day teaching; as such, it occurs in many different contexts and takes different forms with each teacher. The third question encouraged us to investigate the various roadblocks teachers encounter in their attempts to work with other teachers to reflect seriously on their teaching. It also led us to attempts to understand some of the specific conditions that foster reflective activity. Finally, the fourth question elicited examination of how reflection can have both positive and negative consequences for teachers. Collectively, we used the four questions to create a composite view of reflection as it occurs in normal teaching contexts.

The focus of this chapter is primarily on experienced teachers in their role as mentors to beginning teachers. We collaborated with them to promote examination of their own teaching and helped them develop ways to support their novice colleagues as they attempted to learn the complex art of teaching. Essentially, our goal with veteran teachers was to determine ways in which their knowledge, experience, and values could be effectively utilized to support their inexperienced colleagues. We started with the main idea that mentors would be most effective within the context of reflective practice. Reflection was an important concept for us for several reasons. First, we wanted the experienced teachers to activate and make explicit what they knew and believed about teaching. As Schön (1983) points out, so much of what experts do is "dependent upon tacit recognitions, judgments, and skillful performances" (p. 50). Much of teachers' knowing about teaching is thus embedded within their actions. It is often not consciously available to them, and certainly not to their inexperienced colleagues. We wanted to see if the tacit understandings of teachers could be revealed and made available for critical analysis. We believed their own growth as professionals would benefit from such a reflective posture. Second, for similar reasons, we wanted the experts (mentors) to bring their inexperienced colleagues into the reflective process by modeling problem solving and providing judicious feedback.

PROGRAM BACKGROUND

The context of our work on reflection was a five-year effort to develop a statewide plan for beginning teacher induction that could be adopted by the Virginia Department of Education in conjunction with its Beginning Teacher Assistance Program. Our goals during the five years were to (1) develop an in-depth understanding of beginning teachers' socialization into teaching, (2) investigate ways that expert teachers can work with beginners in a mentoring role, and (3) develop a model or models of induction that could be applied throughout Virginia. It was in the pursuit of these goals that our interest in teacher reflection emerged as a major theme. In 1983, when we first began to conceptualize an agenda for teacher induction, the literature on teacher improvement seemed to pull program developers in two directions at once. On the one hand, educators were just beginning to feel the effects of a major push in classroom research that was yielding for the first time a coherent database on effective teaching practices. Notable achievements under active discussion at that time were the Beginning Teacher Evaluation Study (BTES) (Fisher et al., 1980), the Missouri Mathematics Effectiveness Studies (Good & Grouws, 1983), work on teacher expectations (Good, 1983), and the various studies from which Rosenshine synthesized his model of direct instruction (Rosenshine, 1983). Educators and policy makers, many of them eager for quick results from the emerging educational reform movement, advocated wholesale adoption by teachers of the behaviors and practices derived from such research. Pressure to conform to the emerging knowledge base on teaching effectiveness came in the form of teacher tests (both state and local) and top-down staff development practices designed to change teachers' behavior.

At the same time, others were concerned that, in the rush to improve practice, teachers' voices were being ignored in the suggested formulas for reform. Analysts such as Fenstermacher (1979), Sykes (1983), Wise (1979), and Zumwalt (1982) all argued that the power of research lay more in its usefulness in informing and improving teachers' deliberation about their practice than in providing rules and regulations through which practice could be scrutinized and governed. Their arguments called for considerably more freedom and autonomy in teachers' use of research than policy makers seemed willing to give. The tension of reform, then, was between a conception of teaching as a technical enterprise, which would improve only as the research base improved, and teaching as a deliberative, or reflective, activity, which would improve as teachers became increasingly empowered and skilled at conducting inquiry into their own practice. Our work was influenced and guided by the belief that meaningful reform could best be achieved through this latter stance.

PROGRAM DEVELOPMENT AND CONTENT

Two main functions composed our work on teacher reflection during this project. First, we wanted to develop a set of training tasks and procedures that could reliably stimulate in veteran teachers (1) an attitude of inquiry and reflection, (2) a sharpened ability to look at teaching and talk about it with colleagues, and (3) the confidence that they could effectively influence their own professional lives as well as those of novice colleagues. Second, we wanted to identify those factors in the

(text continues on p. 144)

FIGURE 8.1 Tasks Used to Stimulate and Build Reflective Values

TASKS	PHASE 1		PHASE 2	
→	*1. Talking about Teaching*	*2. Classroom Awareness*	*3. Critical Analysis*	*4. Critical Analysis with Colleague*
Task description	Discriminating judgments versus observations	Comparing importance of classroom events based on own values and beliefs	Building on Task #1, using observation instruments to record classroom events	Building on Tasks #1–3, role-playing teacher/observer dyads with observations and conferences
Task purpose	Allowing the teachers to discover the nature of their talk inductively	Encouraging teachers to use increased awareness of classrooms in self-reflection about their own teaching	Integrating the self-awareness into self-reflection by identifying biased versus less biased descriptions of teaching	Providing practice and developing strategies that could be used to initiate collaborative reflection about teaching
Trainer concerns	Difficulty of initial task; creating a task that would allow discovery at an easy level; time	Getting teachers to "unpack" and reveal their conceptions of teaching in terms of values and beliefs	Reflecting on own teaching in negative light; withdrawing from participation; developing a negative attitude toward training	Timing of role-playing (do teachers "have" the tools to conference and reflect together); making sure teachers know the difference between evaluation and analysis
Teacher reactions	Surprised, mildly uncomfortable; quickly turned positive with sense of accomplishment	Difficult due to loose structure; requirement to justify comments forced them to reveal own beliefs and values; developed a broader conception and appreciation of teaching	Difficulty with narrative tools; frustrated with application of observation-versus-judgment delineation; revealed their vulnerability	Mixed, some enjoyed the practice while others felt it was too contrived and removed from real life

Artificial to real contexts
Focus of agenda from ours to the teachers'
Time
Level of complexity

142

| | PHASE 3 | | 8. Planning | PHASE 4 |
5. Looking at Own Students	6. Looking at Own Lessons	7. A Broader View of "Looking"	Reflection with a Colleague	9. Reflection Day and Evaluation
Developing a case study of selected students to increase sensitivity to complexity of own classroom	Analysis, description, and interpretation of 3 of their own audiotaped lessons	Using *Looking in Classrooms* instrumentation, examination, and practice with a variety of ways of looking at one's own lessons	Building on all prior tasks, planning and development of a professional "reflection" day with their beginning colleague	Implementating and evaluating plan developed in Task #8.
Revealing the complex yet implicit nature of teaching	Focusing attention on the interactive nature of the classroom environment	Providing a number of choices of ways to look at teaching	Developing a plan for reflection with the beginning colleague	Providing a "learning day" for the beginners, while the mentors served as brokers for the beginners' reflection
Use of own beliefs and values to exclusion of other interpretations or other points of view	Completion of task; their ability to develop a focus for observation and reflection	The number of "ways" would be overpowering	The experienced colleague may be too directive; administrative permission to allow teachers' plan	Success and/or learning emanating from the plan; positive reaction from administrators to ensure future reflection days
Positive, the task was do-able; were able to develop detailed notes that were beneficial to interpreting the meaning of events in their own classroom	Discovered positive and negative aspects of their lessons; interested in the analyses of own and others' lessons; more sensitive to power of systematic reflection	Enjoyed seeing the number of equally valid and important aspects of classroom life; enjoyed being able to modify instruments to meet their own agendas	Positive; a variety of activities were planned that met the beginner's needs; facilitated discussion about teaching and individual interests	Extremely positive, served as a focal point for year's activities; both the beginning and experienced colleagues reported learning a lot about themselves and their teaching, as well as each other

$\longrightarrow$ $\longrightarrow$ $\longrightarrow$ $\longrightarrow$

workplace that contributed positively and negatively to collaborative reflection and to develop profiles of reflective work as it occurred in natural settings.

The data that inform the following discussion were obtained primarily from fifteen pairs of beginning and veteran teachers with whom we worked for three years. The data sources were semistructured interviews with the teachers and monthly reports summarizing the collegial activities of experts and beginners. Audio- and videotapes of the training activities were also used to better understand the nature of our training activities and the effects of reflective training tasks on the veteran teachers. These data were later augmented by similar information from approximately seventy pairs of beginners and experts who participated in the program when it expanded during 1987–88 to serve the entire school division.

Tasks That Stimulate and Shape Reflection

Many teachers demonstrate a naturally reflective style in their daily work. However, their reflection may be unintentional as well as unfocused and unsystematic. The creation of tasks that were challenging, yet supportive, was an important aspect of our development of training to encourage reflection. In addition to promoting reflection as an action-oriented enterprise, we found that a progression of tasks could be designed to allow for a gradual transition from a less to a more systematically reflective posture. This transition could be handled by varying both the degree of complexity and uncertainty of the task, as well as the extent to which the task focused on a teacher's own teaching or that of another. Moreover, through tasks that allowed for practice and immediate feedback, skills important to reflective practice could be activated, shaped, and refined. Finally, tasks assigned outside the immediate training context and oriented to each participant's own teaching situation helped teachers bring some structure and relevance to what could otherwise be an overwhelming and amorphous request (i.e., go and reflect on your teaching!). Figure 8.1 shows the entire training sequence, revealing important aspects of the tasks themselves, their developmental sequencing over time, and the orientations, concerns, or reactions that both the trainers and participants brought to the training.

In describing these tasks and participants' reactions to them, it is important to note the context in which the tasks were introduced. The mentors were bound to the project primarily through their commitment to helping beginning teachers and their desire to continue their own professional growth. The small honorarium and minimum release-time provided for mentors was helpful but was not a powerful incentive. Thus much depended on the initiative of each individual teacher. Our major expectations were that they would be active participants in the training and that they would help their beginning colleagues as best they could. Beyond that, the extent of their reflective activities was left to them.

Descriptions and Purposes of the Training Task

We began to engage mentors in the systematic analysis of teaching by looking first at their language. The day-to-day professional discourse of teachers is often loaded with fuzzy terminology, imprecise description, and a distinctly judgmental flavor. Consequently, one of the first tasks we devised was one designed to sensitize teachers to the nature of their discourse. As shown in Figure 8.1, this initial phase of the training was seen as foundational in nature, aimed at getting teachers to talk about teaching and look at teaching more systematically and precisely than they normally would. Mechanically, the tasks required teachers to read vignettes of teaching episodes and then write down descriptive and interpretive comments. One of our goals was to sensitize teachers to the distinction between objective observations and judgments. Another goal, pursued more directly in the classroom-awareness tasks shown in Figure 8.1, was to force the experienced teachers to "unpack" their conceptions of teaching and to construct more detailed analyses of teaching than they typically used in their daily professional lives. These activities were designed to enable experienced teachers to be more aware of their own teaching as well as to make them more sensitive to events in their beginning colleagues' classrooms. Through these tasks, primarily involving the analysis of written classroom vignettes, they began to see that many important events occur during classroom instruction and that no one observer (or reader) can attend to everything at once. They also began to understand that what one attends to in the classroom environment depends on values and intentions.

The next set of tasks (phase 2—critical-analysis tasks) were designed to continue to develop classroom awareness and to help participants integrate this awareness into self-reflection about their own teaching. Here we had teachers watch short videotaped segments from normal teaching settings and, again, prepare descriptions of what they saw. During this phase teachers experimented with various ways of preparing qualitative descriptions of the teaching episodes. We continued to focus on their problems in distinguishing between observations and judgments, on ways of isolating particular features of the classroom environment to examine in detail, and on the role of beliefs, values, and intentions in both teaching and looking at teaching. Near the end of this phase, teachers worked in pairs to begin the process of learning how to analyze teaching episodes with a colleague. From these discussions a variety of issues concerning conferences emerged, and we discussed strategies that mentors might use to initiate reflection about teaching, particularly concerning problems that might be of a sensitive nature.

Phase 3 represented the move from looking at "neutral" teaching episodes to an examination of each participant's own teaching. In the first task in this phase of the training, the teachers developed case studies of two students in their classrooms. The purpose of this task was to develop their appreciation of (1) the amount of information that is available in the classroom setting; (2) how difficult it is to be aware of all this information; and (3) how important this information is in managing a classroom that provides equal opportunity to all students. Developing an understanding of these factors increased teachers' sensitivity to the looking process, which we think is fundamental to constructive reflection.

Following the development of the case studies, we asked the mentors to examine their own instructional lessons. They audiotaped three lessons or lesson segments from their own classrooms. The purpose of this task was to focus their attention on the interactive nature of the classroom environment and to allow them to practice choosing their own focus for reflection in the lesson analysis process. Thus the teachers were instructed to listen to their tapes at least three times, write a description of what they heard, and then prepare an interpretation of the lesson. The final task in phase 3 introduced participants to a range of analysis activities from *Looking in Classrooms* (Good & Brophy, 1984). The intent of this task was to give the mentors a number of choices in terms of how and what they could look at in their teaching. They were encouraged to look at the menu of activities provided in the *Looking* book and select any that made sense at that time. If they felt they had an analysis agenda of their own, they were encouraged to use it.

The final phase of training involved getting the mentors started working with their new colleague. Our project had purchased one day of release-time for each member of the pair to use specifically for reflection on teaching. The first task was to develop a reflection plan. Prior to the scheduled "reflection day," each mentor met with his or her beginning colleague and decided on one or more reflection activities they would try. Thus they decided collaboratively what made sense for them.

The pairs then planned when and how the reflection would take place. This resulted in a wide range of scheduled activities. For example, one pair decided to exchange classrooms for a day and then use part of their time talking about the experience each had. Another pair chose to do formal observation and audiotaping and then conduct an analysis that focused on particular aspects of the lesson. Others decided to visit classrooms that represented interesting and sometimes contrasting examples of good teaching or curriculum practices. In some cases the pair went together; in others, they worked separately. In all instances, the colleague pairs engaged in extensive discussion about teaching before, during (when appropriate), and after their experiences.

Teacher Reactions to Tasks

Throughout the series of training episodes, teachers demonstrated a variety of reactions to the tasks. The "talking-about-teaching" activities seemed to affect many of the experienced teachers profoundly. For most, this was the first time they had had the opportunity to engage in an activity that revealed their values and biases so clearly. They commented repeatedly on how unaware they were of the value-laden and judgmental nature of their typical discourse. However, they were quick to distinguish between their own objective and judgmental comments. They seemed pleased with their prospects for differentiating observations and judgments during future interactions with their new colleagues. Interestingly, many reported that this was the first time they had focused to this extent on their talk about teaching.

As the training progressed to the classroom-awareness and analysis tasks, teachers initially found the relatively unfocused "looking" somewhat difficult and unsettling. Most reported that this was the first time they had been asked to look at teaching in such a manner. We were somewhat surprised at this, since the median number of years of experience for the group was at least ten. Apparently, their classroom experiences across those years had caused them to form quite idiosyncratic ways of looking at classroom behavior. These tasks, aimed at discriminating among classroom events, began the long process of opening up the classroom environment for more extended critical analysis. It is important to note that at this particular point, the teachers seemed to be at a very vulnerable stage. The training had to progress slowly and be sensitive to the participants' feelings of competence as professionals.

The activities during phase 3 continued to awaken teachers to the complexities of meaning in their classrooms. Some began to recognize and modify the egocentric interpretations of classroom events to which teachers are often so vulnerable. That is, they stopped attaching meaning to events in their classrooms primarily through their own perceptions without considering others' points of view. Finally, the constructive nature of the reflective tasks was manifested in the specific actions teachers took to enhance the classroom lives of their learners and to improve the quality of their lessons based on their deliberations.

The last phase of the training activities, the reflection day described earlier, was equally as beneficial. As one of the beginners commented: "I cannot begin to tell you the ideas, content, projects, and management ideas that are excitedly running through my head. The benefits of today are numerous." Another confirmed that her reflection day "was the most productive day of learning for me this school year." For the beginners, the day enabled them to focus on their learning without the competition of being in the role of teacher. The mentors served a vital role in this process as "brokers" for the beginners' reflection. Their positive and helpful attitude toward inquiry was the force that helped guide the beginners' experiences. Later, through extended discussions with the mentors, the beginning teachers could specify, elaborate, and evaluate the ideas and feelings that emanated from the experience.

REFLECTIVE PROCESSES AND OUTCOMES

In this section we use the four questions introduced earlier to organize what experts and beginners have taught us about reflection over several years. In telling their stories we will focus particularly on the ways in which three mentor–beginning teacher (BT) pairs managed to work together. Brenda and Karen (BT) are high school English teachers. Karen, a second-year teacher, is primarily responsible for ninth-grade classes, while Brenda teaches eleventh-graders. Robin and Lou (BT) are elementary teachers, having fifth- and fourth-grade assignments respectively. Diane and Ellen (BT) teach special education at the elementary level. All the mentors were trained as described above.

Forces That Stimulate Reflection

Reflection, as we argued earlier, is an active, effortful enterprise; it does not just happen. As we read and reread the interviews and periodic reports of how mentors and beginners managed to work together, reflective activities seemed to arise naturally in at least three kinds of situations. Specifically, we distinguished among reflective behavior that was (1) oriented toward the solution of a problem or dilemma faced by one or more teachers; (2) directive in nature, involving modeling or coaching; and (3) internally driven, involving a more private deliberation with either a personal or professional flavor. Across the mentor–beginner pairs that we observed, some talked primarily about one category, while others demonstrated activity in each category.

Brenda and Karen, who were both teaching high school English and especially interested in composition, were fighting a common problem. Brenda described the situation as follows:

> We . . . at the beginning of the year . . . both picked up a substantial number of students who had test scores between the 35th and 60th percentile. Most come from economically deprived homes . . . and really don't have any social life. They are antagonized by each other, and you have to work very hard to get them [to work] in small groups.

Both Brenda and Karen tended to set high standards for students, even those identified by the school's tracking system as not likely to perform well. Their difficulty in reaching the less motivated and less academically adept students presented them with a powerful dilemma. Both believed that students can learn much about writing from each other, but their plans to involve these students more actively in the writing process had been thwarted by classroom management problems. As Brenda related, they "have a tendency to kill each other." She went on to elaborate:

> We were real distraught and tried to figure out all these plans that we could implement. It upsets us in the sense that she and I have so many ideas on composition that peer editing is important, and feel that once in a while it's nice to deviate from them working alone or just in pairs . . . so that's one thing that early on we wanted to do and try to manage and were unsuccessful doing it.

Their attempts to do a good job teaching under very difficult circumstances provided Brenda and Karen a natural and compelling context for reflection. Both teachers had definite ideas about the best way to approach their subject, and both were unwilling to give up on students who were difficult to teach.

Diane and Ellen presented us with a somewhat different relationship and type of reflective collaboration. At first, Ellen (the beginner) put herself almost totally in Diane's care. According to Diane: "Ellen came to teaching real eager. She wanted to learn. The first couple of weeks of school I just told her what to do and she did it." Diane went on to explain that in special education Ellen was immediately confronted with "six different levels to teach within six different subjects." Moreover, Diane pointed out that "there are even more rules related to special education than there are regular school rules."

Diane's directive influence on Ellen was especially important in such areas as preparing individualized educational plans, developing daily lesson plans, working with mainstream teachers, and handling parent conferences. However, Diane explained that she did not hold onto her strictly directive posture very long:

> After the first nine weeks, after she got her feet wet and tried it my way, then I said now you use your own personality and your own teaching methods and figure out what you like . . . and make it fit you.

As we will show later, Diane's way of working with Ellen provided her with a gradual, low-risk, and progressively less directed and protected way to begin thinking autonomously and reflectively about her own teaching.

In the case of Robin and Lou, we saw a variety of situations that drove their reflection. In their interactions, they discussed issues and problems related to the curriculum, individual students, and working with parents. Robin, drawing from her five years of experience, commented: "I'll give her anything of mine that she needs. When I do research sometimes, I run across something I know she's doing, and I give it to her." What comes across most clearly with this pair of teachers, however, is the extent to which their working together stimulated self-reflection. Lou, the beginner, was unsure of her future direction in teaching and very much involved in examining alternatives. During her reflection day, Lou visited another school in the county, which had a large proportion of minority children. During that day she had an opportunity to work and talk with the school psychologist and interact with the students. Upon her return, she was actively considering the possibility of another assignment, which involved working with underprivileged children. Robin at one point commented that "Lou [sometimes] gets more confused now that she has found these other interests; she starts to question what she's doing and that makes it confusing for her."

Robin also admitted to a certain amount of self-questioning and analysis of her own professional life. Having just moved to the fifth grade for the first time, combined with having to deal with a split class, "put a lot of pressure on me, caused me to be less organized and that's not my nature." Robin went on to say that the situation "upsets me, because I'm not producing at a level I'm capable of producing . . . so that's caused a lot of conflict for me."

In looking at these three pairs of teachers, we see at least three kinds of situations, or contexts, in which reflection occurs. Yet in examining these and other cases closely, there seem to be other ingredients at work. Some of the basic conditions for reflection among two or more teachers are:

- shared conceptions of teaching;
- common beliefs about students;
- available time to think and work together;
- physical proximity in the school;
- shared personal and professional respect.

In the first case we discussed, Brenda described explicitly those commonalities that tended to bond Karen and her together. Her description of her colleague's approach to teaching writing provides one example:

> She does have them do quite a bit of writing, and quite a bit of it is done in class. She gives them quite a bit of structure but also allows them to bring in individualism, which is another common denominator she and I share. We like to give enough structure so that they feel comfortable in doing the assignment . . . but let them take it from there.

In their case the bonding went well beyond common interests in technique:

> One of the things that enters into this is that Karen and I come from families that were not really associated very much with people from the walks of life that we [see in this school]. We were both afraid that we would not empathize with students who had problems at home.

In addition, she mentioned that because they both tended to be "mothering types" they worried that they would get "too involved in the home environment and try to help them hurry up, and try to get their needs met." She described their shared dilemma as follows:

> It has been very difficult for us, for both of us, to realize where to stop before we take over the kid's life, or before we provide too much of a crutch for the kid to lean on. So we've been trying to be sensitive to the home environments to the extent that we know more about the student, but we have had to say stop . . . don't go overboard.

Listening to their discussions, we could not miss the obvious respect that each of these teachers has for the other. Both expressed the importance of being on the same wavelength and being in their situation together.

In the case of Diane and Ellen, there was a mutual acceptance of the mentor–beginner role that made their relationship very easy. According to Diane, in "the beginning, during the first semester, she literally let me hold her hand and agreed to all the things that I told her to do." The building of this relationship, which gradually over the year involved shifting more responsibility to Lou, was facilitated by their close physical proximity:

> Our classrooms are right next to each other, so we mentored six hours a day. There was never a time that we weren't talking or discussing things.

Diane also greatly enjoyed working with new teachers and expected to learn from them as well. She related what she told Ellen at one point later in the year:

> Well, what have you figured out? Share it with me because I certainly need all the help I can get. You just got out of college. They taught you some wonderful new ideas. Don't keep them to yourself.

This attitude of being open to new ideas and wanting to learn even after many years of teaching seemed to contribute a lot to the potential for these two teachers to reflect on their teaching.

Robin and Lou also seemed to connect at a variety of levels, which facilitated their deliberations about teaching. As mentioned earlier, both were involved in their own personal speculations about where teaching would lead as a career. Beyond that, however, they were able to work closely in the day-to-day flow of teaching. Although they did not have a common planning time during the school day, they would talk briefly in the mornings and afternoons as they passed each other in the halls and often arranged times to meet. Robin said: "We'll say, OK, Wednesday afternoon, are you staying late? If we're both staying late, we'll say, why don't we devote Wednesday to sit down and talk about this or that problem . . . that's how we've done it."

Their interest in meeting together and talking about their teaching seemed to be based on several factors. Both were involved in a staff development program that involved reciprocal classroom observations among teachers. During the year they each had three opportunities to watch the other teach and then discuss the lesson based on a particular aspect of teaching they had agreed to focus on. Robin also talked about their common interests: "So we kind of relate in a sense that we're seeing . . . maybe we're getting the same type of child from this particular community, that causes us to have a common bond." One of the effects of their bonding, in Robin's words, was that "we're kind of thinking along the same lines, which has really helped." Because Lou could see that Robin, as an experienced teacher, had similar kinds of problems with similar kids, Robin thought that Lou would understand that "maybe these are normal [problems] and we need to talk this over."

The openness that resulted from their bonding encouraged Lou to invite Robin into her classroom to help with specific problems. As Robin said, "We've talked specifically, just individually . . . I'll go in and observe the individual and she might think, is it the teacher–pupil interaction? Is my personality coming on too strong with this child? Give me your truthful observation." Robin concluded, "She's been a neat person to work with because she's real open to everything, whether it's positive or negative." Another feature to their relationship is the social dimension. Commenting on the fact that she and Lou had a good understanding of each other, Robin explained: "We have been able to socialize a little more this year, so we know where each of us is coming from."

To summarize briefly at this point, the reflective activity we have seen has varied widely in its focus, its intensity, and the nature of the relationship between the teachers involved. In all cases, however, teacher reflection has arisen out of contexts in which some force or combination of forces has stimulated, nurtured, or at least allowed the activity to happen. As we examine the nature of the reflective activities a bit more closely, the importance of some of the facilitating factors mentioned here will be further underscored.

Reflective Activities and Processes

We mentioned earlier that our emerging conception of reflection encompasses several different forms and contexts. Here we will try to develop in greater detail the shape that reflection can take in day-to-day teaching.

In the situation facing Brenda and Karen, reflection was a natural response to a very serious problem for each of them. Both of these high school English teachers agonized over the difficulty of getting more, and better-quality, involvement from their students with low motivation, particularly in composition. Their reflective activities were framed by the intense interest each had in her students. Brenda, during one interview, described Karen's approach as follows:

> I have observed her . . . and her handling of things, and her rapport with students. When we sit down [after school] in her classroom, it is loaded, whether they have to be there or not, they're there. They like her, and they like spending time with her, and she has conveyed to them very well that

she is interested in them, so they do seek her out for problems. . . . She provides the coddling and the discipline and the other things you don't associate with protecting them all in one package, and it's obvious that they do appreciate that in her.

In deciding how best to help their students learn, Brenda described the following scenario as a typical way in which the two of them worked:

We both put things on paper . . . looked at advantages and disadvantages, pros and cons, and tried to figure out priorities and what can wait. . . . More or less it's an analysis of the problem, and then we developed some strategies, no more than one at a time . . . because we don't want to be overloaded.

Brenda commented also on the time frame and pressure under which they worked:

As far as using a particular set of questions, or particular strategy or something from the book, we used them in the beginning, but found we didn't have time to go back that far. And, so, we're going . . . OK, we remember this, this, and this. If it doesn't work, we'll go back to the beginning and take another approach.

Brenda was concerned, however, about the lack of "research" that she felt might have strengthened their deliberation:

We've been basically going on instincts and previous experience and just using some common sense, and of course a lot of things we've approached had to do more with personality and individual perspectives rather than something that was fit into some department [approach] or some category from a book. Not to say that we've ignored that, but in the sense of time, the urgency to attack the problem that we've had, we haven't had the luxury of going back [to do the research].

Part of the urgency that both Brenda and Karen felt was the need to reserve some time for their personal lives (both have families) while also balancing the need for their own collaboration with the constant flow of students in and out of their classrooms.

The activities that Diane and Ellen shared also occurred within the context of a very busy school day. The way they worked together was much different, however, from Brenda and Karen's mode. Regarding their work on lesson plans and topics such as discipline, Diane gave the following description:

The students' Individualized Educational Plans are due October 1, thirty days after you walk in the door. We pretty much sat down and wrote them and I said, take it from me, this is what it should say. Next year try it on your own. So she did that. After she had written them that way for the first nine weeks, then I showed her other special education teachers' plans. I said, now you have gotten used to doing it this way, if you like some of it fine, if not fine, here are some other ways, but at least she had a working model to go by. [A]s the year has progressed, she has gotten to where she comes in and tells me this is what I want, this is what I think, this is my goal and this is my plan, and verifies it with me versus the beginning of the year. [Before] it was, you tell me my plan, my goal, and how to do it; so she has come full circle.

In working with mainstream teachers, Diane served as an intermediary, sitting in on meetings to ensure that Ellen had support if she needed it. After the meeting, Diane explained that "Ellen and I went into it further . . . well, what do you think about what she said? Can you accommodate to what she wants? If not, then you need to go back and let her know that."

Working with parents was also a challenge where reflective coaching came into play. Ellen explained:

Parent meetings are real intimidating when you have not had one before. Special education ones more so. Parents are not really fond sometimes when their children are in an ED [Emotionally Disturbed] program. How dare you say he is emotionally disturbed? It must be something else. So I sat in with her on her first IEP [Individualized Educational Program] meetings, and I pretty much just sat in the background. I put my two cents in when I felt like she needed the support, or answered questions that the parents would ask . . . questions she would have no way of knowing what the answer was, having not been in the district long enough to know. She didn't know the policies and procedures, so I just sat in on those for her to be her support person.

Diane also explained how she modified her interaction with Ellen as the year progressed and Ellen gained experience:

It started as, "This is the way that I do it" and she did it. Then I went to, this is the way that other people in the school do it, here are some other examples. . . . Because I am department head, or least I had that information to make available to her. . . . Then we went into a middle stage of, "what did you learn today?" at the end of every day . . . and she tried to pick one thing every day that she could identify as something new. Either it was working with mainstream teachers, working with the kids, working with the administrative policies and procedures, the politics of schools and that kind of thing. Then we got to the point of where she just comes and says, "This is what I want, and this is how I am going to do it. Do you think this is the right way to go?" Now, we are probably at the point where there are many things that she is telling me after the fact. [She would say], "I wanted you to know I did so-and-so, because we talked about this once before and I thought that this was a similar experience."

In the process of working through the first year with Ellen, Diane had many occasions to engage in reflective questioning that allowed Ellen to sharpen her own problem-solving routines. One specific occasion related by Diane serves as a good example of how Ellen learned to solve her own problems:

> I guess the situation that probably comes to mind when I realized that she had made the cross-over was when one of our kids was getting on a bus. There was a conflict with the bus driver, and she was very annoyed at that and thought that the bus driver was unprofessional in the way that [the situation] was handled. She came and asked me what would be the procedure for that, when you think that somebody else has done something wrong. I asked her what was wrong and she told me. I said, "What did you want to have happen?" and she told me. I said, "How would you go about getting that to happen?" and she told me. Now, "Do you think that it would really happen?" and she said no. I said, "Fine, then why bother with it? It is one of those things that you have to live with." I think that was when I realized that she had gone full circuit and realized even though the problem was important to her it was not going to be important to the administration. It was not going to be important to the bus driver. The child was not affected adversely anyway, and so even though she was right, it didn't really matter.

These and other examples we have seen reveal not only the great variety and complexity of problems and situations that teachers face, but some of the subtle ways in which teachers learn to think about their jobs. Reflection in real situations is seldom easy, as we will see in the next section.

Conditions That Constrain Reflection

Teachers who want to reflect seriously on their teaching, especially with other teachers, often encounter a variety of roadblocks. We will briefly illustrate several of the most common problems.

Lack of time would probably appear on any teacher's list as a major constraint to reflection. One problem, of course, is that little, if any, time is officially allocated for reflection. Planning time, to the extent that teachers can protect it, is often taken up with students, administrative chores, or mechanical aspects of preparation not necessarily involving deep thinking about a problem or dilemma. In the case involving Brenda and Karen, time was limited to the point of frustration. As Brenda explained:

> We haven't been able to . . . have reflective time [like we planned] for a good two and a half to three months. We've been trying to do it, and put it on the calendar, and we'll have a doctor's appointment or something will come up. Also . . . we're being strangled by students who have needs and haven't been able to work their schedules around our schedules.

In terms of making choices, teachers such as Brenda, Karen, and many others we have worked with are unwilling to sacrifice time with students to work on their own problems. Especially in high schools, students will gravitate toward teachers who are willing to respond to their needs. Dedicated teachers find it very hard to protect time for themselves. Some teachers, such as Diane and Ellen, are more fortunate in that close physical proximity in the school allows ongoing contact, chances to observe ("I just have to sneak around the corner," Robin once remarked), and the ability to maintain continuity in their reflective problem solving. Otherwise, the effort to communicate can be simply too difficult to maintain reliably over time.

The administrative climate in schools can also be a potentially powerful determinant in teachers' orientations toward reflection. Several of the teachers we worked with commented on how their administrators could not see the value in their taking time to observe, visit, or talk with other teachers. In one case, an administrator actively discouraged two of our project teachers from taking a day for themselves (for which a paid substitute had been provided) to work on their own professional development. The teachers, in relating this event, expressed an understanding of the administrator's perspective but commented also on the compromises that dedicated teachers make routinely to create a little time for collegial reflection and problem solving. Balancing a private life with their overcrowded and often intensely active workdays is not easy, to begin with.

Another problem we have encountered in encouraging teacher reflection is that it involves a degree of personal risk. Robin expressed this as a potential negative in the sense that "you start to question what you're doing." In the context of the difficult year she was having, she admitted that "it started to come out . . . well, is this what I really want to be doing when I'm 45, 50 years old. If not, I need to start thinking about my alternatives." Robin's thoughtful processing of her concerns, as she described the process to us, represents a good example of the self-analysis type of reflective activity that we mentioned above.

> When I reflected . . . on the way things have gone, the year didn't start out well because I taught summer school two weeks before school started. I started listing things that I hadn't done in the past, and there were a lot of firsts in there. Last summer was the first summer I taught . . . and moving to fifth grade for the first time, and my split class for the first time. I also went to graduate school for the first time. So what I did was list things that kept [increasing] pressure, and I thought, I need to get rid of all of it, clean my slate, and come in with a more positive attitude.

In this case Robin did successfully work through her concerns, and she was able to negotiate the remainder of her "difficult" year successfully. As we have described elsewhere (Wildman & Niles, 1987), reflection can involve painful as well as satisfying and enjoyable episodes, and in both experiences teachers can benefit from strong and reliable support from colleagues and friends.

Reflection on teaching is not easy. Brenda once remarked that one of the toughest aspects is "having to admit the truth when you see it." In the next section, however, we will see that teachers see many positive aspects to taking a more reflective posture on their teaching.

The Impact of Reflection

"I used to do a lot more things by trial and error than I have this year." Brenda was describing here some of the effects that the project (the training plus her work with Karen) had had on her approach to teaching. She talked about how in previous years she had usually proceeded at "breakneck speed," whereas her work this year had helped her "put things into perspective, . . . to use some of the things I've been taught, and especially to spend [more] time investigating." She also observed that, "If I hadn't worked with Karen, I wouldn't have [had] the advantage of doing it. . . . It has sobered me to a certain extent."

The sentiments expressed here were fairly common among the fifteen mentors we had extensive exposure to, as well as the others who participated in the expanded program during 1987–88. In accommodating to the fast pace of classroom life, most teachers do not have the opportunity, encouragement, or resources to slow down and really think about what they are doing. The training we designed for them, along with their responsibility for carefully revealing the complexities of teaching to a beginner, afforded many teachers the first opportunity they had ever to really examine their professional lives.

Sometimes the examination of their professional activities and direction produced a great deal of doubt. When asked about this, Robin said: "They [the doubts] bother me because I started to question what I was doing, do I want to be somewhere else, do I want to be doing something else?" Another teacher admitted: "I put in for a transfer from doing this; I've seen that there are other things." As she put it, the combination of the training she had received, the work with her beginning colleague, and a graduate class had "opened up a whole new world."

Perhaps the most frequent comment heard from experienced teachers who have spent a year or more in a mentoring role is "I think I learned more than (s)he did." They liked the opportunity, as one teacher put it, "to work with other people who are obviously very dedicated." Sometimes, the collaborative reflection on teaching resulted in the veteran teachers seeing things in their own teaching that they had not realized. Diane gave a good example of this:

> Ellen started a music program, and every Friday afternoon her children had earned all the points that they needed because their behavior was appropriate, she took them down and sang songs with them and played the guitar and taught them music. It made me realize that I had gotten real academically oriented with my kids. I remembered that I do have them six hours a day. I am the only person they see because they don't go [outside the classroom]. They need to see the human side of me versus the teacher side of me. She reminded me of that.

Diane went on to explain that she thought many educators "got bogged into . . . I got to get this curriculum done . . . I have to go teach this . . . and I have to be at this level. [Ellen] reminded me that that was not [the only thing] that was important."

Finally, one additional impact of the reflective posture our teachers took was their changing view of how the school as a whole operated to solve problems. One remarked: "Look at the amount of time . . . [teachers] bitch and complain in the halls about something, when you could have been doing it in a much more constructive way." Focusing more specifically on the conversations that go on in the teachers' lounge, one of the mentors contrasted her way of working with that of some other teachers:

They don't talk about what we're going to do about it, what do we need.
. . . They don't categorize their thoughts, they just say it, and think it's a
problem and tired of this and tired of that, whereas if something goes
wrong for us, we say how are we going to solve this problem? What can we
do to help [ourselves] survive with this problem?

As we listened to these and other comments, it seemed clear that as
teachers became more comfortable and adept at reflection and self-
examination, they would turn their attention to a wide variety of problems, taking a much more autonomous posture on how these problems
might be solved.

CONCLUSIONS

In preparing these concluding remarks, we reminded ourselves that
teachers perform exceptionally complex functions in carrying out their
daily work. To reflect on the enterprise, either in groups or in private, is
correspondingly complex. We believe our work during the past few
years has revealed much about how teachers learn to be more systematically reflective and how they manage to use reflection on a day-to-day
basis to inform their own teaching as well as that of their beginning
teacher colleagues. Much remains to be learned, however. We therefore
offer the following summary/conclusion statements with the hope that
they will be useful in shaping further inquiry into teacher reflection as
well as promoting a general redesign of the workplace to better facilitate
reflective practice.

1. Systematic reflection is a learned activity. Our experience suggests
   that any effort to promote reflective practice will benefit from a carefully designed set of experiences (tasks) that help teachers develop (a)
   a sensitivity to their ways of looking at and talking about teaching, (b)
   a positive attitude toward inquiry, and (c) a self-analytic approach to
   teaching.
2. Reflection occurs within natural contexts that we need to better understand. We have pointed out how teachers in our project seemed to
   organize their reflective thinking around shared problems, mentoring episodes involving modeling and coaching, and self-analytic
   needs. If these and other contexts are indeed natural driving forces
   for reflection, then attention should be given to how we might use
   them more systematically to promote teacher learning.
3. Teachers seem to reflect on their teaching *together* when circum-

stances such as proximity, common problems, shared theories about teaching, or social compatibility cause a *bonding* to develop between them. Understanding how such relationships develop might be an important factor in facilitating reflection more broadly in schools.

4. The development of cases showing the explicit "moves" that teachers make during episodes of reflective thinking has been an important focus of our recent work. In the abstract, reflection is a difficult concept to talk about and reveal to teachers and administrators. More attention should be given to the development of a literature from which teachers can draw detailed examples of reflective thinking.

5. Probably the least surprising observation we could make is that schools are difficult environments for reflective thinking. Time, compatible colleagues, a conducive climate, and explicit administrative support are just some of the conditions that would figure into a redesign of the workplace to make systematic reflection a more likely event among teachers.

6. Finally, reflection can be an important tool in teachers' growth. We might even argue that growth is unlikely without systematic reflection. As we continue to examine teacher learning, it will be useful to specify further how reflection fits into a more general model of professional learning.

REFERENCES

Fenstermacher, G. D. (1979). A philosophical consideration of recent research on teacher effectiveness. *Review of Research in Education, 6,* 157–185.

Fisher, C., Berliner, D., Filby, N., Marliave, R., Cohen, L., & Dishaw, M. (1980). Teaching behaviors, learning time, and student achievement: An overview. In C. Denham & A. Lieberman (Eds.), *Time to learn* (pp. 7–22). Washington, DC: National Institute of Education.

Good, T. (1983). Research on classroom teaching. In L. S. Shulman & G. Sykes (Eds.), *Handbook of teaching and policy* (pp. 42–80). New York: Longman.

Good, T. L., & Brophy, J. E. (1984). *Looking in classrooms.* New York: Harper & Row.

Good, T., & Grouws, D. (1983). *Active mathematics instruction.* New York: Longman.

Rosenshine, B. (1983). Teaching functions in instructional programs. *The Elementary School Journal, 83,* 335–352.

Schön, D. C. (1983). *The reflective practitioner.* New York: Basic Books.

Sykes, G. (1983). Contradictions, ironies, and promises unfulfilled: A contemporary account of the status of teaching. *Phi Delta Kappan, 65,* 87–93.

Wildman, T. M., & Niles, J. A. (1987). Reflective teachers: Tensions between abstractions and realities. *Journal of Teacher Education, 38*(4), 25–31.

Wise, A. E. (1979). *Legislated learning: The bureaucratization of the American classroom.* Berkeley, CA: University of California Press.

Zumwalt, K. K. (1982). Research on teaching: Policy implications for teacher education. In A. Lieberman & M. W. McLaughlin (Eds.), *Policy making in education: Eighty-first yearbook of the National Society for the Study of Education* (pp. 215–248). Chicago: University of Chicago Press.

9 Shaping the Rhetoric of Reflection for Multicultural Settings

KAREN NOORDHOFF
JUDITH KLEINFELD
University of Alaska

This chapter describes and analyzes efforts of the Teachers for Rural Alaska (TRA) program at the University of Alaska–Fairbanks to prepare what Donald Schön (1983, 1987) calls "reflective practitioners" for multicultural schools in small communities across Alaska. We discuss our experience with the rhetoric of reflective inquiry, the ambiguity and limitations of this concept, and our rethinking of what this concept means in preparation for teaching in multicultural settings. We suggest and explore the fruitfulness of a different term—the heuristic of design. In addition, we highlight the role of teacher-preparation programs in helping prospective teachers understand the various contexts of teaching—an ability that is at the heart of teachers' effectiveness in multicultural settings. Finally, we briefly present an analysis of program data that demonstrates our novice teachers' developing abilities to consider teaching contexts and to create and implement instructional designs for those contexts. We close by raising questions concerning the relationship of reflection and performance in teaching.

THE CONTEXTS OF TEACHING IN RURAL ALASKA

The Teachers for Rural Alaska program prepares postbaccalaureate, noneducation majors to teach in the multicultural and cross-cultural settings of Alaska's small, rural secondary schools. Knowledge and con-

This work was sponsored in part by a contract from the Office of Educational Research and Improvement, United States Department of Education (Contract No. 400-85-1042). The opinions expressed in this chapter do not necessarily reflect the position, policy, or endorsement of that agency.

sideration of context are important for teachers everywhere, but never more so than in the cross-cultural and multicultural situations of rural Alaskan communities. With about 325 schools serving some 8,500, mostly Native American (Eskimo, Indian, and Aleut), students, rural Alaska confronts teachers with a myriad of contextual factors—students' individual personalities, their diverse cultural and linguistic backgrounds, multigrade and multisubject classroom grouping, remoteness and isolation of the schools, and community economic, social, and political organization—that demand consideration in classroom instruction. To help their students learn worthwhile knowledge, teachers need to become effective in their roles as mediators between subject-matter knowledge and the varying contexts of these rural schools. Furthermore, to be effective, teachers in Alaskan rural schools must demonstrate the political skills needed to identify and marshal scarce resources as well as identify potential and actual allies and adversaries in the environment. In sum we consider the term context to include characteristics and dynamics related to students as well as to classrooms, school, school district, and community settings.

The Alaskan Native American communities for which TRA students are being prepared generally range in population from 100 to 600 persons, with 250 to 350 persons being an average size. Traveling to these villages usually requires transportation via small plane from the state's regional population centers. Yup'ik Eskimo villagers tend to speak their native language in the home, with English serving as a second language in the school. In many other communities, persons speak English—often a nonstandard dialect termed "village English."

Traditionally, villages have subsisted on hunting, fishing, and trapping, but some businesses and governmental agencies (e.g., the post office) now provide some cash to the economy. Schools and newly formed land-based corporations resulting from the Alaska Native Claims Settlement Act (1971) bring additional jobs and money into the community. Secondary schools are an institution only about ten years old in such villages. Overall, rapid economic and social change has adversely affected many communities. Such problems as alcohol and drug abuse and youth suicide concern both village councils and school personnel.

Nonnative teachers—including those from Alaska—often find themselves needing to learn about the realities of life in village Alaska. Even those Alaskan Native Americans who become teachers and move to rural sites other than their original villages face similar challenges in finding a place as teacher in a community that is not their home and that may see them as outsiders.

Teachers in rural Alaska work in small schools where their responsibilities extend across subject-matter areas and beyond the confines of the classroom into the community (Kleinfeld, McDiarmid, & Hagstrom, 1985). According to Kleinfeld and colleagues (1985), more than half of all rural teachers are teaching subjects outside their academic specialization. While class size is often extremely small and allows for considerable tutoring, most classes are not only multigrade but may be multisubject as well. For example, a math teacher may have a class with students from all four high school grade levels who are taking business math, algebra, and general math. Although seeing only about twenty students in the day, a teacher might have as many as twelve different preparations each night both in and out of his or her areas of expertise. Additionally, in most small schools, the two or three teachers are responsible for all out-of-class coaching, advising, and chaperoning. They are also frequently expected to provide a variety of community services, such as recreation supervision. As one teacher has said, "The only time I'm not 'the teacher' is when I'm sleeping."

Teachers who enter small communities whose residents have cultural and social backgrounds different from their own find themselves in complex and uncertain situations. These teachers, who are novices to the school and community, are often unable to interpret students' sociolinguistic and affective behavior. They are uncertain about the appropriateness of educational goals—such as developing standard English skills or preparing students for college—that they may have taken for granted in other settings. They misunderstand power relationships, locally appropriate role behavior, and the history behind present educational stalemates.

Preparation for effective teaching in such contexts means much more than learning to apply technical, research-based knowledge to the classroom. It means much more than becoming a subject-matter specialist knowledgeable about the conceptual foundations of a subject and able to represent subject matter flexibly. Teachers must be prepared both cognitively and emotionally to understand and deal with complex and ambiguous educational situations.

While teaching in rural Alaska involves a number of unique features, understanding and dealing with multicultural educational contexts and planning subject-matter instruction in relation to those contexts is a task facing teachers across the country. The rural Alaskan case demands the preparation of teachers who can perceptively comprehend classroom and community situations and flexibly act and reflect. Our case highlights the role of all teacher education programs in helping prospective teachers understand and act in various multicultural contexts.

TESTING THE RHETORIC OF REFLECTIVE INQUIRY
IN THE PRACTICE OF TEACHER EDUCATION

We have attempted to promote a process of practical reflection in our students which centers on (1) understanding contexts; (2) considering educational goals; and (3) making instructional decisions to fit perceived contexts and selected goals. We wanted to extend the subject matter of reflection beyond teaching performance—the focus of models such as Cruickshank's "reflective teaching" (Cruickshank & Applegate, 1981)—to include social, political, and ethical issues embedded in teachers' thinking and everyday practice (Grant & Zeichner, 1984; Zeichner, 1983). We also hoped to keep our students open to future learning by developing their abilities to reflect on and inquire about their practice. Nemser (1980) reminds us of Dewey's words in this vein: "The aim of education is to enable individuals to continue their education . . . the object and reward of learning is continued capacity for growth" (pp. 136–137).

Thus we have steered away from more technical views of teachers and teaching in which teaching is seen primarily as the application of research findings in classroom settings. Schön (1983, 1987) labels such an approach, in which professional problems are seen as givens and are solved by appropriately applying formal knowledge to practical situations, as "technical rationality." This so-called applications view of knowledge in the preservice teacher education curriculum has been criticized by Feiman-Nemser and Ball (1984) as misleading prospective teachers in several ways:

1. It can lead prospective teachers to assume that research findings directly imply courses of action.
2. The applications view does not prepare prospective teachers to detect, weigh, and manage competing and conflicting goals, teacher commitments, and the numerous obligations inherent in the dilemmas of teaching (Buchmann, 1983; Lampert, 1981). Practical situations do not contain the same problems for each teacher.
3. Teachers' personal and practical knowledge is often devalued through the process of applying research knowledge to classroom settings. Indeed, teachers may be limited in examining and learning from their practice.
4. A technical view of knowledge use sets up prospective teachers to be disappointed about how research knowledge *can* help them in the classroom. They reject such knowledge and its proponents and thus

potentially forsake the perspectives and inspirations that can also come from research.

Recall that we chose the conceptual focus of reflective inquiry into the complexities of everyday teaching problems as a means of communicating to prospective teachers that there are no simple recipes for teaching, especially in changing multicultural and cross-cultural communities. Yet the *language* of reflective inquiry has not proved to be as rich a heuristic device as we had hoped. We do want our students to think about the worthiness of their goals, the possible instructional strategies available, the larger school and community culture in which they work, and so forth. However, the commonsense connotations of the term *reflection* make it vague and ambiguous. To our teacher education students, it means little more than thinking about the business of teaching. It does not imply that they should naturally push their thought into new and more productive directions. In addition, the term *reflection* has negative connotations for both practitioners in general and our students, who see the work of teaching as action oriented and reflection as what university professors have time to do. This situation exacerbates perceived and existing discontinuities between formal preparation on the university campus and learning about teaching from practical experience. As a result, prospective teachers are reinforced in their common notions that real learning about teaching occurs exclusively through experience in the trenches.

DESIGN AS A FRUITFUL HEURISTIC FOR REFLECTION

Schön (1983, 1987) argues that professional practice of all types is fundamentally concerned with the issue of design—*that is, ways of transforming present situations into preferred situations*. Specifically, classroom practice requires action that is rooted in making desired things happen (Buchmann, 1984). What skillful and experienced practitioners actually do in attempting to change present situations into more desirable future ones is to impose a design on a problematic situation, work out the implications of this design, judge the fit between their design and what they want to accomplish, and then revise their design.

Design is a powerful metaphor to describe the work of teachers, particularly in the ambiguous, unique educational environments of cross- and multicultural practice. Design aptly describes what our student teachers do as they try to work out a curriculum that fits particular village high school contexts. Design carries interesting and fruitful images—the architect, the building plan, the art graduate with portfolio. It suggests new ways in which to think about teacher education. Indeed, design aptly describes the type of educational thinking we as teacher educators are doing as we reshape programs like Teachers for Rural Alaska.

In short, we have begun to reorient the goals of the TRA program around the concept of design. The language of design has become our operational definition of reflective inquiry. In our view, design encompasses four kinds of activities:

1. naming and framing situations and issues;
2. identifying goals and appraising their worth;
3. sorting images, selecting strategies, and spinning out consequences;
4. reflecting on effects and redesigning one's practice.

The metaphorical language of design makes the thought processes behind the label *reflective inquiry* more accessible to preservice students. For them, it captures a more active sense of teachers' work than the term *reflection* passively connotes. It promotes images of inventing and constructing, with intents, purposes, and goals informing both mental organization and physical activity. Schön (1987) aptly characterizes the process:

> Designing in its broader sense involves complexity and synthesis. In contrast to analysts or critics, designers put things together and bring new things into being, dealing in the process with many variables and constraints, some initially known and some discovered through designing. Almost always, designers' moves have consequences other than those intended for them. Designers juggle variables, reconcile conflicting values, and maneuver around constraints—a process in which, although some design products may be superior to others, there are no unique right answers. (pp. 41–42)

The metaphor of design, then, more adequately describes teachers' everyday practice while preserving the dynamics and values of reflective inquiry into problematic situations.

In the following paragraphs, we describe each of the four elements of design listed above. While we describe these four design elements in the logical order of their occurrence, we are not implying a strict sequence in use. They may happen within preactive, interactive, and reactive phases of teaching, or a combination thereof. Additionally, teachers might begin a reflective design process with any one of the four types of activities. Further, the activities involved in these four elements interact with each other and intertwine in the actual process of reflective design. It is a messier process in actuality than it might appear here. We have tried to sort out and discuss the elements singly so as to better understand them.

Naming and Framing Situations and Issues

Central to professional practice—and so to teaching—is the process of defining the problem to be given attention (Schön, 1983, 1987). This process is required in order to draw on helpful images and strategies from previous experiences and learning and is a precondition to the more technical aspects of problem solving. Activities associated with this element are driven by several questions: What do I know about the situation I'm working in? What do I need to know and how can I find out what I need to know? Is there a problem here, and if so, what is it?

"Problem-setting," argues Schön (1983), "is a process in which, interactively, we *name* the things to which we will attend and *frame* the context in which we will attend to them" (p. 40). In defining problems, teachers select the features of a situation to which they will give attention, set the limits of that attention, and in so doing impose an order on the situation. As in research, where guiding questions shape results, so problem setting influences the approaches to which solutions will be deemed useful and eventually tried. Through this nontechnical process, ends are clarified and means are organized.

Teachers must have a sense of the realms in which to look for information helpful to understanding and setting problems in "unstructured" (Dreyfus & Dreyfus, 1986) situations. Such situations contain "a potentially unlimited number of possibly relevant facts and features and the ways those elements interrelate and determine other events is unclear" (p. 20).

In order to understand such situations, teachers need to examine a variety of contexts ranging from the micro-level of face-to-face interaction with one or several youngsters to the macro-level of the social and political forces influencing what goes on in schools. Between those two extremes lie other contextual factors to be considered at the individual school, school district, and community levels. In attempting to understand and deal with situations of instruction, teachers identify what they know about specific pupils as well as youngsters in general; about classroom conditions such as the number of pupils involved, the time of year, whether the class is multisubject or single subject; about requirements of the school district and desires of the community. They may find themselves thinking hard about the relationship of the situation to larger issues of equality, justice, and so forth.

Framing a problem thus depends on the situational elements and interactions to which a teacher attends. On the one hand, experienced teachers are known to give attention to extremely diverse classroom phenomena. They use ways of seeing in the classroom that are highly situation-specific and contextually embedded, differing according to the kinds of decision and action the teacher thinks are necessary (Erickson, 1986a).

On the other hand, novice teachers tend to see classroom phenomena in ways more like those described by Annie Dillard (1974) as she chronicles her life on Tinker Creek: "Unfortunately, nature is very much a now-you-see-it, now-you-don't affair" (p. 17). They begin by looking at classroom interactions in fragmentary ways, later developing a greater sense of contexts both within and beyond the classroom (Erickson, 1986a). For example, they get to know students; they note patterns of classroom activity that occur at different times of the year; they identify cultures within the school; and they learn of the community's desires for children within the school. This process is, at first, cumulative, but not integrated. Overall, novices lack the background of contextual information that would allow them to make connections, as experienced teachers do, between the phenomena at hand and between those phenomena and previous experiences in similar situations.

Furthermore, prospective teachers are both helped and hindered in making sense of classroom, school, and community contexts by their existing perspectives. Their analyses of situations—and hence their framing of issues and problems—are influenced by their attitudes (Dewey, 1909/1933), role orientations (Schön, 1983), past schooling experiences and personal biographies (Lortie, 1975), nascent pedagogical commitments and philosophies (Erickson, 1986a), and perspectives deriving from disciplinary training. Teachers' emotions also play an important part in the framing of problems; but this is not well understood and is deserving of study.

Thus, in using their often limited contextual knowledge and perspectives, preservice teachers may not adequately see or read the many variables a situation contains. They also are likely to define problems narrowly and, thus, restrict the range of potential strategies for their use.

This phenomenon can have acute ramifications for teachers and students in multicultural educational environments. Consider the extreme (but not unheard of) example of a student teacher who notices that his Native American pupils do not volunteer to answer questions in class. Unconsciously drawing on his own sociocultural background, he might inappropriately define the problem as students' shyness and possible lack of understanding of the material. He might conclude that he needs to ask more direct questions of individuals to elicit their understandings. After having frequently been put on the spot, then, his students might become even less inclined to participate verbally in class.

If, however, this teacher had also noticed that students seemed to perform relatively well on individual written work and that they were animated, cooperative workers in the running of the school store, he might modify his original conclusion. He might define the problem as one of uncomfortable and unproductive classroom social structures or as the absence of personal connections between teachers and students, rather than problems with students' personal characteristics. He might also become motivated to seek more information about his students from other teachers.

Identifying Goals and Appraising Their Worth

This aspect of the design process considers the relative worthiness of various goals teachers implicitly or explicitly hold for students and the criteria by which that worth can be judged. As the process of problem setting clarifies goals (Schön, 1983), teachers become concerned with the ends of education. Zeichner (1983) argues that questions of ethics, morals, and politics legitimately belong in the subject matter of teacher preparation with a (reflective) inquiry orientation. Questions such as the following take on a central place:

> What knowledge should be taught and to whom? How should a teacher
> allocate time and resources among different children? How much con-
> trol do (and should) teachers exert in determining what is taught, how it
> is to be taught, and how it is to be evaluated? (Zeichner, 1983, p. 6)

Working as a teacher in rural Alaska frequently heightens the puzzlement of the query, "What's worth teaching and being learned?" This question has numerous facets for nonnative teachers in primarily Native American communities, but the central concern seems to be worries about whether Western cultural knowledge—the grammar of standard English, algebra, French—and Western worldviews are valuable to members of Alaskan Native American village societies. Potential value conflicts abound. Should the school be teaching knowledge and skills important in the local cultural context, and, if so, in what balance with standard, Western academics? Should schools prepare students for postsecondary options, especially the option of going to college? Should students be prepared to go to college even if parents want them to stay home? What kinds of wage-earning opportunities, if any, await young adults who stay in the village?

Prospective teachers need to be able to discern the variable messages coming from parents and the community at large about the desires they hold for their youngsters and to appreciate the way school issues are related to larger political issues, such as Native American sovereignty. This is not an easy task in settings wherein conflicting community feelings result from the fact that schools are both an imposed and a desired institution.

Sorting Images, Selecting Strategies and Spinning Out Consequences

As teachers define a problem and clarify the worthiness of related goals, they also sort through their past experiences for approaches and images holding possible solutions. The guiding question of this design element is, "What strategies, images, and bridging metaphors are available in my repertoire to teach *this* subject to *these* students?" Hence the design process becomes a "conversation with the situation" (Schön, 1983, 1987) as practitioners engage in a reflexive dialogue between the problem definition, preferred ends, and potential actions. Teachers' framing of the problem, their visions of possible goals, and their beliefs about students and instruction act as lenses in the process of sorting remembered images and strategies.

Teacher-preparation programs usually support this element of the design process by providing their students with opportunities to learn useful instructional approaches (e.g., motivational approaches, reading strategies). These programs less frequently help students recall strategies or images of teaching they have picked up elsewhere and aid them in analyzing and assessing those images and strategies in terms of possible goals and consequences.

Imagine that a TRA student teacher feels bothered that some of her students are not turning in their homework. She thinks about possible problems involved—they do not see homework as important, they view it as important but do not have a quiet place to do it in a small home, the assignments are inappropriate, the students do not like her. Her goals become to increase students' return of assignments and to convince them that the homework is designed to further their learning of content that will make them eligible for postsecondary programs. At the same time, she does not want to alienate any students. Although her students may say at this point that they intend to live a subsistence life-style in the village, the student teacher does not want to foreclose possible un-known future options. She knows the villages are changing rapidly. She wonders what might help her accomplish her explicit and implicit goals? She recalls what other teachers have said about the possibility of setting up an afterschool study program and the value of teachers visit-ing parents to discuss students' progress. She thinks about the incentive value of afterschool gym time and wonders whether she might set up a reward schedule allowing youngsters opportunities to accrue gym time for completing homework. Perhaps, too, she ought to try out the home-work record-keeping system suggested in one of her university methods classes. The student teacher screens and plays out which of the alterna-tives of combinations she thinks will help her transform the current conditions into a more desirable future situation.

Judging the fit between the invented design and what the teacher wants to accomplish further involves spinning out potential conse-quences of possible actions. Designers assess the likelihood that their selected goals will be achieved and whether the problem will be dimin-ished or managed. They also need to relate activities at the classroom level to wider social-structural factors that influence classroom practice (Zeichner, 1981–82). Teachers should try to imagine intended *and* unin-tended consequences along both positive and negative lines. For exam-ple, one goal frequently taken on by rural Alaskan teachers stresses making school relevant to village youngsters. There are substantial costs to student learning in making the *content* of the curriculum continuous with students' everyday life (Zeuli & Floden, 1987), and teachers must weigh them against possible benefits. Additionally, teacher candidates must consider the costs and benefits to their students and to themselves of using culturally congruent teaching *strategies* (for instance, attempt-ing to create congruent participant structures [see Philips, 1983]).

Although individual preservice teachers differ in their cognitive flexibility, we have found that most have difficulties imagining conse-quences. In part, this situation may be due to their lack of contextual knowledge and images developed from past teaching experience. This condition may also reflect their current range of adaptability to different perspectives.

Reflecting on Effects
and Redesigning One's Practice

Practitioners often reframe and revise designs as a result of reflect-ing on the effects of their efforts. In order to do so, they must be able to see the situation with new eyes and reshape their definition of the situation. They rethink the fit between contextual factors, purposes, and consequences of chosen strategies. When confronting problematic situations, teachers may also reconstruct their goals in an effort to achieve their multiple intentions for learners (Barnes, 1987).

At the heart of this activity is the guiding question, "What's going on here?" Teachers reflect generally on what is being taught and learned and what it means to the participants, on the nature of classroom social relationships, and on the kinds of external historical and political influences that shape what goes on inside the classroom. But more specifically the teacher asks what the effects of the strategies on the situation—particularly on the youngsters' learning—seem to be. To answer this often unstated question, teachers watch for youngsters' responses to instructional strategies. They especially watch for students' emotional responses—which may differ across cultures in the ways that they are expressed. Teachers observe the ways students interact with one another and with the subject matter presented. They evaluate students' work.

Teachers' answers to questions of meanings and effects depend on what kind of experimentation they see themselves involved in during design activities. Schön (1987) identifies three kinds of experiments: exploratory, move-testing, and hypothesis-testing. In exploratory experiments, action is undertaken simply to see what follows from it. This action is probing and playful; it helps practitioners to get a feel for things. At this level, an experiment succeeds when something is discovered. With move-testing experiments, teachers undertake action more deliberately and with an end in mind. They watch to see whether or not the intended effect arises. They also determine whether they like this effect in terms of the values, beliefs, and commitments that they hold. Finally, practitioners testing hypotheses are interested in accounting for a puzzling phenomenon. They want to confirm or refute competing explanations. They watch for evidence that refutes their hunches. Certainly, as Schön asserts, the same practical action can function simultaneously in all three manners. We further claim that teachers may also reflect-in-action at one level, or a combination of levels, more than at others. For instance, novice teachers may tend to experiment in design using an exploratory mode more than other kinds of experiments.

For teachers, reflecting on effects occurs in several phases of instructional design. During preactive design—those activities occurring in preparation for actual teaching activities—teachers reflect in imagination on past and possible future effects, as described in the preceding section in terms of spinning out consequences. During what might be called a reactive design phase, they reconsider as the whole the teaching/learning activity that has just occurred as well as the outcomes of specific aspects of the activity. Yet teaching is also an act of perfor-mance. Thus designing and reflecting on the lesson design that is being created in the moment *with* students also occurs. During the moment-to-moment action of teaching lessons, teachers adapt—indeed, impro-vise (Yinger, 1987)—by working back and forth between the difficulty of the academic task and the nature of the current classroom social partici-pation structure, "wiggling" the relations between the two in efforts to increase students' success at the lesson (Erickson, 1982, 1986b).

Finally, in reflecting on effects, teachers develop theories-in-use that shape subsequent designs. They conceptualize lessons learned from their experiences, although these ideas may not be fully or verbally articulated. Van Manen's (1977) levels of reflectivity suggest that the conclusions teachers reach by way of reflection may be based, in part, on which aspects of the practical situation they have viewed as problem-atic—the efficiency of techniques, the worth of competing educational ends, and/or the moral and ethical questions that mediate educational contexts. For example, while teachers assess the educational conse-quences of classroom activities, they develop criteria for what works based on their own value commitments and the worth they see in com-peting educational goals. In these terms, a teacher would be determin-ing what works at Van Manen's intermediary level. In addition to en-larging and/or refining teachers' practical theories, each experience of reflection-in-action also enriches the practitioner's repertoire of images, exemplars, and approaches potentially to be drawn upon in the next unique and problematic situation (Schön, 1987).

CREATING CONDITIONS AND OPPORTUNITIES FOR REFLECTIVE DESIGN

Literature describing conditions that facilitate practical reflection by inservice teachers is growing (for example, Devaney, 1977; Erickson, 1986b; Little, 1982; Pugach & Johnson, Chapter 10, this volume). Yet, except for a very few studies (e.g., Goodman, 1986; Zeichner & Liston, 1987), we know little about the ways in which teacher education pro-grams actually try to encourage the development of reflective practice in their preservice students. We discuss here two activities of the Teachers for Rural Alaska program—the use of teaching cases and the experience of an analyzed apprenticeship—that we think help promote our stu-dents' reflective dispositions and facility in the design process in cross-cultural and multicultural school settings. Both activities set conditions that render practice as problematic and encourage prospective teachers to examine a wide variety of contextual factors. They occur during the on-campus portion of the program and, thus, exemplify ways that university-based activities can contribute to teacher candidates' growing sense of teaching contexts and initial facility with reflection-in-action.

Teaching Cases

To help prospective teachers reflect on central teaching dilemmas, we have commissioned a series of teaching cases, modeled after the case method of the Harvard Business School. Each case, written by an experienced rural teacher, presents a complex, difficult situation as a source of deliberative material. Our students learn how to spot central issues from different viewpoints of the situation and to frame problems. They consider alternative strategies and try to predict consequences. They attend to possible "at the moment" effects of their strategies along with midrange and longer-term results.

This brief vignette, drawn from a lengthy teaching case discussed by students in the Teachers for Rural Alaska program, dramatically illustrates the kind of design and reflection we want to encourage in our students:

> Carl's desk, Carl's book and the young Eskimo student himself suddenly exploded. With an angry curse, Carl attacked Scott Samson, knocking him out of his seat and blindly pummeling the frightened white youth. The teacher, Peter Wedman, hauled Carl off Scott. Scott had hardly thrown a punch, yet it was Carl whose face struggled to hold back tears.
>
> "Out!" Wedman ordered. Keeping an arm around Carl, he sent the other students to the hall.
>
> "I didn't do anything," yelled Scott. "You saw it. He started it."
>
> "Scott, you're not in trouble, but please meet me in the principal's office."
>
> Wedman later asked Scott what had happened. "I just looked at his writing folder," Scott said. "No reason to flip out."
>
> Before Wedman went home, he got a note from Carl via another Eskimo student. It read, "I don't like it when he says I'm dumb because I'm Native."
>
> Wedman spent the weekend worrying about the situation. Why did the Eskimo students always end up at the bottom of his English class? Was his grading system racist? (Finley, 1988)

Our students lay out the chronology of the longer case from the perspective of the individual actors involved and point to the contextual information contained in the case. They consider questions such as:

Why did this experienced teacher send all the students to the hall—
except the Eskimo student who had started the fight? Was his conduct
culturally sensitive and appropriate, or was it patronizing and racist?
What does fair grading mean when an English class consists of Caucasian students, the children of teachers and other professionals, and
Eskimo students, who speak a dialect of English? What should Wedman
try to help students learn in his class?

Further, students consider Wedman's actions. They try to spin out
possible positive and negative consequences of the experienced teacher's plan to set specific objectives for both Caucasian and Eskimo youngsters based on their developmental levels and to grade them in terms of
their attainment of those objectives. They generate other possible approaches to managing this dilemma. They design alternative grading
systems and play out possible results. Finally, they ask: Is Wedman's
management of the dilemma a short-term or long-term solution?

This case presents two learning opportunities for prospective
teachers—first, to learn from Wedman's model of reflection-in-action as
it contrasts with routine action (see Dewey, 1909/1933, for a discussion
of the distinction between reflective and routine action), and second, to
practice in dialogue with other novices the four elements of design
described earlier in this chapter.

An Analyzed Apprenticeship

During six weeks of the fall (on-campus) portion of the program,
students participate in an analyzed apprenticeship at a local middle
school that has a relatively large population of minority students. The
school is known for its excellent teaching staff and principal. This
school's teaming model also exemplifies some of the conditions and best
practices found in Alaska's small, rural high schools. It provides an
example of fine, customary practice from which our students may begin
to stock their repertoire of thought and action images.

The apprenticeship consists of three phases and requires students
to spend a total of about 125 hours in clinical activities at the school. In
the first two phases, students work as participant-observers during the
first days of school (teacher workdays and two student days), followed
several weeks later by a full-week experience of being paired with a
teacher in their subject-matter area. During these periods, TRA students
get to know how expectations are communicated at the beginning of the
year. They learn to observe how the school culture and routines are set
for both students and teachers, how teachers' work is patterned and the
middle school team functions, as well as how selected youngsters of

middle school age perceive the day-to-day significance of school activities. In the third phase, TRA students work each morning for a month as an assistant to a teacher in their subject-matter area. They participate in teaching activities as directed by the teacher in much the same way an apprentice might in learning a craft. Most frequently, the mentor teachers report that the TRA students correct papers and maintain records, monitor seatwork, get materials ready, and teach portions of lessons.

As a central program requirement during the apprenticeship, our students also plan and carry out a three- to five-day mini-unit that follows from their teachers' regular curriculum. This activity reflects the program's continuing emphases on the contexts of teaching and the metaphor of design to define teaching activities. The TRA students prepare three to five days of instruction, using their knowledge of youngsters, justifying their goals and chosen strategies, and adapting their plans according to youngsters' responses. Students' written analyses of their mini-units reveal that they tend to view the experience as an opportunity to:

1. find out about the nature of teaching;
2. learn about their pupils and use that knowledge in planning instruction;
3. discover the value of lesson designs;
4. test instructional strategies;
5. learn craft knowledge and teachers' perspectives;
6. improvise during teaching-in-action.

We view this analyzed apprenticeship as an intensive rather than extensive experience for prospective teachers. It introduces and reinforces for our students the variety of contextual factors in schools (including characteristics of students and teacher/student dynamics) and the need to adapt lessons to contextual factors both in initial planning and in interactive teaching. It also affords opportunities to design and reflect using all three of Van Manen's (1977) levels of reflectivity—the technical, the interpretive, and the critical. For example, our students sometimes observe teachers using external reward systems with youngsters. Our students may learn how to set up and manage such systems from their mentor teachers and may discuss pros and cons of the approach from the teachers' perspective. In seminar, we also explore possible unintended educational goals that are promoted by such reward systems and the power relationships that may be reinforced by their use. Using practical and technical concerns as motivating springboards, we open seminar discussions to higher levels of reflection. We attempt, like

Berlak and Berlak (1981), "to provide a language for examining the macro in the micro, the larger issues that are embedded in the particulars of everyday schooling experiences" (pp. 3–4).

We have consciously chosen the term *apprenticeship* to describe this early practicum experience, although Dewey—whose thinking is seminal to present-day conceptions of reflection—criticized apprenticeship experiences. In an early essay, Dewey (1904/1965) contrasted the metaphors of *apprenticeship* and *laboratory* as orientations to practice in the preparation of teachers. While criticizing the apprenticeship model for its technical focus on the "tools of the profession" and its emphasis on performance, he applauded the laboratory orientation as one that encourages prospective teachers to develop an understanding of underlying educational principles and keeps them open to learning from future experience. Today, we might label the laboratory model as *reflective inquiry.* Although we focus on reflection in the TRA program, we have chosen the label *apprenticeship* to reflect the structure of the early practicum experience. However, we agree with Ball (1987) that "there is nothing *inherent* in apprenticeship as a form of learning . . . that precludes focusing on principles or conceptual understanding of techniques of practice" (p. 14). As we have demonstrated above, experiences in an *analyzed* apprenticeship can provide deliberative material that is rich beyond the technical level.

EVALUATING PROSPECTIVE TEACHERS' SKILL AND REFLECTION IN DESIGNING INSTRUCTION

Data from the program's first two student groups provide some indication that our students have developed in their ability to utilize a design framework to plan and implement instruction that integrates contextual factors with significant subject-matter content. We asked TRA students to teach a ten- to fifteen-minute lesson appropriate to village high school students at three crucial points: (1) when they first entered the program, (2) at the conclusion of the fall academic/practicum experience, and (3) at the end of the spring rural student teaching experience. All three of these lessons were videotaped. At the end of the lesson we asked students why they had chosen the particular lesson, what they had thought about in planning the lesson, and what changes they would make if they taught the lesson again. During the second and third tapings we also asked students to what extent, if at all, they thought the TRA program had influenced their lessons.

Did our students become more skillful and reflective in designing instruction to fit a multicultural context? We have coded our data from the first two years' groups (n=24). Coding was completed by a rural high school teacher well known for her effectiveness in village communities. In our analysis, we have searched for patterns in TRA students' lesson performance and in their responses relating academic and cultural issues in instruction.

Overall, the program's first two student groups expanded their understanding of the scope of problematic issues in instruction (see Table 9.1). Most dramatic was the shift in their concept of teaching and its fundamental problems. Most students conceived of teaching at the start of the program as no more than "telling." They saw the main issue as figuring out how to squeeze as much information as possible into a ten-minute lesson. They viewed instruction as a task entirely under teachers' control. By the end of their first semester—the university-based experience—a much greater proportion of students conceived of the fundamental problem of teaching as how to get students actively involved in the lesson. They began to perceive that instruction is constructed in interaction *with* students. As teachers, they began to share ownership of instruction with their students. By the end of student teaching, an even greater proportion designed lessons that were interac-

TABLE 9.1 Changes in Teachers for Rural Alaska Program Student Teachers' Reflective Teaching Samples: Beginning to End of Program

	Time Interval		
Characteristics of Student Teacher Thinking	Percentage at Start of Program (September)	Percentage after First University Semester (December)	Percentage after Student Teaching Semester (May)
Emphasizes active student learning rather than teacher listening	12%	50%	92%
Takes into account culturally different students			
—background knowledge and frame of reference	28%	62%	83%
—communication styles	4%	39%	67%

Note: $n = 24$

tive developments of concepts and ideas rather than lectures. TRA students were aware of this change. One student put it this way in his self-analysis:

> I see a definite progression from me just talking to getting students more actively involved in the lesson. I believe the program opened my awareness early on to the need for tuning in to students in order to find what motivated them. It shaped my thinking to look at students as puzzles that had to be unlocked. I learned that if you don't involve students and do it in a way that is really significant to them, you will quickly lose any opportunity for learning to go on.

In other words, these novice teachers began to take more account of a primary facet of the teaching context—their students—in preparing and implementing lessons. They shifted from seeing instruction as a certain task under their control to viewing teaching as a more uncertain and problematic act that is dependent on contextual factors.

Analyses of the first two years' teaching samples also suggest that students changed in their sensitivity to culturally different students' background knowledge, frames of reference, emotional needs, and communication styles. By the end of their university-based experience, more students were taking into account their students' background knowledge as they planned instruction than had at the start of the program. Even though the artificial nature of the videotaped teaching sample made adaptation to Native American students difficult, students' papers showed that they were aware of the issues of communication styles:

> Hopefully the videos do not reflect the pacing that would be found in my classroom!! They showed that the pacing was probably the worst area for me, and although I can explain away part of why this might be so under those circumstances, and although I did show some improvement from tape #1 to tape #3, I know I still need to work on this area.

IN CONCLUSION: WHAT IS THE RELATIONSHIP BETWEEN REFLECTION AND SKILLED PERFORMANCE IN TEACHING?

The current enthusiasm for reflective inquiry in teacher education needs to be tempered by examination and discussion of *what* is to be reflected upon, *how* that reflection is to occur, and to *what ends* it is to be directed. In particular, this effort needs to explore the relation of reflection—especially active, verbalized reflection—to skilled performance in teaching. We have noticed that in programs with a strong reflective inquiry focus, such as Teachers for Rural Alaska, more emphasis may be placed on verbal analysis of teacher thinking than teaching performance. For instance, we have observed that many teachers— including master teachers whom we invited as presenters—instruct in highly appropriate and effective ways but find it difficult to verbalize the conceptual bases of their teaching.

We are concerned that the reflective inquiry focus as it is being played out in many recent teacher education programs—including our own—may not give sufficient recognition either to performance or to the intuitive knowledge that characterizes highly expert performance (Dreyfus & Dreyfus, 1986). Indeed, teacher education programs and faculty often dichotomize reflective activity and teaching performance.

The separation of reflection from performance appeals to those who see the development of reflection as an activity of more worth than the development of teaching skill. In this view, teacher education programs should indeed educate, not train. The rhetoric of reflective inquiry responds to a set of beliefs held by many teacher educators that teaching is a complex professional activity requiring expert judgment, rather than primarily a technical act demanding the performance of skilled behaviors. Promoting teaching as a professional activity raises the stature of teaching and teacher educators. Moreover, some teacher educators—particularly those coming from a critical-theory perspective—contend that teacher education has fostered, in the main, a technocratic, skill-oriented approach to teaching. These critical theorists argue that everyday teaching acts contribute to the reproduction of inequality and injustice in society. Advancing reflective inquiry as a comprehensive approach to teacher education potentially elevates teachers' concerns beyond the mundane, such as implementing discipline systems, to include the consideration of ethical questions, such as equal access to school knowledge. This approach attempts to change patterns in society at large by raising the level of teachers' thinking.

We contend that teachers cannot hope to provide their students with equal learning opportunities without the skills to provide effective, appropriate instructional activities. Rather than place aspects of reflection and teaching performance into hierarchical levels, or set them in contrast with one another, we prefer to interweave them. Such an approach potentially prepares *effective* and *reflective* teachers for multicultural settings.

The separation of reflection from performance also appeals to those who see reflection as an activity indicating less skill than actual expert teaching performance. This view leads us to wonder whether the kind of thinking teachers do in instructional interaction counts as reflective inquiry. Casting design as operationalized reflection occurring variably in all phases of instruction may run counter to perspectives that separate design and skilled performance from reflection (e.g., Dreyfus & Dreyfus, 1986; Yinger, 1987). In such conceptions, reflection is viewed as a relatively analytic act, with little room for intuitive knowledge to be played out. For us, both reflection and design are not only deliberative in character but also constitute creative and somewhat intuitive acts. Teachers synthesize reflective knowings into thought and action improvisationally in the moment of teaching. They quickly and tacitly assess changing instructional contexts, judge actions against their educational objectives, predict potential consequences and possible tradeoffs, while also watching for the effects of their instructional moves in the moment. This is reflective inquiry and design in the act of improvisation; this is a kind of "reflection-in-action" (Schön, 1983, 1987).

The field of teacher education is not yet clear about its views on the relationship between reflection and performance. Can we see reflection-in-action in the fine performances of skilled teachers? Or is reflection an act amenable only to preactive and postinstructional thought? Is it a characteristic of less accomplished professionals, as Dreyfus and Dreyfus (1986) suggest? Is reflection rooted in deliberative analysis? Can it also be conceived as a synthetic act?

In sum, then, many teacher education programs downplay or discount teaching performance and reflection on performance for ideological and political reasons. Teacher educators may also disregard the role of reflection in performance based on a view of improvisation by experts as a step beyond reflection. As these conceptions of the relationship between teaching performance and reflection on the work of teaching are played out in teacher education programs, they tend to keep acts of reflection and performance at a distance from each other. In calling for the serious exploration of reflective inquiry in terms of its content, processes, and ends, we urge the adoption of an integrative stance. We need to explore the question of how we can integrate reflective inquiry focusing on contextual and ethical issues in teaching with expert and intuitive performance so that prospective teachers and their students in multicultural settings will benefit.

REFERENCES

Ball, D. L. (1987, April). *"Laboratory" and "apprenticeship": How do they function as metaphors for practical experiences in teacher education?* Paper presented at the annual meeting of the American Educational Research Association, Washington, DC.

Barnes, H. (1987). *Intentions, problems and dilemmas: Assessing teacher knowledge through a case method system* (Issue Paper No. 87-3). East Lansing, MI: National Center for Research on Teacher Education.

Berlak, A., & Berlak, H. (1981). *Dilemmas of schooling: Teaching and social change.* London: Methuen.

Buchmann, M. (1983). *Role over person: Justifying teacher action and decisions* (Research Series No. 135). Institute for Research on Teaching, Michigan State University, East Lansing.

Buchmann, M. (1984). The use of research knowledge in teacher education and teaching. *American Journal of Education, 92*(4), 421–437.

Cruickshank, D., & Applegate, J. (1981). Reflective teaching as a strategy for teacher growth. *Educational Leadership, 38,* 553–534.

Devaney, K. (1977). Warmth, time, concreteness, and thought in teacher's learning. In K. Devaney (Ed.), *Essays on teachers' centers* (pp. 13–27). San Francisco: Teachers' Centers Exchange, Far West Laboratory on Educational Research and Development.

Dewey, J. (1965). The relationship of theory to practice in education. In M. Borrowman (Ed.), *Teacher education in America* (pp. 9–30). New York: Teachers College Press. (Original work published 1904)

Dewey, J. (1933). *How we think: A restatement of reflective thinking to the educative process.* Lexington, MA: Heath. (Original work published 1909)

Dillard, A. (1974). *Pilgrim at Tinker Creek.* Toronto: Bantam.

Dreyfus, H., & Dreyfus, S., with Atanasiou, T. (1986). *Mind over machine: The power of human intuition and expertise in the era of the computer.* New York: Free Press.

Erickson, F. (1982). Classroom discourse as improvisation: Relationships between academic task structure and social participation structure in lessons. In L. C. Wilkinson (Ed.), *Communicating in the classroom* (pp. 153–181). New York: Academic.

Erickson, F. (1986a). Summary and conclusions (pp. H-1–H-32) and Implications for future work (pp. I-1–I-17). In F. Erickson, D. Boersema, M. Brown, B. Kirschner, B. Lazarus, C. Pelissier, D. Thomas (Eds.), *Teachers' practical ways of seeing and making sense: A final report.* East Lansing, MI: Institute for Research on Teaching.

Erickson, F. (1986b). Tasks in times: Objects of study in a natural history of teaching. In K. K. Zumwalt (Ed.), *Improving teaching: 1986 ASCD yearbook* (pp. 131–149). Alexandria, VA: Association for Supervision and Curriculum Development.

Feiman-Nemser, S., & Ball, D. (1984, April). *Views of knowledge in preservice curriculum.* Paper presented at the annual meeting of the American Educational Research Association, New Orleans.

Finley, P. (1988). Malaise of the spirit: A case study. In J. Kleinfeld (Ed.), *Teaching cases in cross-cultural education* (pp. i–52). Fairbanks, AK: Rural College, University of Alaska–Fairbanks.

Goodman, J. (1986). Making early field experiences meaningful: A critical approach. *Journal of Education for Teaching, 12*(2), 100–125.

Grant, C., & Zeichner, K. (1984). The teacher. In C. A. Grant (Ed.), *Preparing for reflective teaching* (pp. 1–18). Boston: Allyn & Bacon.

Kleinfeld, J., McDiarmid, G. W., & Hagstrom, D. (1985). *Alaska's small rural high schools: Are they working?* Anchorage, AK: Institute for Social and Economic Research.

Lampert, M. (1981). *How teachers manage to teach: Perspectives on the unsolved dilemmas in teaching practice.* Unpublished doctoral dissertation, Harvard University, Cambridge, MA.

Little, J. (1982). Norms of collegiality and experimentation: Workplace conditions of school success. *American Educational Research Journal, 19*(3), 325–340.

Lortie, D. (1975). *Schoolteacher: A sociological study.* Chicago: University of Chicago Press.

Nemser, S. (1980). Growth and reflection as aims in teacher education: Directions for research. In F. Hord & G. Brown (Eds.), *Exploring issues in teacher education: Questions for future research* (pp. 133–152). Austin, TX: Research and Development Center for Teacher Education.

Philips, S. U. (1983). *The invisible culture: Communication in classroom and community on the Warm Springs Indian Reservation.* New York: Longman.

Schön, D. (1983). *The reflective practitioner: How professionals think.* New York: Basic Books.

Schön, D. (1987). *Educating the reflective practitioner: Toward a new design of teaching and learning in the professions.* San Francisco: Jossey-Bass.

Van Manen, M. (1977). Linking ways of knowing with ways of being practical. *Curriculum Inquiry, 6*(3), 205–228.

Yinger, R. (1987, April). *By the seat of your pants: An inquiry into improvisation and teaching.* Paper presented to the annual meeting of the American Educational Research Association, Washington, DC.

Zeichner, K. (1981–82). Reflective teaching and field-based experience in teacher education. *Interchange, 12*(4), 1–22.

Zeichner, K. (1983). Alternative paradigms of teacher education. *Journal of Teacher Education, 34*(3), 3–9.

Zeichner, K. M., & Liston, D. P. (1987). Teaching student teachers to reflect. *Harvard Educational Review, 57*(1), 23–48.

Zeuli, J., & Floden, R. (1987). *Cultural incongruities and inequalities of schooling: Implications for practice from ethnographic research?* East Lansing, MI: Institute for Research on Teaching.

10 Developing Reflective Practice Through Structured Dialogue

MARLEEN C. PUGACH
University of Wisconsin–Milwaukee

LAWRENCE J. JOHNSON
University of Alabama

Current discussions of reflection most often cast it as a personal and isolated act that typically occurs while teachers engage in their craft within the classroom. In contrast, our research has led us away from this individualistic notion of reflection. Rather, we find that the acquisition of and continuing support for a reflective disposition among teachers can be mediated and substantially enhanced by peers, whose role might be described as helping to stretch the limits of their colleagues' capabilities for reflection. Our concern in the arena of reflective teaching is the social and collegial nature of the act of reflection and, specifically, the role of collegial dialogue in advancing the development of a reflective stance among teachers in practice.

In conceptualizing this work, we viewed reflection as a fundamental means by which teachers themselves, working collegially, might differentiate between problematic student situations they could accommodate effectively and those they could not. Through reflection, teachers might develop new patterns of thinking with which to approach the complex environment of teaching as a whole. Specifically, the development of reflective patterns might enable teachers to step back from their routine ways of approaching problematic classroom dynamics and consider alternative instructional and management choices in the classroom and the impact those choices might be expected to have on students struggling with learning and behavior problems. Consistent with

The preparation of this paper was sponsored in part by a grant from the Office of Special Education and Rehabilitative Services, U.S. Department of Education (Grant No. GOO8530153). The opinions expressed in this chapter do not necessarily reflect the position, policy, or endorsement of that agency. The authors would like to thank Patricia D'Auria for her helpful comments on earlier drafts of this manuscript.

theoretical concerns regarding the function of community and dialogue in reflective teaching raised elsewhere in this volume (see Cinnamond & Zimpher, Chapter 4, this volume) was our belief that in working closely with their peers, teachers could be encouraged to draw on their own expertise in developing creative, alternative ways of intervening with students in their classrooms. In this manner, teachers might be encouraged to rely less on specialists for so many classroom problems and gain confidence in their own strength as professionals.

The background for this particular work differs somewhat from the current literature and thinking on reflection as a goal within the field of teacher education. This research was concerned with the relative absence of reflection on the part of teachers. Teachers have typically responded to students who exhibit mild, chronic instructional or behavior problems by making direct referrals to specialists, usually special education teachers or school psychologists. Thus referral, not reflection, on classroom problems has become an institutionalized norm.

The term *referral* is used in the broadest sense here. It may include formal referral, in which a teacher, parent, or someone else indicates that the student may need special education services. This approach invokes the resource-intensive identification procedures mandated by Public Law 94-142, which typically relies on expert testing, not teacher reflection, as a means of diagnosing the problem (Pugach & Johnson, 1988). Or referral may include the more recent, informal practice by special educators and school psychologists of providing expert consultation to teachers. This approach is based on the assumption that without the intervention of a specialist, teachers are able neither to reflect accurately on the relationship between teaching practice and the emergence of classroom problems nor use their own expertise to develop interventions (Johnson, Pugach, & Hammitte, 1988). In either case, we see reflection on the part of teachers being implicitly devalued in the context of referral to specialists precisely at a time in teacher education when preparing teachers to look within, to self-monitor, and to make alternative teaching choices are values and goals receiving serious and worthy attention.

It was within this context that a source for specific strategies to promote reflection as a means of developing interventions for classroom problems was sought. The practical orientation of our work meant that an approach was needed to both advance the act of reflection and facilitate collegial interaction between teachers as they developed a reflective orientation toward intervening in problems of classroom practice. In specifying reflection as an act of thinking mediated by colleagues, the most logical place to turn seemed to be the recent, compelling body of work on the acquisition of metacognitive strategies. This research, based upon the Vygotskian perspective that self-regulation through speech is a precursor to the internal regulation of thinking (Wertsch, 1979), suggests that complex and more reflective patterns of thinking are fostered in socially interactive settings characterized by spoken dialogue between more and less skilled individuals (Palincsar, 1986). Explicit dialogue as a training technique can provide practice for the kinds of internal dialogue that naturally, or intuitively, appear to characterize individuals who engage in strategic thinking. For example, "strategic" thinkers might ask themselves such questions as: What information do I have about this problem? What have I done in the past? Has it worked or not? Of what other problematic situations does this remind me? How is it similar or different? What additional information might I need before I can consider a response?

With its fundamental concern with the development, internalization, and regulation of thought processes, metacognitive training applied to the development of reflective thinking for teachers appeared to have the potential to bridge the gap between reflection as narrow technique (Cruickshank, 1987) and reflection as an overriding moral responsibility (Tom, 1984; Zeichner & Liston, 1987). Critics of the former interpretation have cited the trivialization of the central role of reflection and its oversimplification of the complexities of teaching (Trumbull, 1986), as well as a lack of focus on educational issues themselves (Gore, 1987). The latter interpretation may fail to address the acts of reflection adequately as regards pedagogical means, assumptions of instructional and management choices, and precise ways of encouraging reflection on the moral issues involved in teaching (Liston & Zeichner, 1987). Since metacognition is concerned with strategies of thinking, its application with prospective teachers might lead to reflective thinking both specifically on day-to-day instructional and management choices (see, for example, Neely, 1986) and, more broadly, on curricular and philosophical choices. Research on metacognition seemed to be an apt response to the suggestion raised by Schön (1983) that it should be possible to identify a singular structure of inquiry to promote reflection not only on "the best way of solving specific problems, but about what problems are worth solving and what role the practitioner should play in their solution" (pp. 129–130).

The particular strategies considered for adaptation included those employed by Palincsar and Brown (1984) in reciprocal teaching dialogues as a method of improving reading comprehension. These included clarification, summarization, and prediction. In addition to the conceptual focus provided by this work, research in the acquisition of metacognitive strategies also delineated highly specific direction for developing training components that could lead to the internalization of reflective thinking (Brown & Palincsar, 1982; Palincsar, 1986). The general characteristics of such training should include:

- rehearsing new strategies through self-questioning in a guided, dialogic learning situation;
- providing instruction regarding the rationale for the strategies, or "informed" training;
- providing instruction in monitoring the effective use of the strategies, or "self-control" training.

In the work of Palincsar and Brown (1984) and Palincsar (1986), teacher/ student dialogue was used to construct the meaning of text jointly.

ACQUIRING REFLECTIVE DISPOSITIONS THROUGH PEER COLLABORATION

With this general framework as a guide, a structured, interactive process was developed in which teachers rehearse specific reflective, strategic thinking patterns in a structured dialogue with their colleagues. This structured interaction, called peer collaboration, pairs teachers in the rehearsal of new strategies of thinking. One teacher takes on the role of "initiator" and follows each strategy incorporated into the dialogue in addressing a particular problem of practice, and the second teacher takes the role of peer "facilitator" and guides his or her partner in utilizing each strategy appropriately and in proceeding from step to step, modeling that strategy as needed.

The four steps that make up the peer collaboration process include:

1. clarifying problems of practice by self-questioning in a guided learning situation, a strategy in which particular questions are posed and responded to as a means of reframing the nature of those problems;
2. summarizing the redefined problem;
3. generating possible solutions and predicting what might happen should they be utilized;
4. considering various ways of evaluating the effectiveness of the solution chosen.

In the context of teacher reflection, peer collaboration allows the meaning of problematic classroom situations to be constructed jointly by teachers through the process of dialogue. The collaborative construction of new meaning is intended to be the reflective act that can lead to alternative classroom interventions.

The notion of strategic problem solving similarly characterizes the work of Schön (1983, 1987), who is fundamentally concerned with the development of strategies for problem intervention as well as strategies of inquiry for professional practitioners. As professionals confront problems in daily practice, the proper stance, according to Schön, is one of "exploratory experimentation." In exploratory experimentation, professionals are encouraged to consider problems from different perspectives, or frames, and to act deliberately to produce an end, recognizing from the outset that the outcome may or may not be successful. Inquiry, then, is the willingness to engage in reframing the problem in light of its idiosyncrasies and to view all solutions as potentially, but not absolutely, appropriate.

Each of the steps of peer collaboration illustrates a specific strategy by which reflection may be fostered for the purposes of inquiry into problems and development of potential interventions. To begin a cycle of the process, the initiating teacher writes a brief description of the problem of concern as a departure point for discussion.

Reframing through Clarifying Questions

In the first step, teachers engage in explicit self-questioning and self-responding to clarify the particular problem of practice. The purpose of this step is to assist teachers in exploring problems from different viewpoints and in identifying conditions or factors specific to the problem that might previously have gone unconsidered in attempting solutions. The facilitating teacher's role is to model appropriate topics for the initiating teacher's self-questions and to provide feedback on the use of the self-questioning strategy itself. Facilitators must recognize general aspects of the situation their partners may not be taking into consideration fully and guide the process of self-questioning in those directions. The facilitator does not suggest specific questions to be asked but rather stimulates teacher partners to ask themselves questions about that general area of concern.

Clarification can be thought of as a process of taking on a new perspective about a problem or practice through internal deliberation made explicit. This step offers a means of operationalizing the concept Schön (1983) supports, in which professionals "engage in a conversation with the situation they are shaping" (p. 103). It is within this internal yet public reflective conversation that professionals can explore problems from multiple perspectives, consciously stepping back from the daily routines of practice. Schön (1983) calls these routinized patterns "overlearning" and sees them as resistant to correction in the absence of reflection. The conscious act of self-conversation represented by engaging in clarifying questions provides a deliberate structure for that correction to take place.

It is also in this step that multiple contributing factors can be explored and particular ones selected as more or less important to the eventual development of an intervention, or change, in teaching behavior. Schön (1983) states:

> When we set the problem, we select what we will treat as the "things" of the situation, we set the boundaries of our attention to it, and we impose upon it a coherence which allows us to say what is wrong and in what directions the situation needs to be changed. (p. 40)

Given the intense information-processing demands of the classroom (Clark & Peterson, 1986), teachers may be especially vulnerable to failing to access all the knowledge that may need to be brought to bear on problems of practice. Without access to relevant aspects of a problematic situation, teachers may become stuck on a narrow band of information; this would result in restricting their abilities to engage fully in problem setting. In order to practice the central task of problem setting, which entails framing a problematic situation in a way that leads to a tentative, exploratory solution, specific prompting of individuals may be necessary to access inert but important information (see Bransford, Sherwood, Vye, & Rieser, 1986). The format for clarifying questions, which incorporates the peer as a guide in broadening the kinds of questions posed, provides such prompting as an explicit reflective task for teachers.

Without engaging in some form of specific problem clarification, professionals would find it difficult to accomplish this kind of reframing, to resist regularized responses, to recognize that things are not always as they first appear, and to reconsider the assumptions upon which their previous understandings of the situation have been based. Clarification is the process through which professionals come to see those aspects of the problem they value as important; it also broadens their conceptualizations of teaching-learning situations and sources of difficulty that may be affecting problems of practice.

Problem Summarization

In this step, the initiating teacher gives closure to the process of clarification by redefining the problematic situation using a specified format for summarization. The act of summarization includes the identification of a pattern of classroom behavior, the teacher's affective response to the situation, and the identification of specific variables over which the teacher has control. Similar to the first step, the facilitator's role is to ensure that each part of the summary is completed appropriately and to model summarizing strategies as necessary.

Summarization provides teachers with the opportunity to recast the situation in light of the clarifying questions and to begin considering the range of potential responses based upon specific classroom and teacher variables. It allows the initiating teacher to compare the problem definition as initially conceptualized to that arrived at after the process of clarification, thus drawing attention to the role of reflection in redefining problems. Finally, it points the way to action by specifying variables that may require the teacher's attention.

Generation and Prediction

The next strategy requires the initiating teacher to generate at least three potential action patterns for use in the classroom, to predict the outcomes of each, and to select one for actual implementation. In this step, the facilitator focuses the initiator's thinking on the relationship of potential responses to those variables identified in the previous summary. Once the problem has been redefined, it may still be possible to intervene in various ways, but through clarification the professional has more narrowly identified the field in need of attention; he or she must then reflect on potential hazards and benefits of approaching the redefined problem in a particular way. At this stage, all solutions are potentially, but not absolutely, appropriate (Schön, 1983, 1987).

By defining a range of potential interventions, the third step is designed to promote flexibility and creativity in developing responses, thinking through plans before their implementation, and understanding that previously successful solutions may not fit the particularistic nature of the new problem configuration.

Evaluation and Reconsideration

The final step in the process of peer collaboration requires the development of a plan to evaluate the proposed change in teaching behavior, that is, the intervention that was selected for implementation. The purpose of this step is threefold. First, teachers are encouraged to examine the degree to which their plan is workable given the constraints of the classroom and the degree to which those constraints can be overcome or can preclude the intervention's implementation. Thus prediction plays a part in this step of the process as well. Second, teachers develop a means of monitoring how well they are adhering to the plan. This self-evaluative, self-monitoring requirement further encourages and reinforces reflection on their own changes in teaching performance. Finally, teachers develop an evaluation plan to determine the effectiveness of the change. They are encouraged, however, to recognize from the outset that the outcome may or may not be successful, that the need for reflection is not over or complete in a finite sense, and that the worth of the new approach needs to be monitored and reconsidered over time. Once again, the facilitator prompts his or her partner to follow the planning strategy and models planning for evaluation as needed.

If the action produces a successful outcome, the teacher has created a new response, affirming the redefined understanding of the problem reached through prior strategies in the process. If the action is unsuccessful, the pair of teachers will meet again to engage in further clarification—in short, to continue the cycle of inquiry and reflection, now taking into consideration the new information resulting from the unsuccessful experiment. Thus the process described above is closely aligned with Schön's (1983) description of the cycle of inquiry:

> It is initiated by the perception of something troubling or promising, and it is determined by the production of changes one finds on the whole satisfactory or by the discovery of new features which give the situation new meaning and change the nature of questions to be explored. (p. 151)

RESEARCH ON PEER COLLABORATION

As an initial step toward providing teachers with a structured means of developing alternatives to accommodate students with mild learning and behavior problems, research on peer collaboration began in 1985 and continued for three years. In the first year of the project, emphasis was placed on exploration and the development of the process. In the second and third year of the project, emphasis was placed on determining the effectiveness and replicability of the peer collaboration process.

First, an exploratory, descriptive study was conducted to gain a better understanding of the intervention strategies teachers believed were useful and practical for students with chronic instructional or management difficulties (Johnson & Pugach, 1988). A modest pilot study was also conducted during the first year to (1) refine the specifics of each step of the peer collaboration process, (2) examine the feasibility of peer collaboration as a means of aiding teachers in dealing with problems of practice, and (3) develop a standardized set of training procedures for teachers. Results of the pilot study were encouraging: After six hours of training, teachers began to develop far more complete understandings of the problems they were encountering. They were able to shift from emotional responses and reactions to the identification of factors within their control that could contribute to alternative teaching approaches and behaviors (Pugach & Johnson, 1987). At the end of the first year all training procedures had been developed, and emphasis shifted to determining the effectiveness and replicability of the process.

Training in Peer Collaboration

Training for peer collaboration has undergone only slight shifts over the three years of the project. These shifts were largely a function of the unique needs and characteristics of specific sites and teachers. Essentially, teachers attended two four-hour training sessions grouped in two phases. The first phase consisted of two two-hour group sessions, usually taking place on consecutive days after school. In the second phase, pairs or triads of teachers met for two two-hour sessions with trainers who closely monitored their practice of peer collaboration. These training sessions focused on existing problematic situations from teachers' classrooms rather than fictitious situations.

Phase 1 began with a discussion of the goal of strategic thinking and the relationship between the specific strategies to be learned and that goal. A general overview of peer collaboration was given, followed by a description of the relationship of peer collaboration to research in the acquisition of metacognitive skills. This was followed by demonstration, practice, and feedback on each of the four component steps. Subsequent activities took the general format of viewing one step of the process on a videotaped session from the previous pilot study, followed by both a presentation of specific guidelines for each step and demonstrations of potentially confusing aspects of the process. Participants learned to record their interactions in a specified format in a booklet designed to provide written reminders of the guidelines discussed during training. At the end of the training period, each pair had completed the process for one situation; as a result, the initiating teacher was ready to begin implementation.

In phase 2, pairs of teachers worked through existing classroom problems, with trainers guiding them through each step of the process, modeling as needed for initiating and facilitating teachers alike, and using prompts only as needed when difficulties arose. Teachers participated in two such two-hour sessions, with one teacher serving as the initiator and one as the facilitator. When teachers were grouped in triads, three sessions were scheduled. Thus, each teacher participated in both roles. Subsequent sessions were scheduled with trainers only on an as-needed basis; by the time each pair had gone through the complete process twice, little monitoring was requested or required.

Data Sources

Both qualitative and quantitative indicators of the effectiveness of peer collaboration were derived from studies conducted during the second and third year of the project. The peer collaboration sessions themselves generated a rich set of qualitative data for analysis. All sessions were tape-recorded and transcribed verbatim. Transcripts were studied to identify (1) the kinds of situations teachers selected as problematic, (2) the comparison of problem descriptions before and after clarifying questions were posed and answered, and (3) the kinds of interventions teachers generated and selected for implementation. These issues were analyzed through the development of categories of problems and interventions derived from a content analysis of the transcripts. Following the constant comparative method suggested by Glaser and Strauss (1967), tentative sets of categories were developed and reworked through multiple readings of the transcripts. Transcripts also provided the opportunity to analyze the relative roles of initiating and facilitating teachers and the progression from greater to lesser reliance on various aspects of the structured dialogue. Additionally, the tapes themselves provided the opportunity to gauge similarities in teachers' tone of voice and pacing during problem clarification. Finally, teachers participated in large-group debriefing sessions following the completion of four problems per pair or triad of teachers.

A quasi-experimental design was used to generate quantitative data. In the second year, ninety-one teachers from the elementary and junior high school levels participated, with forty-eight in an intervention group and forty-three in a comparison group. The quantitative measure used was the Teachable Pupil Survey (Kornblau, 1982), an instrument designed to identify teacher preferences for thirty-three attributes of idealized teachable pupils in three categories: cognitive, social, and school-appropriate behavioral dimensions.

Data from the initial use of this measure indicated that teachers in the intervention group increased their range of tolerable cognitive behaviors significantly, suggesting that they were more tolerant of students with a wider range of cognitive abilities. Teachers were able to solve 86 percent of problems addressed through the use of peer collaboration. Furthermore, 91 percent of teachers' initial descriptions of problems changed following problem clarification, frequently shifting their focus from student-centered problems to teacher-centered problems. These findings suggested that the peer collaboration process facilitated self-reflection on the part of the teachers (Johnson & Pugach, 1988).

In the third year of the project, which was just being completed at the writing of this chapter, research conducted during the second year was replicated in Alabama, Illinois, and Wisconsin with a group of 78 elementary teachers in the intervention group and 77 in the comparison group. In addition to Kornblau's Teachable Pupil Survey, quantitative measures included the Teacher Efficacy Scale (Gibson & Dembo, 1984); the Classroom Questionnaire (Johnson, 1987), which utilizes a semantic differential approach to access a teacher's affective outlook toward his or her classroom; and the Classroom Problem Questionnaire (Johnson & Pugach, 1987), which contains descriptions of thirty-three classroom problems and asks the teacher to indicate levels of confidence in handling given problems. Preliminary analyses of these data indicated that, as in the previous year, teachers increased their tolerance of acceptable cognitive competence. Scores on the Classroom Questionnaire indicated that teachers in the intervention group became more positive toward their students after training, whereas the comparison group became less positive. Both groups increased their scores on the Teacher Efficacy Scale, but there was no differential impact from the intervention. Finally, teachers trained in peer collaboration became more confident of their ability to deal with classroom problems as measured by the Classroom Problem Questionnaire.

AN EXAMPLE OF REFLECTION THROUGH COLLEGIAL DIALOGUE

Transcripts of peer collaboration sessions illustrate the different ways in which training for strategic thinking encourages reflection on the part of teachers. The following example portrays one pattern of teacher reflection regarding a specific classroom problem with an individual student. This excerpt was taken from the first step of the process, that of self-questioning for the purpose of problem clarification. The teacher (I) in this excerpt has multiple concerns about Molly, a first-grade student. Molly had dropped three reading levels and had had difficulty keeping on task. The facilitating teacher (F) began with a question prompted directly from the description, namely, Molly's reading difficulty.

F: Is there a question you can ask about Molly's ability to do her reading work?

I: Is there a question I can ask myself about Molly's reading ability? Molly, when she is working in a structured reading group with me at the table, she can read the work. We go through the vocabulary, introduce it one day; we then go through and read the story the second day. So when she does read with me, yes, she can do the work that I'm expecting of her within a group situation.

F: Is there a question you can ask about the type of material she's reading compared to what you have found in her cumulative file?

I: Is there a question I can ask myself about the information in her cumulative file? To be honest, I've not looked at her cum file, because she came in and, because she was placed with Mr. Brown . . . I guess because Mr. Brown placed her in her reading group, I felt that Mr. Brown had gone for the reading folder. Uh, the other thing, when she came in, in October, at that point we were just beginning to develop sounds and building those sounds into words, so as far as actually doing any reading, she was not doing a lot when she transferred to this school. That's a good point; I really . . .

F: Is there a question you can ask about why she has the behavior of being sneaky and trying to get away from her work and not being responsible for it?

I: Is there a reason why Molly is being sneaky and trying to get away from things? Or getting out of doing her work? The sneakiness, I guess, I think of more with taking things like off of my desk, more so than I do than I think of her reading work. I find that she likes to socialize during her reading time; she likes to bring in like a lot of pens and markers; her dad is an artist, and so she likes to take, and loves taking, you know, great effort at any type of art work, you know, that she does. And so we've had to remove the colored markers and the crayons, and they stay at my desk until I feel that there is a project that she needs them.

F: Is there a question you can ask about Molly's preference for the reading she would like to do?

I: Is there a question I can ask myself about the types of reading that Molly likes to do? I . . . don't know for sure. I know that when we were sending reading books home, her parents would write back—we'd ask for comments—and her mom would write back on how they enjoyed it, but I'm wondering if with Molly, if it was not more, you know, that being able to be close to mom—she's an only child, and this is an opportunity for her to have all of mom or dad's attention.

F: What types of reading did she do, then, would you say?

I: The kinds of reading that she did then, was reading that I supplied home to her. Something that I should consider doing is asking Mr. Brown for me to see her . . . [testing] sheets. That would give me an idea, also, of the kinds of reading that she's doing at home. I am supplying some books to the kids, but not all of them.

F: And are they on a variety of subjects?

I: The ones that she first sent home were more phonetic readers. Right, and we're now sending home the primers or the pre-primers of different reading series; so as far as going to the library and choosing different books, no, we aren't. If we did, they would, you know, be the picture books or, you know, the easy-to-read books, which to me you don't get the variety that you do at the upper levels.

F: Is there a question you can ask about Molly's emotional behavior?

I: Is there a question I can ask myself about Molly's emotional behavior? I see Molly as being very immature. I see her wanting to be accepted by her peers. And one of the points . . . I guess, some of the things that are going through my mind as far as beginning to summarize just a little bit, I can see where I had mentioned with the recess times, that she doesn't want to come in. I'm wondering if she is in such need of wanting the approval and the acceptance of her peers that she is wanting to get outside, or at least become a part of that group, and not to be left out. If she's so in need of . . . acceptance among her peer group.

F: Is there a question you can ask about what she does during the time that she is to be at her seat, on-task, doing her reading?

I: What does Molly do at her . . . What does Molly do during her reading seatwork time? . . . It's hauling her back to task . . . It's coming up, you know, wanting some direction, you know, from me—"What do I do here? What do I do there? Can I go to the bathroom?" There will be times if it's, you know, if it's an art-related project that she will sit down and work. The reading that I'm having her do . . . requires a lot of . . . writing activity; I should say, I include a lot of writing activities with their reading this year, and she enjoys being able to take the books home that we make through the writing activities, but it's, I don't think she enjoys the writing aspect of it, either. So it might be, you know, the writing is another area . . .

F: Is there a question you can ask about a difficulty that might be keeping her from writing?

I: Is there a question I can ask myself about Molly's—I'm going to include her handwriting, as well as her ability to write in complete sentences? The handwriting is a weak area for Molly, however, I don't feel that I put a lot of emphasis on that during the writing activities that she's doing; I am expecting that to be done neatly, but it's not that every letter has to be made, you know, perfectly. With her ability to write a complete sentence, the writing that she has to do, there's been a lot of background-building that's been going on; we do a lot of brainstorming, and I write all of the ideas on a sheet of paper, ditto those off, and so she has the sentence, and the information right there in front of her, so it's not that she has to really do a lot of generating herself, or do a lot of spelling on her own; it's right there and it's primarily a matter of copying.

I: I guess a question that I need to ask myself is about her seating placement in my classroom. In talking to Mr. Brown, he has now placed her in the front of her classroom. In my room, she is sitting three rows back from the front.

F: Three rows back?

I: Yes. Also, I think there's a question I can ask myself about, who do I have her . . . who do I have sitting around her?

F: OK. Those sitting around her . . . What question do you have to ask for that?

I: What influence do the friends around her have, and in thinking about her seating placement right now, I can see where she is with girls that she wants to be accepted by and wants to be a part of that group, and I'm beginning to think that some of the off-task behavior may be that she is wanting to become such a part of that group that she's wanting to be spending time with them instead of concentrating on her reading work.

F: Is there a question you can ask about how she is accepted within that group?

I Is there a question I can ask about how she is accepted within that group? I feel that she is not well accepted. I feel that she is tolerated by that group of girls, and not just that group. I'm just . . . in general, I see her as being tolerated by the kids. Not that she does anything to really ignore . . . to irritate them . . . but she has not been . . .

F: . . . genuinely accepted?

I: Right. I don't see her as being a very outgoing person; she's very quiet and part of it can also be that she's, you know, an only child. And I see her parents as being very caring and very loving parents, but also very, very protective.

F: Is there a question you can ask about . . . I'm thinking of her parents. Is there a question you can ask about their concern that she is somewhat isolated?

I: Is there a question I can ask myself about Molly's parents' concern for her being alone? I am unaware of anything, you know, that they are, you know, to do. Molly, as far as I know, is not a member of, like the Brownies, or I don't know what, you know, she is . . . what her involvement with church and things is. I do know that they're going to be living . . . near the downtown, and I would assume that it's an older neighborhood; that there would not be many children. The other thing that I see happening at home is that mother wants to protect her because of a situation that we had where Molly took something off of my desk, and I called mom to tell her that there had been a mix-up, and I needed to find out whose [ring] this really was. And come to find out, it belonged to another student, but her mother said that . . .

another student had given it to her the day before, and she brought it home, and said that this boy had given it to her. She then comes into my room and I put it on . . . she put it on my desk, and I mentioned to mom that she'd taken it off, and mom's response was, "Well, she probably thought that it was hers since the boy gave it to her last night." She felt that she had the right to take it, and so we had to talk about that. No, she doesn't have the right to take things off of my desk; that if I let Molly do it, there would be other kids who would also want to have that same freedom. So I think that, you know, mom wants to do the protecting of Molly.

F: Have you a question you can ask about this affecting Molly's reading, perhaps?

I: Is there a question I can ask about how the peers, and being an only child, and her parents' protectiveness—how is that influencing her reading? I feel that they are really the influencing factors on her reading right now. After going through and talking about it, I really feel that that's where the focus maybe needs to be. In summarizing the problem, I feel that there is some emotional need that she is trying to meet during reading time, and that the inability to complete the assignments is not that she can't do it, but she is trying to fulfill an emotional need.

In this dialogue, the initiating teacher primarily responded to her partner's prompting questions in a one-to-one correspondence. This kind of repetition of the questioning phrase seemed to characterize early use of the process. Once teachers began to feel more comfortable with the goal of self-questioning, they were encouraged to do so without repeating the phrase "Is there a question . . . " Within this particular excerpt, the initiating teacher did begin to generate questions herself a number of times, using such phrases as "I guess a question that I need to ask myself . . . " Since the teachers in this pair were in a very early stage of skill acquisition, the dialogue generally remained highly structured, with the facilitating teacher using the stylized questioning stimulus and the initiating teacher following the same stylized format. During clarification, deliberation on the part of the initiating teacher is represented by such terms as: "some of the things that are going through my mind," "I'm wondering," "after going through and talking about it," and "I'm beginning to think that . . . " to indicate her consideration of the situation from a new or broadened perspective. Such adherence to a stylized mode of questioning reflects the early phase of strategy acquisition; as greater levels of skill are developed, this kind of adherence fades.

The initiating teacher moved back and forth from thinking she might be ready to summarize to the asking of more clarifying questions. In finally summarizing the problem, she eventually came to understand

Molly's difficulty as being more of an emotional and social problem rather than the inability to do the work. With this particular teacher, it is interesting to note that she was identified by her principal as being one of the strongest teachers in the school, one known for her skills as well as her sensitivity to her students. Nevertheless, focused reflection on her part resulted in a far different set of understandings regarding Molly than had occurred when she employed her genuine interest but less reflective approach in conceptualizing the problem.

Teacher Responses to Peer Collaboration

It was the step of learning to ask oneself clarifying questions that took the greatest amount of time during training and proved to be the greatest training challenge—primarily due to the level of discomfort raised by the structure and formality of this phase of the process. However, this step also proved to be the pivotal point in the entire process and provided the anchor for teacher reflection. Reflection through clarification proved to be hard work, and the most effective method of dispelling the discomfort associated with learning the structure for clarifying problems was to provide teachers with a clear understanding of the relative time it would probably take to acquire each step and the disproportionate time needed to acquire clarification skills.

Prior to the clarifying questions phase of the process, teachers' initial descriptions often reflected their frustration over problems of practice. In contrast, specific summaries arrived at subsequent to clarification seemed to serve as springboards for teacher action. The process of reflecting by asking clarifying questions put teachers in the position of generating alternative explanations for classroom dynamics, and this freed them to identify alternative forms of action. The immediate frustration expressed with problems of practice was, as a result, diffused. While in the end many reconceptualizations may appear to be simplistic, such knowledge did not seem to be accessible to teachers in the absence of structured reflection through dialogue.

The value of asking clarifying questions in such a structured format is perhaps best characterized by the following teacher's comments:

> Another thing about the structure of it is that—it was sort of a byproduct of the fact that we need to learn to ask questions—but also because it's awkward, it demands your attention. It causes your thinking caps to be on a little more than if it were a very comfortable, ordinary way of saying something. You would be in your comfortable, ordinary frame of mind, and it might actually be more difficult for you to think of questions if you

weren't already thinking about the structure that you had to adhere to initially.

In this example, the teacher had stepped back from a routine way of thinking about problems and identified a new way of framing a troubling professional situation. Such a response is typical of teachers who learn the peer collaboration process. As a formal and self-conscious act, the asking of clarifying questions seems to promote rethinking the problem in a way that encouraged responsive teacher behavior.

On the tapes themselves, the pacing and tone of teacher self-conversation would suggest a definite stepping back from the issues and a slow and conscious consideration of each aspect of the problem being clarified. Pacing was measured and deliberate, with self-conversation taking greater time and almost always occurring more slowly than interactive conversation. Further, the reflective stance taken by teachers as they engaged in self-conversation was evident in their voice tone as well as their pacing. These tonal and pacing qualities were consistent across nearly all sessions, indicating that reflection as represented in the step of clarification cannot be expected to be a hurried or automatic task but requires focused time in which to sit back and consider the situation purposively.

As teachers became more skilled in peer collaboration, the time it took to complete the four steps lessened progressively. Once teachers had worked through their questions, they were already thinking of alternative ways of responding or reorganizing or were ready to seek out additional information. During the debriefing that followed the project one teacher commented: "I think a lot of the questions can be cleared up prior to going through the sessions because, now that we've been through it, we know which kinds of questions to ask ourselves before we even approach a problem." However, despite increasing familiarity, the pacing of the first step did not change. Engaging in question clarification clearly appeared to be the pivotal deliberative and reflective point in the process.

Teachers spoke about two other outcomes of their experiences. First, the issue of teacher tolerance was raised during debriefing conversations. One teacher observed that anytime a problematic situation in the classroom is minimized, it helps the entire classroom setting and, thus, the other children's environment as well. Another teacher noted that if more time is spent "being interested in what you can do to help a kid, you spend less time being aggravated at what they're doing, and it improves the tone in the classroom. Instead of looking at what's happening and getting immediately angry, you look and you think, 'now why?'

or 'what happened?' and the anger turns off." In this context, reflection may provide the means by which teachers can begin to spend their emotional as well as intellectual energy wisely in the classroom.

A final issue raised regards time itself as a resource and its relationship to an organizational structure in which reflection might take place. Teachers spoke directly to the issue of needing time for reflection. They commented about being unconvinced at the outset whether anyone would use what initially seemed to be a very time-consuming process. Once they had learned the strategies, however, a peer collaboration session began to take from approximately forty-five minutes to one hour for its completion. This time expenditure seemed far more reasonable, with teachers commenting that the structure of the process forced them to use their time to think constructively rather than merely to complain to a colleague. Meeting times had a definite purpose, and with a colleague that purpose was shared. At the same time, however, teachers also indicated that "you have to take time because it isn't there unless you take it. It isn't even there when you take it. You take it from something else." As we talked with building principals who were interested in institutionalizing this particular means of reflection, time also appeared to be the major obstacle to doing so.

TIME, STRUCTURE, AND REFLECTIVE PRACTICE

The goal of peer collaboration is not to arrive at a prescribed solution; rather, it is to engage each initiating teacher in a guided, supportive, and collegial process of reconsidering professional problems in order to encourage new approaches to them. In this sense, strategic processes such as peer collaboration can be thought of as evocative rather than prescriptive; new understandings are evoked that lead to new solutions. It can also be thought of as proactive rather than reactive. When teachers work on problematic situations before the problems escalate, they minimize the potential for formal special education referral. The structure of peer collaboration serves and respects the individual's experience of the situation, bringing to the surface through collegial dialogue its nuances and missed characteristics. Solutions are neither correct nor incorrect but are arrived at through the pairing of time and structure within which reflection can take place.

The disposition to engage in reflective practice, then, is acquired through peer collaboration when internal dialogue or conversation is made explicit, and thus available, to the teacher. Listening to one's own processes of thinking and having those processes modeled provides a structured means for encouraging reflective practice among teachers. It is precisely this ability to carry on internal conversation, moving from problem framing to solution to implication to reconsideration, that eventually must be achieved by professionals.

Although in the literature of professional reflection such a practice is supported in principle (Schön, 1987), the way the requisite explicit explanation and demonstration is communicated is not defined. Experienced professionals are encouraged in Schön's reflective practitioner model to be explicit in sharing with their students more of the internal self-conversation they may hold; it is the disclosure of self-conversation that allows a novice to begin to imitate the reflective process (Schön, 1983, 1987). But despite his calls for public reflection with regard to what may to the novice appear to be implicit processes, Schön has failed to provide a specific structure within which this disclosure of self-conversation might be achieved.

Among practicing teachers there is little tradition of engaging in this type of dialogic interaction. More typically, when problems are encountered, information or advice is passed on from one teacher to another without putting teachers in the position of engaging in any type of reflective, self-conversational process. This type of prescriptive advice giving, while perhaps efficient in the short run, can discourage teachers from actively reflecting on problems in their intricacies (Pugach & Johnson, 1988).

Helping teachers at any level to reflect appears to be a labor-intensive process characterized chiefly by dialogue and deliberation. For those who play the role of facilitator, it is also characterized by restraint in allowing teachers to think aloud and to stumble and approximate verbally. Patience is required in modeling one's own thought processes for one's peer. Such activities take time and are not common to either preservice or inservice practice as they are currently conceptualized. Although dialogue is common enough in preservice teacher education, typically it is dialogue about what is read or seen, not about how one proceeds to think about the classroom and the need for accommodating many types of students. Also, neither teacher educators nor practicing teachers who train novices typically model their own thinking processes for their students. The requisite dialogue provides an opportunity to work collegially toward the goal of reflection, and it is precisely this kind of professional dialogue that is largely absent in the act of teaching as it currently exists. These are dynamics that require time.

Given the contrast between the existing conditions of work for teachers and the time a reflective approach demands, a major issue for teacher educators interested in promoting reflection is the extent to which it can ever be expected to occur regularly without changes in the conditions of work. Reflection is not likely to be a natural outgrowth of a system in which time is an unavailable resource to classroom teachers. In our studies of peer collaboration to date, it is clear that time is one of the critical elements in the reflective process. Reflection is unlikely to take place unless the conditions of work are adapted to support its occurrence.

As we move toward the goal of preparing teachers to be reflective in all aspects of their work, we are obligated to recognize the depth of change its use requires. Time in and of itself is not an adequate resource; specific structures, of which peer collaboration is one example, are needed to help even the most skilled teachers consider their practice in a reflective manner. And since such structured interactions tend to engender discomfort (Sternberg & Martin, 1988), structures distinguished by dialogue are not likely to be engaged in easily in the absence of prompting for their use. The central role of structure has important implications for the way teacher education, at both the preservice and inservice level, is delivered. In the particular case of peer collaboration, studies to date have been limited to reflection on problems of classroom practice by experienced teachers. However, the nature of the strategies would suggest that the process is likely to hold promise for reflecting on problems related to broader educational issues as well, issues such as curriculum choices and the multitude of ethical and moral dilemmas teachers face. While as teacher educators we would expect our students to engage in reasoned, deliberate consideration of such broad educational issues, we must recognize that explicit prompting of reflection at this level too is likely to be needed if the habit of reflection is to be promoted systematically. The development of appropriate structures will require learning new, interactive, and dialogic ways for adults to work together in schools.

REFERENCES

Bransford, J., Sherwood, R., Vye, N., & Rieser, J. (1986). Teaching thinking and problem solving: Research foundations. *American Psychologist, 41*, 1078–1089.

Brown, A. L., & Palincsar, A. S. (1982). Inducing strategic learning from texts by means of informed, self-control training. *Topics of Learning and Learning Disabilities, 2*, 1–17.

Clark, C. M., & Peterson, P. L. (1986). Teachers' thought processes. In M. Wittrock (Ed.), *Handbook of research on teaching* (3rd ed.) (pp. 255–296). New York: Macmillan.

Cruickshank, D. R. (1987). *Reflective teaching*. Reston, VA: Association of Teacher Educators.

Gibson, S., & Dembo, M. H. (1984). Teacher efficacy: A construct validation. *Journal of Educational Psychology, 76,* 569–582.

Glaser, B. G., & Strauss, A. (1967). *The discovery of grounded theory: Strategies for qualitative research*. Chicago: Aldine.

Gore, J. M. (1987). Reflecting on reflective teaching. *Journal of Teacher Education, 38*(2), 33–39.

Johnson, L. J. (1987). *Classroom Questionnaire*. Unpublished manuscript.

Johnson, L. J., & Pugach, M. C. (1987). *Classroom Problem Questionnaire*. Unpublished manuscript.

Johnson, L. J., & Pugach, M. C. (1988). *Accommodating the needs of students with mild learning and behavior problems through peer collaboration*. Manuscript submitted for publication.

Johnson, L. J., Pugach, M. C., & Hammitte, D. (1988). Barriers to special education consultation. *Remedial and Special Education, 9*(6), 41–47.

Kornblau, B. (1982). The Teachable Pupil Survey: A technique for assessing teachers' perceptions of pupil attributes. *Psychology in the Schools, 19,* 170–174.

Liston, D. P., & Zeichner, K. M. (1987). Reflective teacher education and moral deliberation. *Journal of Teacher Education, 38*(6), 2–8.

Meichenbaum, D. (1980). Cognitive behavior modification with exceptional children: A promise yet unfulfilled. *Exceptional Education Quarterly, 1*(1), 83–88.

Neely, A. M. (1986). Planning and problem solving in teacher education. *Journal of Teacher Education, 37*(3), 29–33.

Palincsar, A. S. (1986). The role of dialogue in providing scaffolded instruction. *Educational Psychologist, 21,* 73–98.

Palincsar, A. S., & Brown, A. L. (1984). Reciprocal teaching of comprehension-fostering and comprehension-monitoring activities. *Cognition and Instruction, 1,* 117–175.

Pugach, M. C., & Johnson, L. J. (1987, April). *Systematic teacher dialogue as a prereferral intervention: Self-appraisal through peer collaboration*. Paper presented at the annual meeting of the American Educational Research Association, Washington, DC.

Pugach, M. C., & Johnson, L. J. (1988). Rethinking the relationship between consultation and collaborative problem-solving. *Focus on Exceptional Children, 21*(4), 1–8.

Schön, D. A. (1983). *The reflective practitioner*. New York: Basic Books.

Schön, D. A. (1987). *Educating the reflective practitioner*. San Francisco: Jossey-Bass.

Sternberg, R. J., & Martin, M. (1988). When teaching thinking does not work, what goes wrong? *Teachers College Record, 89,* 555–578.

Tom, A. R. (1984). *Teaching as a moral craft*. New York: Longman.

Trumbull, D. J. (1986). Teachers' envisioning: A foundation for artistry. *Teaching and Teacher Education, 2,* 139–144.

Wertsch, J. V. (1979). From social interaction to higher psychological processes: A clarification and application of Vygotsky's theory. *Human Development, 22,* 1–22.

Zeichner, K. M., & Liston, D. P. (1987). Teaching student teachers to reflect. *Harvard Educational Review, 57*(1), 23–48.

11 The Potential for Research Contributions to Reflective Practice

W. ROBERT HOUSTON
RENEE T. CLIFT
University of Houston

The merits of providing teachers with a practical, technically oriented education as opposed to a liberal, issue- or problem-oriented education have been debated for decades (e.g., Borrowman, 1965; Haberman & Stinnett, 1973; Richardson, Chapter 1, this volume). Scholarly inquiries into the processes and effects of such teacher education programs, however, have only begun to provide empirical data within the past twenty-five years (Lanier & Little, 1986; Peck & Tucker, 1973). Paraphrasing Santayana, teacher education has been condemned to repeat the past because it has failed to learn from earlier successes and mistakes, or even to remember them.

Once again, teacher educators are debating the relative merits of technical training versus reflective problem solving. Given this renewed interest in reflective educational practice, we believe it is especially important to understand more about the nature of reflection in teaching, the development of reflective practice, the effects of such practice on teachers and teacher educators, and the relationships between reflective practice and the experiences of students. In this chapter we invite those who are interested in the image of the teacher as reflective practitioner to move from rhetoric to active inquiry so that future teacher educators might learn from our experiences, not merely repeat them.

It would be naive for us, or anyone else, to assume that a few courses at a university or a few workshops at a school could make a reflective individual out of someone whose current practice consists of

This work was funded in part by a contract from the U.S. Department of Education, Office of Educational Research and Improvement (Contract No. 400-85-1039). The opinions expressed in this chapter do not necessarily reflect the position, policy, or endorsement of that agency.

primarily mindless, automatic actions. Neither can we assume that teachers do not think back on their teaching and attempt to improve upon their actions in subsequent lessons. Such an assumption performs a grave disservice to both the teaching profession and to the academic researcher or teacher educator. Reflection is a normal activity, often mentioned as one form of metacognition (Clark & Peterson, 1986; Peterson & Comeaux, 1988), that occurs both spontaneously and deliberately in adults and in children.

The authors of the preceding chapters advocating reflective, inquiry-oriented teacher education argue that the process of reflective activity can be encouraged throughout teacher education and that the content to be reflected upon can (and possibly should) be expanded to include much more than classroom behaviors. The assumption underlying all of these chapters is that a habit of reflective thinking and educational inquiry is of more value than an incidental, occasional retrospection on one's day. Beyond this assumption, the chapter authors provide a rich, wide-ranging array of issues related to the broad topic of reflection.

Currently, the goals of reflective practice lack clarity. For example, Tom (1985) identifies more than twelve terms that refer to teachers as persons engaged in reflective inquiry, and it is possible to identify even more. The nuances among different names are often subtle; but subtle or not, they refer to different assumptions concerning the processes and outcomes of reflective practice. We agree with Tom that the "parameters for what counts as inquiry teacher education are fuzzy" (p. 36), and we would add that what counts for reflective teacher education does nothing to clarify the situation. Indeed, different scholars, all using the label *reflective*, could be referring to any of the aspects of reflection referred to by Clift and Houston (1988), Van Manen (1977), or Zeichner and Liston (1987). A technical orientation toward reflection, for example, can be seen in Freiberg and Waxman (Chapter 7, this volume). Their discussion presents a sharp contrast to Valli's (Chapter 3, this volume) discussion of forms of reflective practice as defined by the Catholic University teacher education program.

We contend that the language of reflection is central to its practice. Language can either facilitate or limit our ability to reflect. The language we learn as children is supplemented by the professional terms we use as adults. It frames our thinking as we define and study problems, speculate on life, search for the meaning of our existence, and accomplish the daily routines necessary for survival. Our language grows from our experience, but it also controls our experience through the powerful labels we have learned to give certain experiences. To illustrate, let us consider differing conceptions of the concept of time.

Primitive peoples' conception of time was cyclical (for an extended discussion, see Hawking, 1988; Toffler, 1980, pp. 119–121). Spring followed winter as the seasons changed; the harvest was sown, then gathered in; people were born, lived, and died as generations followed one another. Today, most people think of time basically as linear, often portrayed as a number line (our own calendar being based on the Christian epoch of some 2,000 years ago). This change from a cyclical to a linear conception of time causes different thought patterns and poses different interpretations of natural phenomena.

Scientists today conceptualize time in relativistic terms. As individuals we may have felt that time moves more slowly on some occasions than others. Toffler (1980) elaborates on this concept by quoting astrophysicist John Gribben:

> [Time] can be warped and distorted in nature, with the end product being different depending on just where you measure it from. At the ultimate extreme, supercollapsed objects—black holes—can negate time altogether, making it stand still in their vicinity. (p. 313)

The proliferation of meanings surrounding usage of common terminology can create problems in communication, as illustrated by Lewis Carroll (1865/1946):

> "When I use a word," Humpty Dumpty said in rather a scornful tone, "it means just what I choose it to mean—neither more nor less." "The question is," said Alice, "whether you can make words mean so many different things." (p. 238)

In education we tend to act like Humpty Dumpty, manufacturing new terms and defining other terms to meet our own specific conceptions. This leads to confusion about the meaning of certain terms and to inarticulateness and lack of precise communication among professional educators. It may also lead to confusion among our students, sending an unintended message that professional education is more interested in the rhetoric of quality than in the quality of practice (Ginsburg & Clift, 1990).

We have begun to formulate several working hypotheses concerning the connections between reflection, inquiry, and the education of teachers. They are not to be interpreted as conclusions; they are hunches drawn from practice, study, speculation, and some preliminary research that is still young, tentative, and fluid. Our goal is to encourage the spirit of open inquiry based on a careful examination of learning experiences that can be labeled *reflective practice.*

WORKING HYPOTHESES
ABOUT REFLECTIVE TEACHER EDUCATION

Hypothesis One

Current definitions of reflection are strongly influenced by the Western cultural heritage, which emphasizes analysis and problem solving as opposed to negotiation, contemplation, or enlightenment.

The language of reflective practice is dominated by Western analytical philosophy, particularly the philosophy of John Dewey. Cinnamond and Zimpher (Chapter 4, this volume) and Yinger (Chapter 5, this volume) caution that educational researchers have been too narrowly focused in their observations of teaching practice in general and of reflective practice in particular. We would add that teacher education practitioners have been too narrow in their conceptions of encouraging reflective practice among prospective teachers and experienced teachers.

It is relatively easy for us to locate and reference discussions on the reflective method by Plato, Socrates, Descartes, Kant, and Dewey, because liberal education for many of us meant that we studied the Western cultural heritage (Bitting & Clift, 1987). The educational philosophy we studied during graduate education often emphasized Dewey's conceptions of the science of education and his ideas that reflection begins when one defines the arena of the problematic.

We learned the importance of an analytical method that stresses objectivity and emotional detachment. The implication for reflective practice is that the practitioner stands back from the situation, analyzes it, recognizes nuances within it, and proposes solutions that are then tested. This implication is called into question when we are urged to consider the student as a *subject* (Noddings, 1984), not an object, and to base our interpretations and our decisions on the subjective natures of our students. Reflective thinking then becomes a process of trying to understand the subject and to see the world through his or her eyes. Our schooling traditions, holidays, stories, poetry, drama, and music are Western, primarily European. These traditions are so powerful they often overwhelm any attempt to explore any other tradition. And, in so doing, they limit our ability to use our minds and bodies more fully to understand our world.

The concept of reflection is an ancient one. The elders and prophets of old were revered for their wisdom and counsel. That wisdom was based not only on knowledge but also, more importantly, on the ability to analyze situations, to recognize the nuances of problems, to be able to think divergently, and to propose solutions to problems that plagued the people. About the sixth century B.C., a wave of philosophers, scientists, and religious leaders independently, and in all parts of the planet, proposed reflective ideas and taught new ways of thinking that continue to shape thought and action to this day. In Greece these reflective inquirers included Plato and Aristotle; in China, Confucius and Lao Tzu; in Israel, Solomon; and in India, Gautama, the Buddha. They exemplified different conceptions of reflection, but all are revered for the lasting strength of their ideas.

When one begins to recognize that reflection can take an Eastern as well as Western approach, to recognize its long and distinguished history, and to recognize that it is not a method nor a technique but a way of life, then one begins to sense the paucity of thought that has too often gone into the conceptualizations of many teacher-preparation programs. One begins, too, to question a conception of teaching that links reflective activity only with problem solving without an equal emphasis on understanding the totality and the unity inherent in the teaching context.

Such an understanding is crucial if teachers are to adapt to societies, schools, and classrooms that are unlike those which they experienced as students. Change is perhaps the only constant in our lives and in the world. Reflection enables one to appreciate changes in context, meaning, and usefulness not only day by day but also minute by minute. The quality and character of reflection also changes, varying with age and the maturity of individuals, as well as the norms and values within a culture. While the beauty of the passage is somewhat lost in translation, the meaning of an ancient Persian story expresses this so very well.

> Just there, where people imagine the world to be stable, just there its reality slips away instant by instant. Think of the shadow of a tree, which the traveler reaches at last, after miles of walking in the blazing sun. He desires only to rest in its shade, which to him seems permanent and immobile (for its motion cannot be perceived by the senses). But no sooner has he fallen asleep than the shadow moves on and passes over him, and he wakes to find himself in the heat of the sun. (Nasir al-Din Tusi [thirteenth-century poet] quoted in Beny, 1975, p. 90)

The concept of reflective inquiry will continue to be a part of teacher education. The challenge is not only to implement this vision but to study other visions and to broaden the concept so that it can form a powerful framework for improving the education of teachers and the practice of teaching.

Hypothesis Two

Programs attempting to develop reflective practitioners are enhanced through freedom and empowerment.

Freedom and empowerment are twin assumptions of reflection. Constraints on the scope of thought lead to constraints on freedom and thus on reflection. To reflect, an individual must not only be free to think but also feel empowered to think.

We have only begun to identify those contexts that encourage reflective activity, but we suspect that both preservice education and school-based teacher education will need to be restructured if they are to support either individual or communal reflection. Policy mandates can either enhance or inhibit university and school initiatives in developing such structures.

The *extent of constraints* and the *scope of reflective inquiry* are complementary concepts; the greater one becomes, the lesser becomes the other. When a legislature or a state education agency limits the time or the content of a teacher education program, it limits the extent to which the program can emphasize reflection. Similarly, alternative certification proposals may place teachers in classrooms without providing safe spaces in which they can discuss their experiences, thus emphasizing action while leaving reflection up to the individual. Exit examinations and assessment instruments specifying certain rules or behaviors may also define what processes are expected to occur in a classroom, therefore implicitly labeling that which is not important.

With few exceptions, mandates limit the freedom of the teacher to reflect and speculate on conditions at a particular moment in time and on the actions that might be most effective in bringing about positive change. When legislatures, state boards of education, regulatory bodies, and local school district administrators require a specific process or content, they reduce the teacher's degrees of freedom. This is a major factor that distinguishes the professional from the craftsperson or layperson—freedom to act as one's professional judgment dictates. It also distinguishes a professional preparation program from a training and indoctrination program.

Hypothesis Three

Reflective inquiry–oriented teacher preparation programs require more time than other types of programs.

The purpose of reflective inquiry is to bring disparate data, ambiguous situations, and conflicting perceptions into focus. Schön (1983) notes that professional practice involves conflicts over many issues, including values, goals, purposes, and interests. Simple solutions to complex problems are not appropriate for teachers in any context. Reflective inquiry requires two kinds of time. First, it requires time to be able to reflect on the complexity of the classroom and to formulate ideas for teaching. Second, it takes time to learn and to strengthen the use of reflective inquiry in professional settings (see Sugarman, 1985).

Recognizing this need and this reality, Noordhoff and Kleinfeld (Chapter 9, this volume), emphasize instructional design as the time for reflective inquiry. Rather than focusing on the actual teaching process, they are preparing teachers who are reflective in planning lessons and curriculum. Such a perspective provides the time needed to review broad implications of practice and to modify strategies before implementing them.

The second time requirement, time to learn to use reflective inquiry, was noted by Wildman and Niles (1987) following a study of beginning teachers who were asked to review their own instruction and reflect on ways it might be improved: "Systematic reflection takes time. Developing descriptions, examining beliefs, and contemplating changes in one's practice are not automatic routines" (p. 29). Wildman and Niles conclude that when teachers took time to audiotape or videotape their classes, they heard and understood things about which they were previously unaware.

As Pugach and Johnson indicate (Chapter 10, this volume), those learning the process stumble, speculate badly, and reconsider problems and actions. Instruction in the process is labor intensive and time-consuming; it also requires considerable patience.

Hypothesis Four

Community and tradition enhance reflective activity.

Teaching is primarily an isolated profession. A supportive environment and close associates facilitate the reflective inquiry process. "[R]eflection is primarily driven by the individual, but we have found that collegial groups provide both the emotional and technical support that is often necessary for professionals reflecting about their practice" (Wildman & Niles, 1987, p. 29). The experience of other professional groups supports this.

For example, teams of physicians, residents, and interns in a hospital meet regularly to "staff" their patients. Data on each case are reviewed, with emphasis on current conditions and recent changes.

Individual professionals bring to the discussion their expertise and perspective; plans for actions grow out of these discussions (Becker, Geer, Hughes, & Strauss, 1961). Indeed, medical educators are calling for even greater emphasis on supervisory structures to encourage professional reflection throughout a prospective physician's training.

Attorneys work together to consider the approach to be used in a particular case. Legal Aid Services, Inc., is a national, government-sponsored organization that represents people who are not financially able to employ an attorney. Their cases are primarily related to problems with landlords (rent or housing conditions), problems related to employment, and actions by social agencies. There are always too many needs—some more deserving than others, some with broader implications than others, and some with greater repercussions than others (Korman, 1988).

Determining priority among and considering how to expend scarce resources is always a problem. In Springfield, Massachusetts, the attorneys, social workers, and legal aides in a Legal Aid Services office meet regularly to decide which cases to emphasize, how to approach each, and who will take the lead. Even though their time is very limited, they have found that the different perspectives of the staff increase the effectiveness of strategies that are selected and decrease the time ultimately expended on cases (Korman, June 1988, personal communication).

Curriculum projects in schools are enhanced when teachers with varying experiences and expertise work together to develop a new program or revise an existing one. The broader the range of perspectives, the longer the process requires, but the ultimate product typically is better. When persons from several organizations—such as schools, universities, and business—collaborate, the range of viewpoints and values becomes even broader, the process more complex, and the outcomes potentially more effective.

Collaboration is not an aimless exercise. It is goal-directed, and the goal often is multifaceted, embedded in a complex situation that can be enhanced with consideration by various persons. Yinger (Chapter 5, this volume) points out that specialization of professionals can be a major problem, for it inhibits conversations among persons with similar goals and needs and leads to isolation.

Hypothesis Five

Breadth of knowledge improves both the process and the outcome of reflective inquiry.

Resnick (1987), in a discussion of higher-order thinking, identifies several characteristics that also apply to reflective inquiry. Synthesizing and modifying her list, we would hypothesize that reflective inquiry is nonalgorithmic (path of action not fully specified in advance), complex, and yields multiple solutions. It involves nuanced judgment and interpretation, the application of multiple criteria (which sometimes conflict with one another), uncertainty, and self-regulation of the thinking process. It requires considerable effort and finding structure in apparent disorder.

Reflective inquiry is dependent upon the teacher's having a broad and in-depth understanding of what is happening in the class. Wildman and Niles (1987) found that teachers were not able to articulate reliable descriptions of classroom life: "Their understanding is more utilitarian than analytical and not rich or detailed enough to drive systematic reflection. . . . [T]heir language [is] highly judgmental and often not consistent with the actual events" (p. 26). Training in making and discussing such observations improved the teachers' ability to do so.

The problems teachers face are rarely as straightforward and clear as they are described in preparation programs, research reports, or professional papers. Teaching conditions are highly complex. What teachers are asked to do is to "suspend judgment" and "consider alternatives to established practice" (Tom, 1985, p. 37) as they reflect on their options and alternatives.

Hypothesis Six

Depth of content knowledge enables teachers to reflect upon their students' understandings of subject matter and therefore their ability to adapt instruction to meet students' needs.

Shulman (1986) observes that professional competence is specific to domains; that is, to make the right decisions, there are no global algorithms per se. One needs detailed knowledge both of one's speciality and of how to employ that knowledge to help others. Shulman (1986; 1987) and colleagues have conducted two-year case studies, following student teachers into their first year of teaching. These studies included teachers who were misassigned to content areas other than their area of expertise (Ringstaff, 1987) and comparisons of teachers who began teaching with and without teacher preparation (Grossman, 1988). These cases demonstrate the dilemmas novices faced as they struggled to teach material they had not yet learned. In the absence of detailed content knowledge or of pedagogical knowledge of classroom procedures, teachers cannot make content as accessible to students.

The quality of reflective inquiry is dependent upon content-specific knowledge, upon pedagogical knowledge, and also upon the two other commonplaces identified by Schwab (1973)—knowledge of students as groups and as individuals and knowledge of the milieu of individual schools and communities. The practice of reflective inquiry in education is enhanced not only by depth of knowledge in any or all of these areas but also by a knowledge of the interrelationships among areas.

Hypothesis Seven

Programs that promote reflective thinking cannot rely on a single set of prepackaged experiences.

Some advocates have equated reflective inquiry with the scientific method. For them, using the five-stage model for solving problems is the only way to proceed. Yet we know that most people, even scientists, do not use this model when reflecting and conducting inquiries. It is a mythical model, generalized but not practiced, simple but of little value. The essence and strength of reflective inquiry is lost when all persons, in all situations, dealing with any problems or considering any field, are expected to speculate on the situation in the same way.

Subotnik (1988) quotes Barthes to the effect that: "Through the mythology of Einstein, the world blissfully regained the image of knowledge reduced to a formula . . . [and of] the universe [as] a safe of which humanity seeks the combination" (p. 69). He then attacks the scientific method as the only approach to reflective inquiry, pointing out that all paradigms for research are but metaphors. While metaphors can expand our thinking, their unexamined use may also limit our thought.

Mirga (1984) describes several models that rely on specific procedures to carry out reflective inquiry. These models include the "Successful Decision Making" course, designed by Charles Wales and Anne Nardi at West Virginia University, wherein students are "encouraged to solve problems by taking the following steps: stating a goal, gathering pertinent information, identifying what can be changed, examining possible solutions, considering constraints and assumptions, making a choice, re-examining the choice, then implementing it" (p. 10).

The CORT Thinking Program, developed by Edward de Bono of Cambridge University in England, represents a very different approach, with its emphasis on "lateral" thinking, a process that encourages students to look at a situation holistically. Students include values and emotional responses as they move from thought to action. The Learning to Learn program is almost a direct contrast to this, in that students are urged to raise and test hypotheses. Because questions are keyed to instructional objectives, students learn to generate questions that help them sort out irrelevant information. The program is based on the psychological theory, investigated by Thune (1950) and further studied by Hogan (1978), that practice on a variety of tasks leads to improved performance on subsequent tasks. Practice in formulating hypotheses and testing them leads to greater ability to do so.

There is considerable doubt as to whether any program can train a person in thinking, including use of reflective thought. Mortimer Adler opposes the specification of particular procedures: "[I]n the case of critical thinking, devising a special program to produce the desired result is a chimerical effort. It cannot be done" (1986, p. 28). The way to improve critical thought or reflective thinking is to involve students in situations that require such thinking and to help them realize that different types of problems necessitate different types of strategies.

The social and behavioral sciences are concerned with values as well as experimental findings, and these are inextricably linked together. Social scientists approach problems differently from natural scientists. Value and cultural context are considerations in the research paradigms of social scientists and are reflected in their findings. Engineers approach problems differently from attorneys, social workers, architects, and teachers. Their general beliefs about what is important, how to solve problems, and what is legitimate authority all vary. Adler points out that instruction throughout is that of coaching. Student performances are corrected when mistakes are made, and instructors insist on the correct mode of performance. Skills are inculcated until they become a stable habit of operation.

Reflective inquiry is not learned by listening to a lecture or reading a book. Rather, it becomes a habit through use and further reflection on such use. The emphasis in Adler's program is not so much on the specific content taught, particular skills demonstrated, or prescriptive formulas for effective teaching; it is not an information-processing model of instruction. Advocates of reflective inquiry in teacher education believe that students learn to teach most effectively when programs provide them opportunities to practice inquiry and they are coached in the Adlerian sense.

In such programs, instructors present activities and current events to be analyzed, dilemmas to be considered, questions to be answered, simulations and case studies to be examined, curriculum and instruction to be analyzed and developed, research to be undertaken, and values about which to speculate. It is an action-oriented process that is open-ended, ever-broadening, and made more effective with use.

Ross (Chapter 6, this volume) quotes Copeland (1986) in suggesting reflective writing as an important part of reflective inquiry programs. Writing permits the student to practice reflective inquiry, and it also provides others with knowledge of each student's current level of understanding. Keeping a journal is one method of stimulating reflection. The journal may be based on specific questions or a conceptual framework; it may also be completely open-ended.

Interpersonal process recall (IPR) is another technique used to help students speculate on their actions (Kagan, 1980). Following a lesson they were taught, students view a videotape of it and are interrogated by a counselor concerning their thoughts, feelings, and achievement. The teacher of the same lesson is also queried while watching a videotape or listening to an audiotape of it. The teacher considers why he or she took specific actions, what his or her goals were, and how instruction might be improved. In the third phase, the teacher is told of students' reactions and uses that information in thinking further about how to improve practice.

Supervision is yet another strategy to help students become better reflective inquirers. Simmons and Sparks (1987), Zeichner and Liston (1987), and Pugach and Johnson (Chapter 10, this volume) discuss the approaches used in supervision that emphasize reflective inquiry. Broader than clinical supervision, instructional supervision, or administrative supervision, *reflective supervision* considers cultural contexts, unintended consequences of actions, and the teacher's values as each *influences* impacts on the flow of instruction.

Reflective inquiry is not form, and the substance changes. Each individual has his or her own mode of inquiry. A teacher education program can provide the challenges needed to sharpen skills used in reflection as well as the opportunities to consider alternatives. But specific formulas or definitive algorithms for reflective inquiry hinder rather than help persons in using it.

CONCLUSIONS

The purpose of professional education is to provide sufficient background knowledge to enable a teacher to frame questions, to investigate answers, and to evaluate those answers. Those of us who are involved in programs that educate teachers at all points in the practical and the academic arenas are concerned with questions of the content, extent, context, and intent of professional reflection. That is, what are the salient problems for professional reflection as opposed to routines or improvisations that are automatic or spontaneous? To what extent is it desirable to engage in reflective activity, and at what point does reflective thought debilitate action? Is professional reflection best accomplished alone, or does the presence of a reflective community enhance the reflective process? Finally, what is (are) the goal(s) of professional reflection? The improvement of teaching? An increased ability to understand complex educational phenomena? The improvement of one's ability to work within school settings? An increased awareness of self as a practitioner? These questions, and more, are implicit in the preceding chapters.

Reflection and inquiry are more than code words, more than the latest educational fad. We who are attempting to develop teacher education programs based on the notion are concerned that they may be treated as such because the investment in carefully coordinated program development and systematic evaluations of programs is costly and labor intensive. Pragmatic legislators, business leaders, and educators seeking measurable results from standardized tests are restricting experimentation. They do not adequately fund evaluation research or basic research in teacher education.

Reflective inquiry–oriented teacher education programs are only beginning to become programmatic realities in preservice teacher education; more contemplative variations based on Eastern concepts have yet to be examined at all. As yet, there are no programs that provide a complete program for encouraging reflective practice—beginning with university training and continuing as teachers move into school settings that structure systematic occasions for communal reflection among faculty. Engaging in reflective teaching implies more than familiarity with the Western, rationalist, scientific method, as well as more than a course or two in "how to reflect." Inquiring into and reflecting upon the programs, processes, and outcomes of teacher education determine the degree to which we actively practice what we advocate for our students. A commitment to research and evaluation by teacher educators, followed by spirited discussions of the results and implications of that research, may provide substantive reality to the image of teachers as reflective practitioners.

REFERENCES

Adler, M. J. (1986, September 17). Education Week, p. 28.
Becker, H. S., Geer, B., Hughes, E. C., & Strauss, A. (1961). The boys in white: Student culture in medical schools. Chicago: University of Chicago Press.
Beny, R. (1975). Persia: Bridge of turquoise. Canada: McClelland & Stewart.
Bitting, P. F., & Clift, R. T. (1987, October). Reflecting upon reflection: Classical and modern influences. Paper presented at the Reflective Inquiry Conference, Houston, TX.

Borrowman, M. (1965). *The liberal and technical in teacher education.* Westport, CT: Greenwood.

Carroll, L. (1946). *Through the looking glass.* New York: Grossett & Dunlap. (Original work published 1875)

Clark, C. M., & Peterson, P. L. (1986). Teachers' thought processes. In M. C. Wittrock (Ed.), *Handbook of research on teaching (3rd ed.)* (pp. 255–296). New York: Macmillan.

Clift, R. T., & Houston, W. R. (1988, February). *Making reflection a reality: Reflective practice begins at the university.* Paper presented at the annual meeting of the Association of Teacher Educators, San Diego, CA.

Copeland, W. D. (1986). The RITE framework for teacher education: Preservice applications. In J. V. Hoffman & S. A. Edwards (Eds.), *Reality and reform in clinical teacher education* (pp. 25–43). New York: Random House.

Ginsburg, M. B., & Clift, R. T. (1990). The hidden curriculum of preservice teacher education. In W. R. Houston (Ed.), *Handbook of research on teacher education.* New York: Macmillan.

Grossman, P. L. (1988, April). *Learning to teach without teacher education.* Paper presented at the annual meeting of the American Educational Research Association, New Orleans, LA.

Haberman, M., & Stinnett, T. (1973). *Teacher education and the new profession of teaching.* Berkeley: McCutchan.

Hawking, S. W. (1988). *A brief history of time.* London: Bantam.

Hogan, J. C. (1978). *Trainability of abilities: A review of nonspecific transfer issues relevant to ability training (ARRO Technical Report R 78-1).* Washington, DC: Advanced Research Resources Organization. (ERIC Document Reproduction Service No. ED 150 428).

Kagan, N. (1980). *Interpersonal process recall: A method of influencing human interaction.* East Lansing, MI: Michigan State University.

Lanier, J. E., & Little, J. W. (1986). Research on teacher education. In M. C. Wittrock (Eds.), *Handbook of research on teaching* (3rd edition) (pp. 527–569). New York: MacMillan.

Mirga, T. (1984). Emerging interest in reasoning skills marks meeting on "critical thinking." *Education week, 3*(41–42), 1, 10.

Noddings, N. (1984). *Caring: A feminine approach to ethics and moral education.* Berkeley: University of California Press.

Peck, R. F., & Tucker, J. A. (1973). Research on teacher education. In R. M. W. Travers (Ed.), *Handbook of research on teaching (2nd ed.)* (pp. 940–978). Chicago: Rand McNally.

Peterson, P. L., & Comeaux, M. (1988). Assessing the teacher as a reflective professional: New perspective on teacher evaluation. In A. Woolfolk (Ed.), *Beyond the debate: Research perspectives on the graduate preparation of teachers* (pp. 132–152). Englewood Cliffs, NJ: Prentice-Hall.

Resnick, L. B. (1987). *Education and learning to think.* Washington, DC: National Academy Press.

Ringstaff, K. (1987, April). *Teacher misassignment: The influence of subject mat-*

ter knowledge on teacher planning and instruction. Paper presented at the annual meeting of the American Educational Research Association, Washington, DC.

Schön, D. (1983). *The reflective practitioner.* New York: Basic Books.

Schwab, J. J. (1973). The practical three: Translation into curriculum. *School Review, 81*(4), 501–522.

Shulman, L. (1986). Those who understand: Knowledge growth in teaching. *Educational Researcher, 15*(2), 4–14.

Shulman, L. (1987). Knowledge and teaching: Foundations of the new reform. *Harvard Educational Review, 57*(1), 1–22.

Simmons, J. M., & Sparks, G. M. (1987, October). *The need for a new model of teacher supervision and evaluation: The implications of identifying reflection as an explicit goal of teacher education.* Paper prepared for the Reflective Inquiry Conference, Houston, TX.

Subotnik, D. (1988). Wisdom or widgets: Whither the academic enterprise? *The NEA Higher Education Journal, 4*(1), 67–80.

Sugarman, J. (1985, June 12). Teaching teachers to be critical thinkers. *Education Week,* p. 23.

Thune, E. L. (1950). The effect of different types of preliminary activities on subsequent learning of paired-associate material. *Journal of Experimental Psychology, 40,* 423–438.

Toffler, A. (1980). *The third wave.* New York: Morrow.

Tom, A. R. (1985). Inquiring into inquiry oriented teacher education. *Journal of Teacher Education, 36*(5), 35–44.

Van Manen, M. (1977). Linking ways of knowing with ways of being practical. *Curriculum Inquiry, 6*(3), 205–228.

Wildman, T. M., & Niles, J. A. (1987). Reflective teachers: Tensions between abstractions and realities. *Journal of Teacher Education, 28*(4), 25–31.

Zeichner, K. M., & Liston, D. P. (1987). Teaching student teachers to reflect. *Harvard Educational Review, 57,* 23–48.

ABOUT THE EDITORS
AND THE CONTRIBUTORS

INDEX

About the Editors
and the Contributors

Jeffrey Cinnamond is currently at Indiana University of Pennsylvania, in the Counselor Education Department, where he teaches research design and higher education administration. He received a Ph.D. in Educational Policy and Leadership from Ohio State University. His research includes explorations into relationships between the "self" and the "other" within the educational context.

Renee T. Clift (Editor) is Assistant Professor of Curriculum and Instruction at the University of Houston, where she has helped develop the Reflective Inquiry Teacher Education Program. Her research concerns the social and psychological process of learning to teach. She is the first to receive the Conference on English Education, National Council of Teachers of English, *Richard A. Meade* Award for English education research. Currently, she is studying the potential for creating time for reflection in public school contexts.

Gaalen L. Erickson is Associate Professor in the Department of Mathematics and Science Education and Associate Director of the Centre for the Study of Teacher Education at the University of British Columbia. His research interests have focussed first, around developing an instructional perspective that acknowledges the important role of students' prior knowledge and understanding of phenomena in classroom instruction, and second, around developing a theoretical and methodological frame for viewing professional knowledge, such that this perspective can inform both preservice and in-service programs in teacher education.

H. Jerome Freiberg is Professor of curriculum and instruction in the College of Education at the University of Houston. He is also Director, Institute for Research on Urban Schooling, and editor of the *Journal of Classroom Interaction*. He has published in more than 50 books, chapters, monographs and journals, including *Educational Forum*, *Journal of Teacher Education*, and *Educational Leadership*. Dr. Freiberg is listed in the 1988–89 edition of *Who's Who in American Education*.

Peter P. Grimmett is Assistant Professor in the Department of Administrative, Adult, and Higher Education and Director of the Centre for the Study of Teacher Education at the University of British Columbia. His research interests focus on ways in which teachers develop professionally through school improvement, staff development, and instructional supervision initiatives, and on the relationship between such development and reflective practice.

W. Robert Houston (Editor) is Professor and Associate Dean for Academic Affairs, College of Education, University of Houston. He has been principal investigator of 24 major multi-year research and development projects that have explored competency-based teacher education, teacher centers, needs assessment for staff development, school-based teacher educators, mid-life career changes to teaching, and reflective inquiry in teacher education. He has authored or co-authored 37 books and nearly 100 chapters and journal articles. Dr. Houston has received numerous awards for his contributions to teacher education, and has served as President of the Association of Teacher Educators.

Lawrence Johnson is Associate Professor and Chairperson of Early Childhood Education for the Handicapped (ECEH) at The University of Alabama. He also currently co-directs two training projects, one for ECEH supervisors and the other for ECEH teachers: RISE–TEC, a technical assistance center for teachers of young handicapped children; ACTLab, a laboratory to demonstrate adaptive technology for young handicapped children; and RISE-Tran, a demonstration project for transition procedures between infant/toddler programs and preschool programs. In addition to his interests in early childhood special education, his research interests have focused on methods to enhance the ability of classroom teachers to accommodate the needs of students experiencing mild learning and behavior problems.

Judith Kleinfeld is Professor of psychology and Head of the Department of Education, Fairbanks Faculty, College of Rural Alaska, University of Alaska—Fairbanks. She received master's and doctoral degrees from the Harvard Graduate School of Education. Her research specialties include teacher preparation and secondary schools in rural Alaska. Currently, she is directing Teachers for Alaska—an innovative program designed to prepare high-quality teachers for Alaska's rural and urban high schools.

Allan M. MacKinnon is Assistant Professor in the Faculty of Education, University of Toronto, and a doctoral candidate in the Department of Mathematics and Science Education, and the Centre for the Study of Teacher Education, at the University of British Columbia. His research investigates ways of conceptualizing reflection about science teaching, and the means for evoking reflection among beginning science teachers in preservice and practicum experiences.

Susan G. Magliaro is Assistant Professor of educational psychology at Virginia Polytechnic Institute and State University. Her professional interests and research are focused on how individuals attempt to solve problems in educational contexts. Two populations of her current study are beginning teachers and reading diagnosticians.

Ruth Anne McLaughlin is a research associate at Virginia Polytechnic Institute and State University. She works on three projects that deal with beginning teachers. Her professional interests and research are on issues related to teacher induction.

Jerome A. Niles is Professor of curriculum and instruction at Virginia Polytechnic Institute and State University, and program leader for elementary education and reading. His research and practice are focused around issues that relate to promoting researcher learning at the preservice, induction, and experienced stages of teachers' careers.

Karen Noordhoff is Assistant Director of the Teachers for Alaska program and an instructor of education at the University of Alaska—Fairbanks. Her present scholarly interests focus on teacher preparation, especially the role of preservice field experiences in the process of learning to teach. She is currently a doctoral candidate at Michigan State University.

Marleen Pugach (Editor) is Associate Professor in the School of Education at the University of Wisconsin–Milwaukee. She is a faculty member in the Center for Teacher Education, where she is involved in the establishment of urban professional development schools. Her research interests include the role of collegial dialogue in teachers' development of classroom interventions for students who are having difficulty in school, and the relationship between the preparation of classroom teachers and the preparation of specialists for the schools.

Virginia Richardson is Associate Professor of teaching and teacher education, College of Education, University of Arizona. She has just completed a three-year editorship of the *American Educational Research Association*. Her recent books include *Educators' Handbook: A Research Perspective*, and *School Children At-Risk*. Prior to her academic position at the University of Arizona, she managed the research initiative of the U.S. Department of Education in the areas of effective teaching, effective schools, and teacher education. Her research interests include teachers' beliefs and practices, teaching and teacher education policy, qualitative methodology, and the relationship between research and the improvement of practice.

Theodore Riecken is Assistant Professor in the Faculty of Education, University of Victoria, British Columbia. A faculty member in the Department of Social and Natural Sciences, he teaches curriculum and instruction classes in elementary social studies to preservice teachers. A recent graduate of the Centre for the Study of Teacher Education at the University of British Columbia, his research interests include reflection in teaching, and the interaction of school culture and programs for school improvement.

Dorene Ross is Associate Professor in the Department of Instruction and Curriculum at the University of Florida. In both research and teaching, her primary interests are preservice and in-service teacher education and the development of reflective practitioners. She has been active in the development and evaluation of the elementary PROTEACH program at the University of Florida. Her recent articles concerning teacher education and reflection appear in the *Peabody Journal of Education* and the *Journal of Teacher Education*.

Linda Valli is Associate Professor and Director of Teacher Education at the Catholic University of America in Washington, D.C. She is the author of *Becoming Clerical Workers*, a critical social analysis of gender, schooling, and workplace relations, and is editing the forthcoming *Curriculum Differentiation: Interpretive Studies of U.S. Secondary Schools* with Reba Page. Her primary areas of interest include gender issues in education, school cultures, and reflective teaching.

Hersholt C. Waxman is Associate Dean for Research and Associate Professor of curriculum and instruction at the University of Houston. He received his doctorate in educational research and evaluation from the University of Illinois at Chicago, and his postdoctoral fellowship was from the Learning Research and Development Center at the University of Pittsburgh. He is currently President of the Southwest Educational Research Association. He has been involved in many nationally funded school-based research projects in the areas of effective classroom instruction and learning environments. Dr. Waxman has published many articles in journals and books such as *Journal of Educational Research*, *Educational Leadership*, and the *International Encyclopedia of Educational Research*. His areas of expertise include research methods, classroom instruction, educational productivity, and cognitive psychology. He is currently writing an introductory educational psychology textbook and co-editing two books on classroom learning environments, and equity, leadership, and school effectiveness.

Terry M. Wildman is Professor of educational psychology at Virginia Polytechnic Institute and State University. His professional interests and research are focussed on teacher learning and staff development, as well as applications of learning theory to educational practice. Currently, he is studying aspects of beginning teacher induction.

Robert J. Yinger is Associate Professor of Education at the University of Cincinnati. His research has been in the areas of design and interactive performance in teaching and other professions, instructional theory, the nature of skilled practice, and professional education. He has held appointments as Senior Researcher at the Institute for Research on Teaching at Michigan State University, Distinguished Visitor at the University of Calgary, and Visiting Professor at Stanford University.

Nancy L. Zimpher is Associate Professor in the College of Education at The Ohio State University. She offers graduate instruction in the area of professional development for teachers. Her research interests and publications focus on inquiry into the nature of initial programs of teacher preparation, entry-year programs and characteristics of teacher mentors, and purposes and formats for staff development for teachers in schools. She is a member of the Research and Information Task Force of the American Association of Colleges for Teacher Education, which conducts longitudinal studies of teacher preparation. In addition, she is the book review editor for the *Journal of Teacher Education*, and chairs the membership committee of Division K of the American Educational Research Association.

Index